BILLS OF RIGHTS IN AUSTRALIA

history, politics and law

ANDREW BYRNES
HILARY CHARLESWORTH
GABRIELLE McKINNON

UNSW
PRESS

1005727052

A UNSW Press book
Published by
University of New South Wales Press Ltd
University of New South Wales
Sydney NSW 2052
AUSTRALIA
www.unswpress.com.au

National Library of Australia
Cataloguing-in-Publication entry

Author: Byrnes, Andrew.
Title: Bills of rights in Australia: history, politics and law/Andrew Byrnes, Hilary
       Charlesworth, Gabrielle McKinnon.
ISBN: 978 1 921410 17 8 (pbk.)
Subjects: Civil rights – Australia – Legislation.
       Human rights – Australia.
       Constitutional law – Australia.
Other Authors/Contributors: Charlesworth, H. C. (Hilary C.)
       McKinnon, Gabrielle.
Dewey Number: 342.94085

Design Josephine Pajor-Markus
Cover Fairfax Photos
Printer Ligare

BILLS OF RIGHTS IN AUSTRALIA

ANDREW BYRNES is a Professor of International Law at the University of New South Wales, and Chair of the Australian Human Rights Centre. Previously, he was Professor of Law at the Australian National University (2001–05) and prior to that was Associate Professor of Law at the University of Hong Kong. His research interests include international law and human rights law (particularly gender and disability issues), and he is a leading academic commentator on the Hong Kong Bill of Rights.

HILARY CHARLESWORTH is an Australian Research Council Federation Fellow and Director of the Centre for International Governance and Justice, Australian National University. She also holds an appointment as Professor of International Law and Human Rights in the ANU College of Law. Professor Charlesworth chaired the ACT Bill of Rights Consultative Committee in 2002–03, which was instrumental in the development of the ACT *Human Rights Act 2004*.

GABRIELLE MCKINNON is the Director of an Australian Research Council linkage project at the Australian National University examining the impact and implementation of the ACT *Human Rights Act* over its first five years. Prior to this Gabrielle was an accredited specialist children's lawyer, practising at Marrickville Legal Centre in New South Wales. Gabrielle has been a member of the Juvenile Justice Advisory Council of NSW and worked on the Non-government Report on the Implementation of the United Nations Convention on the Rights of the Child in Australia 2005.

Contents

Abbreviations *vii*
Foreword *by Philip Alston* ix
Introduction *xv*

1 **What are human rights?** *1*
   The idea of human rights *2*
   Theories and critiques of human rights *9*
   The international protection of human rights *13*
   Australia's approach to international human rights *20*

2 **A short history of Australian bills of rights** *23*
   An Australian bill of rights? *24*
   Protecting human rights in Australia *36*
   State and Territory bills of rights *41*

3 **Bills of rights: models and controversies** *44*
   Models for an Australian bill of rights *44*
   Themes in the Australian debate *54*

4 **The ACT *Human Rights Act 2004*** *73*
   History *74*
   The *Human Rights Act 2004 (ACT)* *79*
   The ACT HRA in operation *86*

5 **The Victorian *Charter of Human Rights and
   Responsibilities 2006*** *108*
   History *109*

The Victorian Charter *114*
The Victorian Charter in operation *123*

6 **Towards an Australian bill of rights** *139*
State consultation processes *141*
A national bill of rights *146*

Notes *170*
Select Bibliography *204*
Table of cases *212*
Table of statutes and bills *216*
Table of international instruments *222*
Index *224*

Abbreviations

AFP	Australian Federal Police
ALP	Australian Labor Party
AO	Order of Australia
CAT	Convention Against Torture and Other Cruel, Inhuman or Degrading Treatment or Punishment
CEDAW	Convention on the Elimination of All Forms of Discrimination against Women
CERD	International Convention on the Elimination of All Forms of Racial Discrimination
CRC	Convention on the Rights of the Child
Cwlth	Commonwealth
DCA	Department for Constitutional Affairs (UK)
HREOC	Human Rights and Equal Opportunity Commission
ICCPR	International Covenant on Civil and Political Rights
ICESCR	International Covenant on Economic, Social and Cultural Rights
ILO	International Labour Organization
OPI	Office of Police Integrity (Vic)

PILCH	Public Interest Law Clearing House
QC	Queen's Counsel
SARC	Scrutiny of Acts and Regulations Committee
SC	Senior Counsel
UDHR	Universal Declaration of Human Rights
UN	United Nations
VEOHRC	Victorian Equal Opportunity and Human Rights Commission

Foreword

In 1994 the Human Rights and Equal Opportunity Commission, in cooperation with the Australian National University's Centre for International and Public Law, published a volume of essays exploring the desirability of an Australian bill of rights.[1] Significantly, many of the contributors lamented the fact that the most important issues arising in that context were 'barely being debated at all' at the national level. The current volume provides eloquent testimony to how far the situation has evolved in the intervening decade and a half.

In 1994 the observation was made that 'two processes, operating partly in tandem and partly quite separately', would, in the absence of any deliberate steps to adopt a bill of rights, 'conspire to bring about a de facto Bill of Rights'.[2] The first was said to be the 'inevitable evolution of the judicial role in protecting individual rights in response to changing attitudes within society, the rapid evolution of human rights jurisprudence in other common law jurisdictions, and the emergence of a range of new or resurgent threats to the enjoyment of human rights within Australia'. That combination of factors does indeed seem to have been a potent force in pushing us to the point where today Australia is almost alone among what used to be called 'civilised nations' (indeed we are almost alone among uncivilised ones as well) in not having any written bill of rights. As noted below, the United Kingdom, which was the other great holdout among common law states, not only adopted a comprehensive Human

Rights Act a decade ago which effectively incorporated (albeit in a qualified way) the whole of the European Convention on Human Rights into domestic law, but is also now debating the adoption of a 'Bill of Rights and Responsibility'.

The second process noted in 1994 was the influence of the international human rights regime and of the commitments which Australia had undertaken *vis-à-vis* the international community, especially through its ratification of the major United Nations human rights treaties. Since that time Australia has achieved the dubious distinction of being the state with the third highest number of formal complaints registered against it before the UN Human Rights Committee. Between December 1991 and January 2007 the Committee adopted decisions in response to 48 cases concerning Australia. It found violations in 14 of the 19 cases in which it adopted so-called Final Views. Thus around one in every 30 of the Committee's total number of registered communications, and findings of violations, have concerned Australia. In response, the federal government consistently challenged or even rejected many of the Committee's Views. The principal explanation for this state of affairs is the lack of a national bill of rights which would have ensured that these complaints would have been taken care of domestically rather than having to be referred to a United Nations body.

This volume gives reason to believe that these lessons have now been learned. A *de facto* bill of rights is the least desirable option. What is needed is a document that reflects the deeply held values of Australian society in a way which is consistent with the international undertakings that it has given to uphold and ensure human rights, even, indeed especially, in times of hardship and threats to those values.

The best starting-point for the debate that is now fully under way is to acknowledge that many of the arguments invoked at the extreme on each side of the debate are overstated and bear little resemblance to the actual experience of other countries which have enacted bills of rights. Some proponents of a bill of rights present it as a bold step which will resolve a great many injustices, rein in government excesses and abuses, ensure a decent standard of living for all, and provide guarantees of the enjoyment of respect for human rights for all individuals living in Australia. In short, it would be a panacea. Opponents have presented almost a mirror-image picture in which the advent of such a bill would be a disaster in a range of ways. Parliamentary supremacy would be undermined, the courts would run riot and the judiciary would be the new Platonic guardians, governments would be empowered across a wide range of areas in which they currently defer to individual choice, and the basic values of Australian society would be dictated by foreign visions of a good and just society.

Fortunately for the rest of us, those who present either of these extreme visions or reactions to a proposed bill of rights have been too busy on the hustings or the blogs to notice that international experience with bills of rights has been rather more nuanced. Most importantly, a great deal depends on the society itself and on the ways in which the different actors choose to respond to the adoption of a bill of rights. Governments will take such a bill seriously to the extent that public opinion compels it to do so, courts too will be influenced in their approach to the bill of rights by their perception of public attitudes. It has been rightly observed that some of the most progressive judgments implementing human rights provisions, whether in the United States, South Africa or elsewhere, were preceded by shifts in public opinion which laid the groundwork for the courts to move boldly to uphold human rights. As political scientist Stuart Scheingold puts it, on the basis of a careful review of a very wide body of recent literature on the dynamics of rights discourse:

> When the courts validate an expansive interpretation
> [of a right] they provide both institutional leverage and
> discursive legitimation. However, without a favorable
> political ethos and a cadre of movement activists to take

advantage of the leverage and legitimation, collective mobilization will not occur.[3]

It is also appropriate to draw attention to another of the key issues which should be debated at the national level. It relates to the scope of an Australian bill of rights, and whether some or all of the economic, social and cultural rights recognised in the International Covenant on Economic, Social and Cultural Rights, to which Australia became a party under the government of Malcolm Fraser, should be included. Proposals for their recognition were made, albeit unsuccessfully, in relation to both the ACT *Human Rights Act 2004* and the Victorian *Charter of Human Rights and Responsibilities 2006*. More recently, the December 2007 *Report of the Consultation Committee for a Proposed WA Human Rights Act* was firmly of the view that such an Act should 'recognise and protect' such rights as the right to education, and the right to have access to adequate housing. The Committee suggested three alternative approaches to the implementation of economic, social and cultural rights. One was to accord them the same means of protection as apply to civil and political rights, another was to provide an administrative rather than a judicial complaints system, and the third was to require what might be termed an 'impact statement approach' as a way of implementing a progressive realisation commitment in the Act.[4]

This is not the place to enter into a detailed analysis of these alternative proposals. It is noteworthy, however, that the United Kingdom is in the midst of a very similar debate. The UK Lord Chancellor and Secretary of State for Justice, Jack Straw, has endorsed a very cautious approach in the context of a proposed British Bill of Rights and Responsibility. He observed that many social rights, such as the right to social security and the right to a minimum wage, are already justiciable. But, he added, 'we would have to look very carefully before making any further economic or social rights justiciable'. He went on to express certainty that there was a consensus, shared by the judiciary, that it would be 'quite inappropriate (and unwanted) if the courts had to make decisions on levels of spending or resources which rightly should be the preserve of Parliament'.[5] But this is a specious argument, not only because courts very often hand down judgments which have major resource implications, but because there are many techniques which the courts in countries such as Canada, South Africa and even the United States have devised to ensure that resource implications as well as the prerogatives of the legislature and the executive are taken fully into account in such contexts. Their judgments are indeed often based upon detailed submissions by governments as to resource feasibility and related dimensions.[6]

The Lord Chancellor sought to invoke some of my own writings on bills of rights to support such minimalism:

> If, for instance, economic and social rights were part
> of our new Bill, but did not become further justiciable,
> this would not in any way make the exercise worthless.
> [Washington, DC, in which this version of his speech
> was presented] is a living testament to the power of
> symbols. As the jurist Philip Alston described, Bills
> of Rights are 'a combination of law, symbolism and
> aspiration'. What he makes clear is that the formulation
> of such a Bill is not a simple binary choice between
> a fully justiciable text on the one hand, or a purely
> symbolic text on the other. There is a continuum. And
> it is entirely consistent that some broad declarative
> principles can be underpinned by statute. Where we
> end up on this continuum needs to be the subject of the
> widest debate.[7]

There is good news and bad news in this formulation. To the extent that the Lord Chancellor is endorsing the importance of recognising economic and social rights within a bill of rights, even if their status is not entirely the same as that accorded to civil and political rights, that would be an encouraging development in the United Kingdom. But if the emphasis is on 'mere' declarative principles which carry no legal weight or clout beyond their statutory 'underpinnings' then it would be very difficult to conclude that the declarative principles represent a step forward from the existing situation in which the Parliament is free at any time to extend or withdraw social benefits. In other words, the difficulty would be to distinguish between forms of symbolism which are empty and rhetorical and those which are essentially empowering. If virtually all aspects of economic and social rights other than social security and labour law are per se excluded from the purview of the courts, the message being sent might well look like empty symbolism.

This volume provides a compelling, insightful and even-handed review and analysis of Australia's protracted domestic debates over bills of rights at the federal, state and territory levels. It makes clear that the time has come to bring Australian human rights policy at the federal level into the 21st century.

Philip Alston, John Norton Pomeroy Professor,
New York University Law School

Introduction

Although Australia is proud of its human rights record, human rights have a precarious foothold in the Australian legal system. In recent years, children and adults have been held in mandatory detention under punitive immigration laws, while the elderly, people with disabilities and those with mental illnesses have often been treated without dignity. In the wake of the events of 11 September 2001, the offence of sedition has been revived to criminalise some forms of criticism of government action and laws have been passed allowing severe restrictions on the liberty of people who have not been found guilty of any offence. Australian law does not provide any mechanism to remedy these breaches of human rights.

The aim of this book is to contribute to the longstanding debate over whether Australia should adopt a bill, or charter, of rights. The debate has simmered in the background of public life for the past fifty years, occasionally coming to the boil, then cooling off again. It is warming up once more because the Australian Capital Territory and Victoria enacted statutory bills of rights in 2004 and 2006 respectively and because of the election of a federal Labor government in 2007.

There are a number of excellent books dealing with the more legal, technical aspects of existing bills of rights in Australia; by contrast, this book is interested as much in the history and politics of these bills of rights as the detailed legal issues they raise. By analysing the idea of human rights generally, and the ways that this idea has influenced Australia since Federation, we hope to provide a broader context for considering the introduction of a national bill of rights. Although we support such a development, we have attempted to present here a full range of arguments and views. While there are many reasons for supporting a *constitutionally* entrenched bill of rights (as well as reasons for opposing one), our primary focus is on the arguments for and against *statutory* bills of rights, and the experience under those instruments in Australian and comparable overseas jurisdictions. This reflects the history of the debate in this country and the current political landscape, in which the adoption of a constitutional instrument is unlikely, and in which the wisdom of introducing even a statutory charter is hotly contested.

In chapter 1 we trace the development of ideas about human rights, and their current embodiment in international instruments. Chapter 2 examines the history of debates in Australia about constitutional or legislative bills of rights, and gives an overview of the legal and other protections of human rights under current legislation. Chapter 3 analyses the arguments often made for and against bills of rights, focusing on the relevance and validity of these arguments in the context of the statutory bills of rights recently adopted in a number of jurisdictions.

In chapters 4 and 5 we consider the experience under the statutory bills of rights in the ACT and Victoria, testing the theoretical arguments about their operation against the actual experience in the only two jurisdictions to adopt such protections. Chapter 6 describes recent developments in Tasmania and Western Australia and seeks to identify the critical issues that should be addressed in the debate over a national bill of rights.

We are grateful to the Australian Research Council for its support of the Linkage Project of which this book forms part (*Australia's First Bill of Rights: Assessing the Impact of the Australian Capital Territory's Human Rights Act 2004* (LP0455490)). Details of the project are at <http://acthra.anu.edu.au/index.html>. The project has been carried out in partnership with the ACT Department of Justice and Community Safety, for whose cooperation we are very grateful. We would particularly like to acknowledge the support for the project of Elizabeth Kelly and Renée Leon. We also thank those officials of the ACT Government who agreed to be interviewed about the effect on their work of the ACT *Human Rights Act 2004*.

Our colleagues at the Law Faculty, University of New South Wales, and at the Regulatory Institutions Network at the Australian National University provided congenial and constructive environments for our work.

Max Charlesworth, Andrea Durbach, Penelope Mathew, Helen Watchirs and George Williams all made helpful comments on drafts of the manuscript and we thank them warmly. We are also grateful to Kim Pham for her excellent research assistance.

As far as possible, the information in this book is current as at 30 June 2008.

A note on citations

In citing court cases we have, with one exception, used only 'medium-neutral' citations (sometimes also known as 'court-designated' or 'vendor-neutral' citations). The exception is cases decided by the High Court of Australia, where we have given parallel citations to the *Commonwealth Law Reports*. All the cases referred to in the book are available through open-access websites, such as AUSTLII or WORLDLII.

1

What are human rights?

Human rights have a powerful presence in the modern world. Embodied in international declarations and national constitutions and statutes, they are invoked both to resist excesses of state and private power and to bolster political claims to the material conditions of a fulfilling human existence.

In Australia, human rights have increasingly become part of the vocabulary of national debates over important political and social issues. Whether it be mandatory sentencing or anti-terrorism laws, immigration law and policy, housing and social security policies and programs, the rights of employees in the workplace, the rights of defendants and victims in the criminal justice process, the rights of Indigenous Australians, or the rights of parents, partners and children in the family law system, the legitimacy of laws and policies is now regularly contested in human rights terms.

The widespread acceptance of the vocabulary of human rights masks considerable debate about the meaning of the term. The history of human rights has seen vigorous argument over whether a coherent and persuasive justification can be offered for human rights and over the desirability of the framework they embody for the organisation of political and social life. This chapter begins by examining the development of ideas of human rights, considers some of the critiques of the human rights movement as a background to an understanding of contemporary controversies over human rights protection in Australia, and goes on to describe the scope of the international law of human rights, which is the basis of both existing Australian bills of rights and of proposals for a national system of human rights protection. The final section considers Australia's approach to international human rights.

The idea of human rights

The notion of rights is a very basic one. Rights and obligations/ duties are defined in terms of people's relationships with each other. If we have an obligation or duty to someone in respect of paying a debt, or in treating her or him as an equal, that person has a right to expect that she or he will be repaid or treated equally.

The animating idea of the modern human rights movement is that individuals have inherent rights by virtue of their humanity. Traces of this notion are found in early texts from a range of cultures. For example, Sophocles' Antigone is often understood as appealing to rights beyond the state, based in divine or natural law, when she refuses to obey Creon's order to leave her brother, Polynices, unburied.[1] The edicts of the Indian emperor Ashoka, promulgated in the 3rd century BC, referred to tolerance and liberty as the basis of society;[2] and the Qin dynasty's government in China over 2000 years ago emphasised the appropriate and fair treatment of all persons, whatever their status, in accordance with the social and moral expectations of the relationship between the persons involved.[3]

Despite these fragments of human rights ideas appearing in early philosophical, religious and political traditions, the form that human rights take today has been heavily influenced by developments in Western Europe over the last few centuries. The Reformation, which began in the 16th century, saw the first major step in the development of modern ideas of human rights.

It can be viewed in a number of ways – as the rejection of the dominion of the Roman Catholic Church in religious affairs and a desire for a Christianity more directly based on scripture and the individual conscience; as a protest against the political role of the papacy; and as an 'intellectual revolution, aiming for liberty in the kingdom of the mind to free science and art from the proscriptions and censorship of dogmatic orthodoxy'.[4] Some scholars see the rise of modern scientific method in the 18th century Enlightenment as grounded in the affirmation of freedom of thought and inquiry that each individual was able to exercise on the basis of rational thought and analysis, free from externally imposed 'authoritative' views.[5] The rejection of religious absolutism paved the way for the rejection of political absolutism and the assertion of the rights of the governed.

The struggle to attain political liberty and freedom from the absolute rule of monarchs was advanced in the fundamental political changes wrought in the English Revolution of the 17th century and the American and French revolutions of the 18th century. The English Civil War, the overthrow of the Stuart kings, and the Glorious Revolution of 1688, which saw the arrival on the throne of William and Mary on terms decreed by the Parliament, represented the rejection of the divine right of kings to rule over their subjects, who had no recourse against misrule. It also marked the ascendancy and sovereignty of Parliament. A Bill of Rights was adopted by Parliament in 1689, but the title of this document disguises its true nature. It did not recognise the rights of individuals generally but, like the Magna Carta agreed between King John and his barons in 1215, acknowledged a limited set of rights as belonging to a restricted, and privileged, class of people. These two documents are best understood as political settlements rather than precursors of modern human rights guarantees.[6]

The political developments of the 17th century were accompanied by, and drew support from, the writings of various political theorists. The English political philosopher John Locke has particular importance because of the way in which his writings were taken up by those who led the American and French revolutions. Locke, like others before him such as Thomas Hobbes, sought to find a justification for political arrangements in terms of a social contract, an abstract notion used to explain why individuals agreed to live together in civil society and thus avoid the predations and violence of the unregulated 'state of nature'. Locke saw individuals in the state of nature as enjoying a series of natural rights and freedoms – to life, liberty and property – and maintained that the purpose of joining civil society was to secure those rights by granting powers to government to protect individuals against the violations of those rights by others.[7] For Locke, the converse of this grant of powers to government was a duty on government to protect its citizens' rights, failing which citizens would be obliged to overturn it and install a legitimate government.[8]

The authors of the American Declaration of Independence and the United States Bill of Rights (comprising the first ten amendments to the Constitution of 1787, proposed in 1789 and in force from 1791) drew heavily on Locke's thought. His influence can be seen in the famous opening words of the Declaration of Independence adopted on 4 July 1776, with their endorsement of inherent rights and the legitimacy of the government depending on its protection of those rights:

> We hold these truths to be self-evident, that all men are created equal, that they are endowed by their Creator with certain unalienable Rights, that among these are Life, Liberty and the pursuit of Happiness. – That to secure these rights, Governments are instituted among Men, deriving their just powers from the consent of the governed. – That whenever any Form of Government becomes destructive of these ends, it is the Right of the People to alter or to abolish it, and to institute new Government, laying its foundation on such principles

and organizing its powers in such form, as to them shall
seem most likely to effect their Safety and Happiness.

The other proclamation of rights that influenced modern human
rights is the French Declaration of the Rights of Man and the
Citizen of 1789. This was shaped not only by the American
Declaration of Independence but also by the writings of Charles
Montesquieu and Jean-Jacques Rousseau. Rousseau's book *The
Social Contract*, published in 1762, argued that the basis of
entering the social contract involved giving up natural liberty
for civil liberty. The Declaration mirrors this account of social
order:

> 1. Men are born and remain free and equal in rights.
> Social distinctions may be founded only upon the general
> good.
>
> 2. The aim of all political association is the preservation
> of the natural and imprescriptible rights of man. These
> rights are liberty, property, security, and resistance to
> oppression.
>
> ...
>
> 4. Liberty consists in the freedom to do everything which
> injures no one else; hence the exercise of the natural
> rights of each man has no limits except those which
> assure to the other members of the society the enjoyment
> of the same rights. These limits can only be determined
> by law.[9]

The Declaration listed specific guarantees, including rights to
freedom of expression and religion, the right to be free from
arbitrary arrest or detention, the presumption of innocence, and
the right to property.

While the 18th century ended with these major statements of individual rights as an essential component of the modern state, the reality belied the rhetoric. The rights of man were just that – women were not viewed as the beneficiaries of those rights or as participants in the political society. Olympe de Gouges prepared a Declaration on the Rights of Women in 1791 as a protest against the male focus of the French Declaration.[10] She was guillotined three years later for her radical political ideas, including championing women's rights.[11] Guarantees of rights were also restricted to certain categories of men, with slavery a lawful institution in the United States until the mid-19th century, and the franchise limited in many countries to those who satisfied property qualifications. Those limitations did not pass unchallenged at the time of the adoption of the proclamations of rights,[12] and the struggle to extend those rights formally and in practice to all human beings continues to this day.

The French and American recognition of rights as the basis of the social order and government were largely based on the protection of political and civil rights. In the 19th century these concepts were expanded, most particularly through the writings of Karl Marx and Friedrich Engels. They saw guarantees of civil and political rights as based in a concept of the individual as an autonomous being, which failed to reflect the reality of human beings as members of social groupings or 'species beings'.[13] Moreover, they argued that these 'rights of man' were the rights of the bourgeoisie – those who already had property and privilege – and were of little use to workers and other marginalised groups. Such rights would simply entrench disadvantage. Political scientist and historian Micheline Ishay has emphasised the significance of socialists in the development of human rights, noting that their position constituted:

> the first historical assertion that all humans, regardless
> of wealth, gender, race or age, were entitled to
> both political and social rights. In this respect, they

broadened the narrow definition of universalism from
the Enlightenment, articulating a broad commitment to
enhance simultaneously, rather than selectively, the rights
of slaves, women, homosexuals, and Jews.[14]

An increase in the political and economic power of the new
middle classes allowed them to invoke their civil and political
rights against the aristocratic elites. At the same time, industri-
alisation brought with it large-scale migration from rural areas
to cities and the emergence of a poor urban proletariat. Those
who were able to find work were often required to labour for
long hours in shocking conditions; children were employed
in factories, mines and other workplaces at very young ages,
ruining their health and wellbeing. The economic and social
deprivation of the working classes was underlined by their
exclusion from the political process. Nowhere was there even
universal male suffrage, and efforts to extend the franchise were
frequently supported by groups who were also at the forefront
of campaigns for better working conditions, access to education,
and other economic and social benefits. Many of these efforts
were supported by socialist groups, as well as groups such as
the Chartists, who worked for a broadened franchise and better
social and working conditions in Britain.[15]

These claims challenged not just the power and influence of
the traditional elites but also the property and power of the new
middle classes. Efforts to extend the franchise more broadly, to
reconfigure elite power structures, and to claim fairer and more
equitable treatment in work and the allocation of the economic
benefits met with considerable opposition – including the violent
suppression of such movements on various occasions, such as the
crushing of the Paris Commune in 1871.[16] There were, however,
some successes: for example, in Britain the employment of children under nine in mines was banned by the Factory Act of 1833
(a ban extended to the employment of women as well as children under ten years of age in 1842) and the working hours for

children and women were set at a maximum of ten hours per day in 1847.[17]

Human rights ideas also animated the national and international campaigns that gained momentum during the 19th century to abolish first the slave trade and then slavery in all its forms.[18] For example, the institution of slavery was formally abolished as a matter of law in the United States by the 13th Amendment to the Constitution, adopted after the Civil War in 1865. This had been preceded by the abolition of the slave trade by Britain in 1807, and of slavery in most of its colonies where the practice existed (mainly the Caribbean) by the Slavery Abolition Act of 1833.[19]

It took another century for the international community to assert an interest in protecting a fuller catalogue of human rights outside the context of slavery. The Covenant of the League of Nations of 1919, for example, did not include human rights generally within that institution's purview, though a number of specific issues were addressed: labour rights (through the establishment of the International Labour Organization, ILO), women's equality in relation to labour rights and the League Secretariat, and protection for various national minorities in the Covenant (and associated peace treaties) and in the mandate system established to govern the colonies of the defeated powers after the First World War.[20] It was not until the adoption of the United Nations (UN) Charter in 1945 that human rights generally were given international status. (These developments are discussed in the final section of this chapter.) International declarations and treaties have now become the major foundation for human rights laws in countries around the globe, although the translation of the international standards has varied significantly from country to country, as we discuss in chapter 3.

Theories and critiques of human rights

There have been many attempts to justify those human rights accepted at national and international level:[21] religious justifications; conceptions of rights derived from the essential nature of humanity or from basic human needs; utilitarian approaches, which seek to show that human rights provide a way of maximising the overall welfare of individuals and the community; approaches that stress that rights are a historical response to particular social wrongs[22] or a preventive strategy against standard threats to human wellbeing;[23] or approaches that see rights simply as the result of decisions about how best to provide the opportunity for human flourishing.[24]

Typically, accounts of human rights, in particular international human rights, underline the claim of human rights to universality. In this respect they show the influence of the writings of the 18th century German philosopher Immanuel Kant. Kant set out to articulate universal moral principles from a 'categorical imperative' – that we should act only according to principles that we would want everyone else to observe.[25] He also insisted that each individual should be treated as an end in her or himself, and never as a means to an end. These ideas support a notion of human rights as inherent and inalienable. Thus, international lawyer Christian Tomuschat writes, '[h]uman rights are rights which a person enjoys by being human, without any supplementary condition being required'.[26] Such an understanding is often associated with natural law philosophies because it bases human rights on natural or universal grounds such as human nature and assumes their existence independent of state action to provide for them in positive law. Some scholars who support a universal theory of human rights also view human rights, perhaps inconsistently, as a product of consensus in international society.[27]

This account of human rights as universal and independent of history or social or political context is seductive. Yet human rights as we know them today are the outcome of particular political, social and intellectual developments in the West over the last five centuries. They are the result of political struggles against historical forms of abuse, disadvantage and exclusion. A major challenge has been to reconcile the historically contingent origins and forms of modern human rights with their claims to universality and their applicability to human beings everywhere.[28] The contention that human rights are those rights that a person possesses merely by virtue of being human does not indicate what particular rights flow from the status of being human.

Critiques of the idea of human rights have been numerous. One strand of criticism has focused on the grand promises of human rights and the failure to deliver on them. On this analysis, there is nothing 'natural' about human rights. They exist in particular political and social contexts and are not above the state, but rather *of* the state. Thus, in the 19th century, Jeremy Bentham debunked the notion of natural rights articulated in the French and American Declarations, declaring that natural rights were 'simple nonsense: natural and imprescriptible rights, rhetorical nonsense, – nonsense upon stilts'.[29] For Bentham, true rights were embodied in positive law. The political theorist Edmund Burke also saw little justification for asserting the existence of the 'rights of man' – only the 'rights of Englishmen' was a meaningful category.[30] A contemporary version of this critique, based on a philosophical and theological rejection of Enlightenment rationality, is that of philosopher Alasdair MacIntyre: '[t]he truth is plain: there are no such [natural or human] rights, and belief in them is one with belief in witches and unicorns'.[31] Similarly, international lawyer David Kennedy has criticised human rights for being the dominant vocabulary for talking about emancipation, and has pointed to its blind spots and limitations.[32]

A second type of challenge to human rights has come from the developing world. Despite their claim to universality, critics charge, human rights reflect the values of individualistic Western

culture and do not respond to the focus on community charac-
teristic of non-Western societies.[33] While there is some merit in
this critique as far as the origins of civil and political rights are
concerned, the claim does not take into account the pivotal role
played by non-Western philosophers and activists in drafting
central human rights documents, such as the Universal Declaration of Human Rights (UDHR).[34] The critique also does not
acknowledge the range of economic, social and cultural rights,
as well as collective rights, that form part of modern human
rights law. The value of human rights principles outside the West
has, moreover, been affirmed by others, for example non-government organisations working to hold governments accountable
for mistreatment of their citizens.[35]

Feminists have provided another set of challenges to human
rights. One claim is that human rights standards tend to be built
on typical male lives and do not respond readily to the oppression of women.[36] For example, violence against women does
not easily fit into traditional understandings of human rights
because it largely takes place outside the public realm of government and inside the private world of the home and family. Indigenous peoples also have criticised the lack of attention to their
concerns in the human rights canon.[37] The particular claims of
indigenous communities, especially to their land, are not well
protected by human rights formulations.

Human rights in their current formulation can thus be understood as flawed, or incomplete in their coverage; but they also
retain considerable force, for example in the imaginative, tran-
scendental power of human rights claims. They offer a framework for debate about basic values and conceptions of a good
society. Brazilian jurist Roberto Unger has captured some of
this power in his claim that human rights provide 'a protective
sphere for vital interests, which people need to persuade them
that they may accept vulnerability, run risks, undertake adven-
tures in the world, and operate as citizens and people'.[38] This
is not to say that human rights should be the only or even the

dominant framework around which persons organise their lives; in legal anthropologist Marie-Bénédicte Dembour's words, they 'offer just one example of the politics of dignity'.[39]

Human rights are a useful set of political and moral ideas to set against oppressive practices. We argue that they are particularly significant in Australian political life, which has long been dominated by utilitarian perspectives, because they offer a new way of understanding the relationship between the government and the governed.

Human rights are, in the first place, rights. In other words, they represent claims that a rights-holder (generally an individual, but possibly also a group) may legitimately make against the bearer of the corresponding duty (primarily the state, but in some approaches non-state actors as well), that the latter take particular actions or refrain from doing so. Rights can, of course, be of different sorts (natural, moral, legal and so on), but here the focus is on their legal expression.

Human rights are a particular category of rights. The term makes clear that it is human beings who are the rights-holders (though in some cases corporations and other entities have been recognised as potential rights-holders). It also suggests that the distinctive grounding of this category of rights in a concept of humanity both gives them a particular value (above, say, a contractual right to have one's newspaper delivered each morning), and provides guidance for what these rights might comprise based on reflection on human nature and social life.

In this book we use the term 'human rights' to refer to the content of the various international declarations and treaties that are the foundation of the international human rights system. The next section of this chapter describes these instruments. One might argue that, given a broad international consensus on a catalogue of universal human rights, it is perhaps not so important to have agreement on the specific justification for them. Indeed, some have argued that while it may be impossible to reach agreement on the justifications for rights, it may still be possible to agree on the importance of specific rights or norms and that the only practical way to proceed is to work with overlapping consensus or 'incompletely theorised agreements' in relation to them.[40] The idea is that different participants in debates over human rights may agree on a specific norm or value that can be included in a code of rights, but justify it in quite different ways, for example, by reference to a religious or ethical system, or a model of human flourishing, or utilitarian assessment.[41]

The international protection of human rights

The international law of human rights has largely developed since the mid-20th century. International law had traditionally regulated the relations between states, the rights they enjoyed and the obligations they owed each other, and did not concern itself with a state's treatment of the individuals who fell within its jurisdiction. One exception was when a treaty conferred a right on an individual citizen of a foreign state or the host state had engaged in conduct that involved a gross denial of justice to a foreigner in its territory, this being viewed as a wrong against the state of the person's nationality. But a state's treatment of its *own* citizens was not a matter of international concern or obligation; this fell within the sovereign powers of the state.

One exception to this was the body of international law relating to slavery, referred to above. Another internationalised concern with individuals developed in the 19th century through what is now referred to as international humanitarian law. Rules about how war could be waged and how non-combatants or captured combatants should be treated are to be found in different cultures and traditions over many hundreds of years. However, concentrated efforts to address the problem in a comprehensive way in the context of modern industrialised warfare can be traced to the US Civil War and various conflicts in Europe during the 19th century. Prominent among them were the Lieber Code commissioned by President Lincoln[42] and the first Geneva Convention of 1864,[43] promoted by the International Committee for the Relief of Military Wounded, later known as the International Committee of the Red Cross. These documents were the precursors of the many treaties that now govern the conduct of armed conflict and the treatment of those who are non-combatants or who are no longer engaged in combat – the wounded, sick or captured. The best known examples are the four Geneva Conventions of 1949.[44] Yet the nature of international humanitarian law is such that, in most cases, the conduct being regulated is the treatment of the nationals of one state by another state in the conduct of hostilities or the treatment of persons who fall into its power, rather than a code regulating a state's treatment of its own nationals.

A further extension of the concern of international law with the treatment by a state of persons within its jurisdiction came with efforts to protect national minorities living within another state. The drawing of political boundaries in Europe (and elsewhere) frequently meant that persons who belonged ethnically, culturally or linguistically to a particular national group ended up in a country where the dominant population belonged to other ethnic groups. At the end of the First World War, a number of states entered into agreements – either as part of peace agreements or in separate treaties – that guaranteed the rights of national minorities.[45] These treaties provided for affected minorities to raise complaints with the Council of the League of Nations, and for any dispute between the states which were parties to the treaties to be referred to the Permanent Court of International Justice.

Another area of expansion of international concern in the early 20th century was in what we today call economic and social rights, in particular through the establishment of the ILO in 1919, as part of the Treaty of Versailles.[46] The goals of the ILO were humanitarian (to alleviate the exploitation of workers and the deleterious consequences for their health and family lives); political (to avoid the possibility of social unrest or even revolution instigated by the ever-increasing number of workers who became disaffected); economic (to endeavour to level the playing field so that states which adopted progressive regulation of their labour markets and protected the rights of workers did not suffer competitive disadvantage in relation to those states who did not do so); and to contribute to 'universal and lasting peace' (which could be 'established only if it [was] based upon social justice').[47] The ILO has adopted a large number of conventions and recommendations on matters relating to labour and work, and has provided technical advice and assistance to states to help them implement human rights standards. Since 1926 it has had in place an effective monitoring system which involves regular reporting to committees of experts, as well as providing for complaints of violations of the right to freedom of association to be dealt with by a specialist committee and for the possibility of inquiries into allegations of violations of international labour conventions.

Notwithstanding these important developments, well into the 20th century a state's treatment of individuals within its own territory was a matter still largely unregulated by international law and not considered to be a matter of international concern. The events leading up to the Second World War and the war itself provided the impetus for the international community to reject the traditional view that international law had no relevance to the depredations carried out by a state against its own citizens, and that the only test of lawfulness was whether actions were authorised under national law. The atrocities committed by the Nazi regime against its citizens – Jews, persons with disabilities, Roma peoples, political opponents and others – made it impossible for the international community to maintain the classical position that what a state did to its own citizens was, by and large, of no concern to the international community. The fact that many of the violations had been lawful under the laws of

Nazi Germany required a response that accepted that there were standards external to a national system of law under which a government could be held accountable, even when it had authorised such actions under its own laws.

International human rights standards as set out in declarations and treaties embody civil and political freedoms, sometimes referred to as 'first generation' rights. These include the rights to life, liberty and due process; the right to be free from torture and other inhuman or degrading treatment; freedom from slavery and forced labour; the right to a fair trial; freedoms of thought, conscience, religion, expression, association and movement; rights to privacy and respect for family life; the rights to vote and to participate in the political process; the rights of members of minorities to use their language and to take part in other communal activities; and rights to equality and non-discrimination.

This category of rights is only part of the picture. The hardships and injustices of the industrial revolution led to the articulation in the 19th century of a further category of rights (so-called 'second generation' rights). These rights were economic, social and cultural rights, including the right to safe and decent conditions of labour, the right to organise, the right to education, the right to health, the right to an adequate standard of living (including access to adequate food, clothing and housing), the right to social support, and the right to participate in cultural activities.

In the 20th century, a third category of human rights has developed – collective or solidarity rights ('third generation' rights). These rights, which include the right to self-determination of peoples and the right to development, were a response to claims by developing countries that their legitimate claims should be reflected in rights terms. The distinctive aspect of these types of rights is their collective dimension.

The protection and promotion of 'human rights and fundamental freedoms' was identified as a fundamental purpose of the United Nations, although these terms were left undefined in the UN Charter adopted in 1945. Definition had to await the adoption of the UDHR, which was drafted by the new UN Commission on Human Rights and eventually adopted by the UN General Assembly on 10 December 1948. The Preamble to the UDHR reflects its debt to the Enlightenment tradition, but in tandem with concerns to ensure the realisation of economic, social and cultural rights and a just and peaceful international order:

> Whereas recognition of the inherent dignity and of the equal and inalienable rights of all members of the human family is the foundation of freedom, justice and peace in the world,

> Whereas disregard and contempt for human rights have resulted in barbarous acts which have outraged the conscience of mankind, and the advent of a world in which human beings shall enjoy freedom of speech and belief and freedom from fear and want has been proclaimed as the highest aspiration of the common people,

> Whereas it is essential, if man is not to be compelled to have recourse, as a last resort, to rebellion against tyranny and oppression, that human rights should be protected by the rule of law.

The UDHR comprises thirty substantive articles. It opens with an affirmation of the freedom and equality in dignity and rights of all human beings (art. 1) and of the right of all to enjoy human rights and fundamental freedoms without discrimination of any kind (art. 2). It then proclaims classical civil and political rights (arts. 3–21), followed by economic, social and cultural rights (arts. 22–27). Article 28 proclaims the entitlement of everyone 'to a social and international order in which the rights and freedoms set forth in this Declaration can be fully realised', while article 29 emphasises the individual's duties to the community and specifies the circumstances under which rights may be limited. Article 30 provides that the Declaration should not be relied on as a justification for the destruction of the rights or freedoms of others.

The UDHR was a declaration of the General Assembly, a statement of principles, ideals and aspirations rather than a treaty formally binding on the members of the United Nations. It was envisaged as the first step in a process that would lead to the adoption of a binding treaty (an International Covenant on Human Rights) which would embody the rights contained in the UDHR, in a form appropriate to a statement of binding legal obligation.[48] Cold War tensions meant that the envisaged single covenant eventually became two – the International Covenant on Civil and Political Rights (ICCPR) and the International Covenant on Economic, Social and Cultural Rights (ICESCR), both adopted by the General Assembly in 1966.[49]

In addition to the UDHR and the two International Covenants, collectively known as the International Bill of Rights, there have been many other instruments adopted within the framework of the United Nations that have sought to apply their principles and norms to other specific groups or specific human rights problems. The two International Covenants have been supplemented by the following major human rights treaties within the UN system:[50]

- International Convention on the Elimination of All Forms of Racial Discrimination 1965 (CERD);
- Convention on the Elimination of All Forms of Discrimination against Women 1979 (CEDAW);[51]
- Convention against Torture and Other Cruel, Inhuman or Degrading Treatment or Punishment 1984 (CAT);[52]
- Convention on the Rights of the Child 1989 (CRC);[53]
- International Convention on the Protection of the Rights of

All Migrant Workers and Members of Their Families 1989
(Migrant Workers Convention);
- Convention on the Rights of Persons with Disabilities
2006;[54] and
- International Convention for the Protection of All Persons
from Enforced Disappearance 2006.

When a state becomes a party to a treaty, usually through signature followed by ratification, it is bound under international law to give effect to the obligations set out in that treaty. In the case of human rights treaties, this means ensuring that the rights set out in the treaty are guaranteed under domestic law, and that remedies are provided for violations of those rights. In general, unless specifically required by the treaty, it is not necessary to incorporate all the terms of the treaty into domestic law *verbatim*. While such incorporation may be desirable and even helpful to the implementation of the treaty, simple incorporation will rarely be enough to achieve this goal – detailed legislation will normally be required, supported by appropriate policies and programs.

For each of these treaties, a committee of independent experts has been established to monitor their implementation by the states that become parties to them ('states parties'). All the treaties require states parties to submit regular reports to the United Nations for consideration by the committees; following discussion with the state, the committees issue concluding observations that set out their assessment of the progress made and the steps that need to be taken in order to implement the treaty fully. Under a number of the treaties (or their optional protocols), states parties may accept the jurisdiction of the committees to consider complaints by individuals of violations of the rights guaranteed by the treaty in question (if the individual has not been able to obtain a remedy within the national legal system); these procedures result in quasi-judicial decisions by the committees that are not formally binding but nevertheless carry considerable weight.

Some of the treaties also confer on committees the power to carry out inquiries on their own initiative when they receive information suggesting there may be serious or systematic violations of the treaty by a state party that has accepted this procedure. The treaty bodies also produce 'jurisprudence' in decisions under individual complaint procedures and in general comments and recommendations, which set out detailed analyses of the obligations of states under the various treaties.

Australia's approach to international human rights

Australia was a founding member of the United Nations and an active member of the Commission on Human Rights during the drafting of the UDHR. Australian External Affairs Minister Dr H V Evatt was President of the UN General Assembly at the time of the adoption of the Declaration and welcomed it as a 'step forward in a great evolutionary process'.[55] Australia was also a consistent participant in the negotiation of the International Bill of Rights, and in the early stages made strong calls for a requirement that states parties incorporate human rights obligations into binding domestic laws.[56]

Australia is a party to most of the major UN human rights treaties and a number of the optional protocols. By June 2008, the only two treaties it had not committed to accept were the Migrant Workers Convention and the Convention for the Protection of All Persons from Enforced Disappearance. Australia has also submitted itself to the individual complaints procedures under the Optional Protocol to the ICCPR, art. 14 of CERD, and art. 22 of CAT, and has accepted the inquiry procedure under art. 20 of CAT.[57] In 2008, Australia announced that it would accede to the individual complaint procedure and the inquiry procedure under the Optional Protocol to CEDAW as well as a system of monitoring visits to places of detention under the Optional Protocol to CAT.[58] Australia is also likely to accept the complaints and inquiry procedures under the Optional Protocol to the Convention on the Rights of Persons with Disabilities (it ratified the Convention itself on 17 July 2008).[59]

Australia has taken a leadership role in seeking to protect human rights in other countries, including East Timor and Zimbabwe, and in the establishment of the International Criminal Court.[60] However, despite its initial support for rigorous implementation of human rights standards, Australia has not systematically incorporated its treaty obligations directly into domestic law, and existing protections are piecemeal. In the late 1990s, tensions emerged over the consideration of some of Australia's reports to the international treaty committees, and the hearing of individual complaints by these committees. The Howard Coalition government took particular exception to concerns raised by the Committee on the Elimination of Racial Discrimination in response to Australia's twelfth periodic report to the Committee in 2000. The government rejected the Committee's findings on Indigenous issues, asserting that '[i]t is unacceptable that Australia, which is a model member of the UN, is being criticised in this way for its human rights record'.[61] Following a review of Australia's relationship with the treaty bodies, the government adopted a more 'robust and strategic approach', effectively limiting its engagement with the treaty system and other UN human rights procedures.[62] The election of the Rudd Labor government in late 2007, however, has generated a more constructive relationship with the United Nations.[63]

Despite their limitations, international human rights represent a significant global consensus regarding the conditions that are fundamental for people to live lives of dignity, and to the freedoms that must be safeguarded to prevent oppression. Australia played an important role in the development of these foundational international human rights instruments, and has at times been a key player in advancing the cause of human rights internationally. However, successive governments have been ambivalent towards the full implementation of human rights obligations by directly enacting human rights treaties as part of Australian law. The next chapter explores the chequered history of attempts to codify human rights into a national bill of rights for Australia.

2

A short history of
Australian bills of rights

A debate over whether Australia should have some kind of bill of rights has proceeded in fits and starts since Federation. This chapter describes the major events in this debate and identifies its main themes, then sets out the current Australian legal framework for the protection of human rights in Australia and analyses the limitations of this scheme.

The terminology used in Australia has varied between 'bills of rights', 'Human Rights Acts' and 'charters of rights'. The latter two are more common today, but there is often little difference in substance in the content of bills, Acts and charters. For example, Australian bills of rights proposed in the 1970s and 1980s, described below, had many similar features to the Human Rights Acts and charters of rights mooted in the 2000s. The change in terminology to Human Rights Acts and charters is often designed to emphasise differences between current proposals and American-style constitutional bills of rights, which have attracted considerable criticism. The change is useful to the extent that it avoids inaccurate comparisons with the US model, discussed in the next chapter. In this book, however, we use the term 'bill of rights' as an omnibus category for formal legal protection of human rights.

An Australian bill of rights?

Federation debates

Rights were on the agenda during the drafting of the Australian Constitution in the last decade of the 19th century.[1] The first formal discussion of Federation took place in Melbourne in 1890. After the 1890 Federation Conference, Andrew Inglis Clark, the Tasmanian Attorney-General, prepared a preliminary draft of a constitution which drew extensively from the Constitution of the United States.[2] He was an admirer of the US Constitution and corresponded with the famous jurist, Oliver Wendell Holmes, Jr. Clark was committed to what he called 'the essentially republican doctrine of the natural, or ... the rational rights of man', which he saw as countering 'the tyranny of the majority, whose unrestricted rule is so often and so erroneously regarded as the essence and distinctive principle of democracy'.[3] Clark was a member of a drafting sub-committee for the 1891 Convention, chaired by Samuel Griffith. The draft included, at Clark's behest, four particular rights with an American heritage: the right to a jury trial; the right to the privileges and immunities of state citizenship; the right to equal protection under the law; and the right to freedom and non-establishment of religion. It may seem surprising today that Clark was so modest in his borrowing from the Americans. Perhaps it was due to the fact that many of the rights in the US Constitution had not yet been invoked in the 1890s and did not appear as central as they do today. The guarantee of freedom of expression contained in the 1st Amendment to the US Constitution, for example, had little prominence in constitutional debate until after the First World War.[4]

Much of the debate about the rights provisions occurred at the 1898 Melbourne Convention. There was considerable scepticism about the inclusion of rights guarantees, especially guarantees that would bind the States. The colonial delegates ridiculed the prospect of the States acting to breach rights and argued that it was offensive to restrain governmental action explicitly, thereby suggesting the possibility of actions in bad faith. There was, however, less concern about limiting the Commonwealth's powers in the name of rights. A limited right to a trial by jury in Commonwealth offences (s. 80), a prohibition on the Commonwealth establishment of any religion or prevention of the free exercise of any religion (s. 116) and the protection of residents of one State from discrimination by another State on the basis of residence (s. 117) were finally included in the Constitution of the Commonwealth of Australia.

No trace of Clark's proposals for a due process clause and an equal protection clause survived, however.[5] These proposals were attacked both on the basis that such guarantees were unnecessary for the protection of the rights of citizens in a polity based on representative and responsible government, and because they were seen as having the potential to restrict colonial laws that limited the employment of Asian workers.[6] With respect to the due process clause, South Australian Alexander Cockburn argued that 'the insertion of these words would be a reflection on our civilisation. People would say – "Pretty things these states of Australia; they have to be prevented by a provision in the Constitution from doing the grossest injustice".'[7]

Some of the drafters took a different view. Richard O'Connor, the NSW Solicitor-General, for example, argued for the inclusion of a due process clause because '[w]e are making a Constitution which is to endure, practically speaking, for all time'.[8] He argued: 'In the ordinary course of things such a provision would be unnecessary; but we all know that laws are passed by majorities and that communities are liable to sudden and very often to unjust impulses.'[9]

At the time of the adoption of the Australian Constitution, its lack of protection of individual rights was regarded by some commentators as proof of the document's modernity and democratic character.[10] In 1942, Sir Owen Dixon, Chief Justice of the Australian High Court, explained to an American audience that a study of the US Constitution 'fired no [Australian constitutional drafter] with enthusiasm for the principle [of guarantees of rights]'. He went on: 'Why, asked the Australian democrats, should doubt be thrown on the wisdom and safety of entrusting to the chosen representatives of the people ... all legislative power, substantially without fetter or restriction?'

It has more recently been suggested that the Australian drafters:

> had no recent memory of a bitter struggle against
> tyrannical devices to make them determine to erect
> permanent protections against their use again. ... [T]hey
> must have felt that the protections to individual rights
> provided by the traditions of acting as honourable men
> were quite sufficient for a civilised society.[11]

The 1944 referendum

The issue of the adequacy of the Australian Constitution's coverage of human rights re-emerged during the Second World War in the context of the Commonwealth Government's powers to manage post-war reconstruction. At the urging of the Commonwealth Attorney-General, Dr H V Evatt, a Constitutional Convention in 1942 proposed the insertion in the Constitution of federal legislative power over the 'four freedoms' articulated by US President Franklin D Roosevelt in 1941: freedom of speech and expression; religious freedom; freedom from want; and freedom from fear. The Constitution Alteration (War Aims and Reconstruction) Bill 1942 sought to give the Commonwealth Parliament 'full power' to legislate to guarantee these rights as well as power over other aspects of reconstruction. The Bill was ultimately not put to a referendum because of the war.

In 1944, the Labor government introduced similar referendum legislation to amend the Constitution to extend the centralised planning powers of a wartime administration into the post-war period in order to allow social reform and restrict the monopoly powers of the banks, although the legislation omitted Roosevelt's four freedoms. The *Constitution Alteration (Post-War Reconstruction and Democratic Rights) 1944* aimed to give the Commonwealth Parliament the power to legislate over fourteen specific areas, including health and family allowances, and Aboriginal people for five years. A provision preventing State and Commonwealth governments from abridging freedom of speech was inserted in order to mollify those who feared that the Labor government might impose a socialist program. The proposed constitutional amendments also extended the guarantee of religious tolerance in s. 116 to the States. There were various arguments raised against the rights amendments, including concerns about the restriction of State powers.[12] The referendum was lost decisively, managing only a slim majority in two States, South Australia and Western Australia.

1959 Joint Committee on Constitutional Review

In 1959, a Parliamentary Joint Committee was established to review the functions and powers of the Commonwealth Parliament in light of changes to the electoral system and High Court decisions on interstate trade. The international movement for civil rights was gaining momentum at this time, and the Committee was strongly lobbied to endorse an entrenched bill of rights. However, the Committee did not perceive such a need, arguing that the absence of an entrenched bill of rights 'had not prevented the rule of law from characterising the Australian way of life',[13] and concluding that democratic elections and the principle of responsible government were sufficient to secure the civil liberties of Australians.[14]

Human Rights Bill 1973

It took almost another 30 years, and the election of a Labor government in 1972, for Australian political debate to return to the protection of human rights. From the early 1960s there were moves within the Labor Party to incorporate into the party platform commitments to enact legislation at Commonwealth and State levels for the protection of civil liberties, and the 1967 platform included a commitment to a constitutional amendment that would protect fundamental civil rights and liberties.[15] In 1969 this section of the platform was rewritten to provide a more detailed plan which included constitutional amendment, Commonwealth and State human rights legislation, and implementation of international human rights treaties.[16] The Labor Party made a campaign promise in 1972 that Australia would become a party to the two major United Nations (UN) human rights treaties, the International Covenant on Economic, Social and Cultural Rights (ICESCR) and the International Covenant on Civil and Political Rights (ICCPR), both adopted in 1966. Shortly after the election of the Whitlam Labor government in 1972, Australia signed both treaties and in 1973 the Commonwealth Government introduced a Human Rights Bill into Parliament in order to fulfil its obligations under the ICCPR. In the second reading speech on the Bill, Attorney-General Senator Lionel Murphy described his ultimate goal as the amendment of the Australian Constitution to provide for individual liberties, and suggested that the legislation was a prelude to this.[17]

The Human Rights Bill 1973 defined fundamental rights and freedoms in terms virtually identical to the ICCPR. This was important because the constitutionality of the legislation was seen as depending at least in part on its being an exercise of the power to legislate with respect to external affairs. It included individual rights to non-discrimination; equal protection of laws; freedom of thought, expression and movement; the right to vote; the right to privacy and to certain procedural rights. The draft legislation applied to both Commonwealth and State governments and also covered private actions. It provided that Commonwealth laws inconsistent with the defined rights would be inoperative unless they contained an express term that they were to operate notwithstanding the Human Rights Bill. State laws inconsistent with the Bill would have been rendered invalid through the operation of s. 109 of the Constitution, which provides for the supremacy of Commonwealth law.

The Human Rights Bill was to be enforced through the office of the Australian Human Rights Commissioner. The Commissioner could investigate actual or imminent claims of breaches of rights, prompted by a complaint or on the Commissioner's own initiative. The Commissioner could secure a settlement of the complaint or bring an action against the offender in the Australian Industrial Court. An individual could also bring a court action directly. The Court had the power to make a declaration that a particular action violated the legislation and it could grant a variety of remedies: an injunction to prevent the action continuing; an order directing a defendant to do a compensatory act; an order cancelling a contract or setting aside a judgment, quashing a conviction or directing a new trial; and the award of damages for any loss, humiliation or injury. The Human Rights Bill also provided that any evidence obtained through a breach of human rights would be excluded in judicial proceedings.

Lionel Murphy's Human Rights Bill provoked great controversy. It was attacked as being unnecessary in Australia's parliamentary democracy, and as likely to politicise the judiciary and to undermine States' rights. Doubts were also raised about the validity of the legislation because the ICCPR, on which the legislation was based, had not yet come into force (it was to do so in 1976). The Bill lapsed with the prorogation of Parliament in early 1974 and was not reintroduced in the new parliamentary session.

The *Human Rights Commission Act 1981*

The Liberal-National Party Coalition returned to power in 1975 and remained in government until 1982. In the course of its term, the Fraser government ratified the two human rights covenants that its predecessor had signed – the ICESCR in 1976 and the ICCPR in 1980. When, in 1979, Prime Minister Malcolm

Fraser was asked whether his government would use the Constitution's external affairs power to implement the ICCPR through a bill of rights, he responded that the proposal 'not only raises some serious legal and constitutional problems but also is at odds with [my] philosophy and policy ... to work in harmony and cooperation with the States, and also in a way that protects the basic rights of the States to the extent that that is possible'.[18] The Fraser government insisted that there was no need for a comprehensive bill of rights to implement the ICCPR on the grounds that 'having regard to the existence of such safeguards as the common law, statutory and procedural remedies ... the system of representative and responsible government, the rule of law, the independence of the judiciary and the freedom of the press, Australia is already in substantial conformity with the Covenant'.[19]

To deal with the few areas it conceded did require attention, the government drew up legislation that created remedies for breaches of rights recognised in human rights treaties. After two false starts, the government enacted the *Human Rights Commission Act 1981* (Cwlth).[20] The legislation provided administrative remedies for violations of some internationally recognised rights by the Commonwealth Government. The legislation created a Human Rights Commission and authorised it to examine Commonwealth laws for consistency with international human rights standards. The Commission was empowered to investigate alleged violations of international human rights and could also receive complaints, but its ultimate sanction was to report the result of its investigations to the Commonwealth Parliament. The Opposition Labor Party criticised the Act as a 'toothless tiger' and called for replacement of the legislation by a judicially enforceable bill of rights.[21]

Labor bills of rights proposals in the 1980s

After the election of the Hawke Labor government in 1983, two further attempts were made to devise an Australian bill of rights. Attorney-General Senator Gareth Evans announced in July 1983 that he would introduce a national bill of rights, first as a legislative measure and later as a constitutional amendment. A draft bill was circulated in early 1984. Senator Evans described his proposal as a general translation of the ICCPR into Australian law. The legislation was designed to differ from the Murphy Human Rights Bill, which the Attorney-General described as 'just too vague and far-reaching'.[22] The Australian Bill of Rights Bill required the interpretation of ambiguous provisions of Commonwealth and State legislation in a manner that promoted human rights. The protected rights were declared to have the status of Commonwealth law, which meant that they would prevail over prior federal legislation and, by virtue of s. 109 of the Constitution, over all prior and subsequent State legislation inconsistent with them. The Bill provided that subsequent Commonwealth legislation could declare that its provisions were to operate notwithstanding the Bill of Rights. The draft Bill also empowered the Human Rights Commission to investigate complaints about State or Commonwealth governmental actions apparently violating the Bill of Rights, and to resolve complaints through conciliation, settlement or reporting to Parliament.

The Attorney-General described the draft law as 'a shield not a sword' with respect to the protection of rights.[23] The legislation did not allow any direct challenge to laws by a person affected by them. It was possible, however, to seek a declaration in the Federal Court that a particular law was inconsistent with the Bill of Rights and was therefore repealed or inoperative, as long as the person challenging the law was not a party to proceedings arising under the impugned legislation. A strong attack was made on the proposals, particularly by the Premier of Western Australia, Brian Burke, on the basis that the law would diminish State legislative power. Queensland Premier Joh Bjelke-Petersen also argued that the legislation would undermine the federal system and 'advance the cause of centralism by light years'.[24]

An early federal election was called in December 1984 and the Labor government lost the appetite for this controversial legislative project.

In April 1985, the Senate referred to its Standing Committee on Constitutional and Legal Affairs the task of inquiring into the 'desirability, feasibility and possible content of a national Bill of Rights for Australia'. The Committee produced an 'Exposure Report' in November 1985, endorsing the idea of a statutory bill of rights,[25] but its deliberations had been overtaken by the introduction of a revised draft bill of rights into Parliament the month before by Attorney-General Lionel Bowen.[26] Bowen's draft legislation was narrower still than the Evans Bill, applying only to Commonwealth laws and excluding all State laws from its scope. The Bill was passed by the House of Representatives, but came to grief in the Senate – attacked by the Australian Democrats for being ineffectual and by others opposed to a bill of rights.[27] Opposition also came from within the Labor Party, particularly from Western Australian Premier Brian Burke, and the Bill was withdrawn in 1986.[28] The Commonwealth Parliament then enacted the *Human Rights and Equal Opportunity Commission Act 1986* to replace the *Human Rights Commission Act 1981*, which expired after five years. The 1986 legislation is discussed further below.

The 1988 referendum

The Labor government set up a Constitutional Commission in December 1985 to report on the revision of the Australian Constitution. One aspect of the review was whether the Constitution adequately protected democratic rights, and an Advisory Committee on Individual and Democratic Rights was established to assist the Commission in its deliberations. The Advisory Committee reported in 1987, making some modest proposals for constitutional amendment to provide a range of guarantees of civil and political rights, derived in large part from the ICCPR.

The Commonwealth Government decided to go to a referendum on the issue of rights before it had received the final report of the Constitutional Commission, in a hasty and politically clumsy bid to achieve constitutional change during the bicentenary of European settlement in Australia.[29] Four groups of amendments were put to the electorate in this 1988 referendum, among which were those contained in the *Constitutional Alteration (Rights and Freedoms) 1988*.[30] These would have extended to the States the existing constitutional right to trial by jury and to freedom of religion. The proposals were defeated by a huge margin, with only 31 per cent of voters approving the rights provisions. In the end, the final report of the Constitutional Commission proposed that a more comprehensive bill of rights be inserted in the Constitution, but all political momentum on the issue had been lost and the recommendations were shelved.

Other proposals

In October 2000, the Australian Democrats released an Australian Bill of Rights Bill for comment. The draft law was based on the ICCPR and the Australian Bill of Rights Bill 1985, but was more extensive in its coverage in that it would have applied to State laws and actions as well as to those of the Commonwealth and Territory governments. It also expressly applied to the common law and to delegated legislation. The Bill, retitled the Parliamentary Charter of Rights and Freedoms Bill, was introduced into the Senate in September 2001 by Democrats Senator Meg Lees.[31] It was subsequently reintroduced into the Senate by Democrats Senator Natasha Stott Despoja in 2005 and 2008. It was not passed in 2005, but as at 30 June 2008 was still before the Senate.[32]

In 2005, a community-based campaign for a Human Rights Act for Australia was initiated with the sponsorship of the independent online magazine *New Matilda*.[33] The campaign, chaired by Susan Ryan AO, a former Minister in the Hawke Labor government, produced a model Human Rights Bill which was formally launched for consultation in October 2005. The *New Matilda* Bill was drafted by Professor Spencer Zifcak, with assistance from other academics and legal practitioners, and included rights drawn from a range of international human rights instruments including the ICCPR and the ICESCR. The draft Bill became a focus for bills of rights supporters during the final years of the Howard government (1996–2007) and stimulated considerable debate. From 2008, the campaign was relaunched as the Human Rights Act for Australia Campaign, independent of *New Matilda*.[34]

The Australian bill of rights debate

The debate over the issue of protecting human rights has waxed and waned in Australian political life over the last century, but two themes have been strikingly consistent throughout. The first is concern over encroachment on States' legislative powers and the consequent undermining of the federal system. The 19th century constitutional drafters were anxious that a guarantee of equal protection of the law would, for example, invalidate State laws that restricted the employment of Asian workers. The bills of rights proposals of the 1970s and 1980s were defeated in large part through successful campaigns based on the slogan of 'States' rights'. The 1988 referendum proposals were similarly attacked as undermining States' rights. Again, in a national debate in 2000 over whether Northern Territory and Western Australian mandatory sentencing laws breached human rights, the major political parties agreed that the Commonwealth Government should not intervene to overturn State and Territory legislation. Prime Minister John Howard, for example, said that such action, while legally possible, would 'upset the federal balance'.[35]

A second major theme in discussions of bills of rights has been the compatibility of such instruments with Australian parliamentary democracy. At Federation, the drafters were confident that the traditions of civilised peoples would ensure that Australian legislatures acted honourably. Alexander Cockburn, for example, argued that the insertion of constitutional guarantees of rights would be an admission of their necessity. They were appropriate, said Cockburn, only in the constitution of a 'savage race'.[36] This type of argument is still heard today, but more often it is couched in terms of the superior capacity of the legislature, compared to the judiciary, to protect human rights. Bills of rights in any form are presented as a fundamentally undemocratic mechanism that will disrupt, perhaps even undermine, the political process. The idea is that parliamentary sovereignty and the tradition of responsible government in Australia – the convention that the executive branch of government is kept in check by being answerable to the elected legislature – are adequate to protect individual rights. Prime Minister Sir Robert Menzies summarised this argument in 1967:

> Should a Minister do something which is thought to violate fundamental human freedom he can be promptly brought to account in Parliament. If his Government supports him, the Government may be attacked, and, if necessary defeated. And if that … leads to a new General Election, the people will express their judgement at the polling booths. In short, responsible government in a democracy is regarded by [Australians] as the ultimate guarantee of justice and individual rights.[37]

The modern-day versions of this critique of bills of rights are discussed in more detail in chapter 3.

Since the early 1970s, a further dimension of the debate about Australian bills of rights has been the influence of the development of international human rights law. International treaties on human rights have provided a focus for activism and political action directed to advocating Australian ratification of these treaties and their implementation in domestic law. The limitations of Commonwealth legislative power have meant that the power to legislate with respect to external affairs – which the High Court has confirmed to include the implementation of international treaty obligations – has been an important factor in the design of the various proposed Commonwealth bills of rights. The catalogues of rights put forward at the Commonwealth level (and in a number of the States) have drawn on, and in some cases essentially reproduced, the rights in the ICCPR. The rights contained in the ICESCR, by contrast, have been largely ignored.

Protecting human rights in Australia

The current system for the protection of human rights in Australia relies on an intricate patchwork of international, Commonwealth and State laws and institutional arrangements. These include rights under human rights treaties; the federal structure (which involves the distribution and thus diffusion of power between the Commonwealth and States); a limited number of express or implied constitutional guarantees at both Commonwealth and State level; legislation explicitly protecting human rights (such as anti-discrimination legislation, privacy legislation, criminal procedural and evidence laws); legislation, policies and programs that in substance protect or promote human rights although not specifically designated as 'human rights legislation' (including extensive systems of Commonwealth and State administrative law); common law doctrines; a system of independent courts and tribunals; and parliamentary and administrative processes promoting the enjoyment of human rights (such as parliamentary scrutiny committees, ombudsmen and other institutions). We cannot give a complete account of these laws, institutions, programs and practices here,[38] but focus instead on the way in which international human rights standards are implemented in Australian law. The overall picture is of limited and selective incorporation of human rights into the Australian legal system.

International remedies

There are a number of avenues for seeking redress before international human rights bodies where a remedy is not available within the Australian legal system. Under the International Convention on the Elimination of All Forms of Racial Discrimination 1965 (CERD),[39] the Optional Protocol to the ICCPR, and the Convention against Torture 1984 (CAT),[40] Australia has accepted procedures which allow individuals who claim that their rights under these treaties have been violated to bring the case before the responsible UN human rights treaty body.[41] This can only be done if the complainant has first exhausted all available remedies within the Australian legal system. The decisions adopted by the various committees are not formally binding as a matter of international law, and do not automatically have effect within the Australian legal system. Nevertheless, these decisions carry considerable weight and states parties to the treaties are obliged to give them appropriate consideration in good faith, since they are the pronouncements of specific deliberative bodies with considerable expertise in relation to the binding legal obligations which the state has undertaken.

A number of cases have been brought against Australia under the various individual communication procedures.[42] As at 30 June 2008, the complainants have been successful on the merits in 19 cases out of a total of 69.[43] The first case taken to the UN human rights treaty bodies was *Toonen v Australia* in 1992.[44] This was a challenge to provisions in the *Criminal Code Act 1924* (Tas) that made homosexual acts between consenting adult males illegal, on the ground that these provisions violated the right not to be subjected to arbitrary interference with one's privacy under article 17 of the ICCPR. The UN Human Rights Committee upheld the challenge, with the support of the Labor government of Prime Minister Paul Keating. When the Tasmanian Government refused to amend the offending legislation, the Commonwealth Government enacted the *Human Rights (Sexual Conduct) Act 1994* to overturn the Tasmanian legislation.

However, the constructive response to international criticism in *Toonen* was to prove atypical, since the subsequent Coalition government of Prime Minister John Howard regularly rejected, or ignored, the views of human rights treaty bodies, particularly in relation to decisions on matters of immigration law and policy.[45]

Commonwealth legislation

Australia's most extensive explicit legislative implementation of its human rights obligations is in relation to various forms of discrimination.[46] At the Commonwealth level, there are a number of statutes prohibiting discrimination on a range of grounds, including race, colour and ethnic or national origin, sex and pregnancy, disability and age.[47] Some of this legislation explicitly refers to the relevant international standards and incorporates their language. This is because the constitutional validity of the legislation is dependent at least in part on its being a proper exercise of the power of the Commonwealth to legislate with respect to external affairs. The *Racial Discrimination Act 1975* (Cwlth) and the *Sex Discrimination Act 1984* (Cwlth) are examples of the constitutional need for a link to international obligations. In addition to anti-discrimination, there are many other areas in which legislation provides direct protection of human rights. Among the most prominent examples are privacy, data protection and freedom of information legislation.[48]

The principal legislation for the institutional protection of human rights in Australia at the Commonwealth level is the *Human Rights and Equal Opportunity Commission Act 1986* (Cwlth) (HREOC Act), which established the Human Rights and Equal Opportunity Commission (HREOC). HREOC has a number of functions, including research and education on human rights, examining existing and proposed legislation for consistency with human rights, reporting to Parliament on the need for laws or other actions to implement international human rights obligations, and examining Acts or practices of Commonwealth authorities for consistency with human rights.[49] It also has the function of receiving and conciliating complaints under a number of Commonwealth anti-discrimination statutes,[50] and carries out inquiries on human rights matters of public importance. In the HREOC Act, 'human rights' are defined as those rights set out in various human rights instruments appended to or declared under the legislation. These include the ICCPR and the Convention on the Rights of the Child 1989 (CRC),[51] but not other major treaties such as the ICESCR. This means the Commission has no formal power to investigate complaints of violations of the latter treaties.[52] The rights contained in the appended treaties (apart from those relating to race, sex, disability and age discrimination, discussed below) are implemented in an indirect way: the Commission may consider and attempt to conciliate complaints of violations of the various human rights instruments by Commonwealth authorities and, if this is unsuccessful, report to the Attorney-General.[53] Its reports and recommendations have no binding force in law.

HREOC and the individual commissioners have the power to participate in court proceedings that raise human rights issues in a number of circumstances.[54] HREOC itself may seek leave of the court to intervene in judicial proceedings where issues relating to 'human rights',[55] discrimination in employment or occupation,[56] or other issues of discrimination (racial, sex, disability or age)[57] arise, a power it has used to some effect.[58] This power applies to any proceedings, civil or criminal, and to any court.[59] In 1998, an attempt was made to curb HREOC's power to intervene by making its exercise subject to approval by the Commonwealth Attorney-General.[60] This draft legislation was ultimately withdrawn, but it emphasises the vulnerability of the system of human rights protection in Australia. An unsuccessful attempt along the same lines was made in 2003.[61]

In addition to the power HREOC itself has to intervene in cases, each of the individual commissioners[62] has had since 2000 the power to seek leave to participate as an *amicus curiae* ('friend of the court') in proceedings brought before the Federal Court or before a federal magistrate under the Commonwealth's *Racial Discrimination Act 1975*, *Sex Discrimination Act 1984*, *Disability Discrimination Act 1992* and *Age Discrimination Act 2004*.[63]

The success of HREOC in bringing human rights issues into the public consciousness over the years has been due to the integrity and independence of its presidents and commissioners, rather than the mandate granted by the legislation. More often than not, however, HREOC's recommendations to Parliament to remedy breaches of human rights have been ignored. The hostility with which its 1997 report into the 'stolen generation' of Aboriginal children was treated by the Howard government illustrates the weakness of our current system in responding to major human rights issues.[64]

State and Territory human rights legislation

The Australian States and Territories have extensive legislative protection against discrimination, which in most States covers a wider range of grounds than Commonwealth anti-discrimination statutes.[65] The State legislation also establishes administrative bodies similar in a number of respects to HREOC and, in some cases, specialised tribunals to consider cases under anti-discrimination legislation. The jurisdiction of those equal opportunity commissions (and tribunals) has until recently largely focused on discrimination, but with the advent of human rights legislation in the ACT and Victoria, the commissions in those States now have an expanded jurisdiction to monitor human rights. Each of the States and Territories also has institutions such as privacy commissioners, ombudsmen and other complaint-handling bodies which provide some oversight of government administration and aspects of the private sector's activities. Some States and Territories have also established specific children's commissioners with investigative and reporting powers.[66]

State and Territory bills of rights

We have noted above that an enduring theme in debates about an Australian bill of rights has been that such an instrument would impinge on State legislative powers. The use of the word 'rights' in the successful slogan 'States' rights' has obscured the fact that the claim is for unfettered governmental power over the human rights of people. In this sense, State rights have often been pitted against the protection of human rights in the debate. It is striking, therefore, that Australia's States and Territories have now become leaders in human rights protection.

Proposals for formal State and Territory protection of human rights date back to a Queensland initiative in 1959,[67] with a number of campaigns mounted during the 1980s and 1990s. All were unsuccessful. They included a 1987 proposal for a Victorian Declaration of Rights and Freedoms,[68] a 1993 discussion of an ACT Bill of Rights,[69] and a 1995 Northern Territory Legislative Assembly discussion paper on a bill of rights.[70] In 1998 the Queensland Parliament's Legal, Constitutional and Administrative Review Committee held an inquiry into whether that State should adopt a bill of rights. The inquiry recommended against such an innovation and proposed instead an educational campaign on human rights.[71] In 2001, the NSW Parliament's Standing Committee on Law and Justice conducted an inquiry into whether New South Wales should adopt a bill of rights and also recommended against such a move.[72]

It was not until 2004 that the first breach appeared in the general Australian scepticism about the value of formal protection of rights. The background to and structure of the two existing State and Territory bills of rights, the *Human Rights Act 2004* (ACT) and the *Charter of Human Rights and Responsibilities Act 2006* (Vic), are discussed in chapters 4 and 5.

Political scientist Brian Galligan has pointed out that the positions of Australia's major political parties with respect to a bill of rights are puzzling at first sight.[73] The Australian Labor Party traditionally sought to strengthen central governmental power to develop collective social policy, while the Liberal Party supported individual autonomy and the federal system. These traditions suggest that Labor should oppose restrictions on governmental power and that the Liberal Party should support individual rights, but this has not proved to be the case. Labor's interest in a bill of rights emerged in the 1960s as a result of the work of reformist and internationally-attuned politicians such as Gough Whitlam, Lionel Murphy and Don Dunstan, frustrated by the lengthy period of conservative government and responding to a changing constituency.[74]

Attitudes to an Australian bill of rights are not determined solely, however, by political allegiance. While Liberal-National coalitions have generally disparaged calls for better human rights protection through a bill of rights, individual members have occasionally shown an interest. Indeed, one of the earliest calls for a State bill of rights was made by Country-National Premier Frank Nicklin in Queensland in 1959.[75] In 2005, federal Liberal parliamentarian Steven Ciobo argued for a statutory bill of rights to balance tough anti-terrorism laws.[76] On the other hand, Labor politicians such as former NSW Premier Bob Carr and NSW Attorney-General John Hatzistergos have been strong critics of the idea of a bill of rights, on the basis that they would reduce parliamentary power.[77] While still maintaining a commitment 'to adhere to Australia's international human rights obligations and [to] seek to have them incorporated into the domestic law of Australia and taken into account in administrative decision making',[78] the Labor Party platform's 40-year commitment to a bill of rights was amended in 2007 to one to consult with the community on the issue.[79]

It is clear that the unpredictable politics of bills of rights in Australia are linked to different understandings of democracy.

In the next chapter, we turn to the substance of the debate about the value of bills of rights to trace various accounts of democracy and its relationship to human rights.

3

Bills of rights: models and controversies

We saw in chapter 2 that discussions about an Australian bill of rights have a long history, dating back to Federation. They have highlighted a national scepticism about the need for formal protection of rights – the sense that such an innovation is unnecessary in our generally peaceful and democratic country. Since the 1970s, debates about bills of rights have centred on Australia's implementation of our human rights treaty obligations, and attempts to translate human rights treaty provisions into the national legal system have encountered sustained opposition. As we discuss in chapters 4 and 5, the States and Territories have now taken the lead in this area. In this chapter, we first consider various models of formal protection of human rights that have informed the debate, then catalogue the major arguments marshalled by proponents and opponents of Australian bills of rights and assess them in light of the way such documents have worked in practice.

Models for an Australian bill of rights

Discussions about the desirability of a 'bill of rights' often proceed on the assumption that there is an agreed definition of what the term means. There are, however, many instruments that could be described in this way. As international human rights expert Philip Alston notes:

> the term is applied in practice to a wide range of documents, from short manifestos detached from any particular institutional arrangements, through to detailed, constitutionally entrenched and legally enforceable charters. It is also used in reference to bundles (or even tiny packages) of norms or principles which are almost nowhere formally stated to constitute such a bill, but which are more typically to be found in constitutional chapters – of greatly varying length and content – under a heading such as 'fundamental rights'. The term is also often used in relation to much more general provisions which, in the view of the observer, are said to function in effect as such bills of rights. The philosophies underlying the different bills are diverse and their significance in practice varies from being unadulterated window-dressing to being the yardstick against which every governmental move is measured.[1]

A number of rights documents have been put forward as candidates for Australian bills of rights. These range from constitutionally entrenched charters to legislative bills of rights to non-binding, symbolic statements of rights. This section provides an overview of the bills of rights from comparable overseas jurisdictions that are most commonly referred to in Australian debates on the subject.

Constitutionally entrenched bills of rights

United States Bill of Rights (1791)

The United States Bill of Rights constitutes the first ten amendments to the United States Constitution, adopted in 1791, including rights to freedom of expression, due process of law, freedom from unreasonable search and seizure, and the right not to incriminate oneself. The guarantees in the Bill of Rights and the Constitution itself have been supplemented by a number of later amendments that contain important human rights guarantees, including the 13th Amendment (1865), which abolished slavery, the 14th Amendment (1868), which guaranteed equal protection of the laws to all citizens of the country, and the 15th (1870) and 19th (1919) Amendments, which guaranteed the right to vote to all citizens without regard to race or sex, respectively.

The provisions of the Constitution and the Bill of Rights are entrenched, in the sense that a normal Act of the Congress cannot override them. The courts (with the Supreme Court of the United States as the ultimate arbiter) may declare legislation invalid if the Court considers that it violates the guarantees of the Constitution. Such interpretations are binding and can only be overridden by constitutional amendment or if the Supreme Court itself changes its views. The adoption of a constitutional amendment requires that a demanding procedure be followed.[2] The power of judicial interpretation of the Bill of Rights has led to considerable political scrutiny of judicial appointments and the judiciary is regularly criticised for usurping legislative functions in the context of protection of rights.[3]

Canadian Charter of Rights and Freedoms (1982)

The Canadian Charter of Rights and Freedoms was adopted in 1982 as part of the revised Canadian Constitution that was 'patriated' from the United Kingdom to Canada. The Charter covers various categories of rights such as 'fundamental freedoms', including the rights to freedom of conscience and religion; 'democratic rights', including the right to vote; 'mobility rights'; 'legal rights' and 'official language rights'. The Charter also affirms the existing rights of Canada's Indigenous peoples. Charter rights and freedoms are made subject 'to such reasonable limits prescribed by law as can be demonstrably justified in a free and democratic society' (s. 1). The Charter is an entrenched bill of rights, with the courts given the power to declare legislation unconstitutional on the ground that it involves impermissible restrictions on the enjoyment of rights guaranteed by the Charter. It is subject to the Constitution's amendment procedure.[4] However, s. 33 of the Charter (known as the 'notwithstanding clause') provides for the possibility of limited legislative override of its provisions: the federal legislature or a provincial legislature may expressly provide that a law will operate *notwithstanding* its inconsistency with a provision of the Charter, an exclusion that operates for five years and may be renewed. Since the adoption of the Charter, apart from its initial use by Quebec in the period 1982–87 when the provincial legislature inserted an override clause into all its laws, the override clause has been used on only a handful of occasions, in each case by provincial legislatures.[5]

South African Bill of Rights (1996)

The South African Constitution adopted in 1996 (which replaced a 1994 interim Constitution) includes a bill of rights. The Bill of Rights covers most internationally recognised civil and political rights as well as economic, social and cultural rights such as the rights to housing, a healthy environment, health care, food, water and security. The protected rights are subject to limitations that are reasonable and justifiable in an open and democratic society based on human dignity, equality and freedom (s. 36). The South African Bill of Rights applies not only to all government institutions, but also in private relations (s. 8). The Bill of Rights is interpreted by the courts, with the Constitutional Court of South Africa the final authority. The Bill of Rights is entrenched in the sense that it can only be amended by a special procedure.[6]

Hybrid constitutional/statutory bills of rights

Hong Kong's bill of rights regime (1991)

In 1991 the UK government enacted a bill of rights for Hong Kong.[7] This was part of the effort to build confidence in the lead-up to the colony's return to the People's Republic of

China following the traumatic suppression of the pro-democracy movement in China in 1989. The legal regime had two elements. The first was the Hong Kong Bill of Rights Ordinance 1991 (BORO), an ordinary statute that requires prior legislation to be construed consistently with the BORO if it admits of such a construction; if earlier legislation cannot be given such a construction, it is repealed to the extent of the inconsistency (s. 3). The BORO also provides that future legislation should, 'to the extent that it admits of such a construction, be construed so as to be consistent with the International Covenant on Civil and Political Rights [ICCPR] as applied to Hong Kong' (s. 4). The second element was constitutional, and involved the insertion of a provision in Hong Kong's colonial constitutional instrument, the Letters Patent, which had the effect that any legislation enacted after 8 June 1991 which was inconsistent with the ICCPR as applied to Hong Kong would be invalid. With the resumption of Chinese sovereignty over Hong Kong on 1 July 1997, the BORO continued on (with some modifications), and the Letters Patent were replaced by a new constitutional document, the Basic Law of the Hong Kong Special Administrative Region of the People's Republic of China (Basic Law). Chapter III of the Basic Law contains a number of specific rights guarantees, and also provides in article 39:

> The provisions of the International Covenant on Civil
> and Political Rights, the International Covenant on
> Economic, Social and Cultural Rights [ICESCR],
> and international labour conventions as applied
> to Hong Kong shall remain in force and shall be
> implemented through the laws of the Hong Kong Special
> Administrative Region.
>
> The rights and freedoms enjoyed by Hong Kong
> residents shall not be restricted unless as prescribed by
> law. Such restrictions shall not contravene the provisions
> of the preceding paragraph of this Article.

Thus, Hong Kong, a common law system, has had a constitutionally entrenched bill of rights for more than 25 years; since 1997, both the ICCPR and the ICESCR have been incorporated as a justiciable part of Hong Kong law. The case law on the BORO and the Basic Law comprises the largest body of English-language jurisprudence interpreting and applying the ICCPR and the ICESCR in any national jurisdiction.

Non-entrenched, statutory bills of rights

New Zealand Bill of Rights Act (1990)

New Zealand adopted a statutory statement of rights, the New Zealand Bill of Rights Act 1990 (NZ BORA), after an unsuccessful attempt to introduce a constitutional bill of rights.[8] It covers a range of civil and political rights (mainly drawn from the ICCPR) and applies to acts of the legislature, Executive and judiciary as well as those of persons performing a public function (s. 3). As an ordinary statute of the Parliament, it requires the courts to interpret laws in accordance with the Bill of Rights if that is possible (s. 6). However, if a statute cannot be interpreted in a human rights-consistent manner, the Act does not confer power on the courts to declare the impugned statute incompatible with human rights[9] or to hold the offending provisions invalid. (However, the Human Rights Review Tribunal and, on appeal, the courts may issue declarations of inconsistency where a statute is consistent with the equality guarantees contained in s. 19 of the Bill of Rights Act.[10]) The Attorney-General is required to inform Parliament when presenting legislation that is inconsistent with the Bill of Rights Act (s. 7), but Parliament retains the power to pass legislation inconsistent with the Bill of Rights, and also to amend or repeal the Act itself.

United Kingdom Human Rights Act (1998)

In 1998, the United Kingdom Parliament enacted the Human Rights Act 1998 (UK HRA), a statutory charter of rights based on the European Convention on Human Rights 1950. It came into force two years later, in order to allow time for all branches of government to become familiar with it. The UK HRA protects the rights set out in the European Convention, which generally mirror those in the ICCPR. The Convention rights protected include the rights to life (art. 2), liberty and security (art. 5), and a fair trial (art. 6); freedoms of thought, expression (art. 10), conscience and religion (art. 9), assembly and association (art. 11); prohibition of torture (art. 3), slavery (art. 4) and discrimination (art. 14); the right to respect for private life (art. 8) and the right to marry (art. 12). The UK HRA also incorporates some of the rights in the later Protocols to the European Convention, namely the prohibition of the death penalty (Protocol No 6) and the right to free elections and limited rights to property and education (Protocol No 1).

The UK HRA is an ordinary statute and can be amended or repealed by the Parliament like any other law. It requires courts 'so far as it is possible to do so' to interpret legislation 'in a way that is compatible with the Convention rights' (s. 3(1)). If it is not possible to do this, the Act empowers certain superior courts to make a formal declaration of incompatibility (s. 4), although the courts do not have the power to declare inconsistent legislation invalid. Courts can, however, refuse to give effect to rights-incompatible subordinate legislation, unless the offending provision is required by its parent statute (s. 3(2)(c)). In the case of a declaration of incompatibility, the government may take advantage of a special, expedited procedure to amend the offending legislation (s. 10), introduce amending legislation in the normal way, or decide to take no action. When a Bill is presented to Parliament, the responsible Minister must make a statement of human rights-compatibility or indicate that the government intends to enact a law notwithstanding its incompatibility with human rights (s. 19). The Act imposes a specific obligation on public authorities to comply with the Convention rights, and makes inconsistent conduct unlawful unless it is specifically authorised by legislation (s. 6). The definition of public authority extends to other entities 'whose functions are functions of a public nature', and includes the courts, but not the Parliament (s. 6(3)). A person who is the victim of an unlawful act by a public authority may bring legal proceedings based on the claimed illegality, and may be awarded damages or other remedies under the same criteria as apply in the European Court of Human Rights (ss. 7, 8).

Non-binding statements of rights

A more limited model of a bill of rights is one that declares a set of human rights as aspirational principles for legislation or public policy, without an explicit mechanism of enforcement or any binding effect on the courts or legislature. Queensland's *Legislative Standards Act 1992* is one example of a non-binding statement of rights, as it includes a set of fundamental legislative principles (including reference to appropriate regard for rights and liberties (s. 4)), but provides only that the Office of the Parliamentary Counsel should 'provide advice' to the relevant Minister or instructing Member of Parliament as to the application of those principles in the drafting of legislation (ss. 7(g)(ii), (h)(ii)).

Creating dialogue through bills of rights

The recent history of human rights in national legal systems reveals a movement away from the US-style bill of rights, which gives significant power to the judiciary, toward a model that preserves the role of the legislature in deciding how best to protect human rights. These modern creations are sometimes termed 'dialogue' bills of rights, as they encourage a 'conversation' about rights protection between the Executive government, the parliament and the judiciary. The dialogue metaphor was first introduced by constitutional lawyers Peter Hogg and Allison Bushell in relation to the Canadian Charter,[11] and was in part an attempt to respond to the criticism that judicial review under the Charter was anti-democratic (or at least anti-majoritarian).[12]

The notion of 'dialogue' has generated extensive academic and judicial discussion in Canada about what is meant by the term, whether the practice under the Charter involves genuine dialogue, and whether the courts' views of the meaning of the Charter still supersede the interpretations of the other branches of government, among other issues.[13]

The original meaning of the idea of dialogue was that 'the court decisions in Charter cases usually left room for a legislative response, and usually received a legislative response'.[14] The legislature could still achieve its original purpose if it disagreed with the court by pursuing its goals in another manner that was consistent with the Charter.[15] The Canadian legislative response to the courts varied; it might involve the use of the 'notwithstanding clause' in s. 33 of the Charter to override the Supreme Court of Canada's interpretation (though this has been used only once in response to a judicial decision),[16] or the repeal or amendment of an offending provision, the redrafting of a statute to achieve the original goals in a manner consistent with the Charter, or simply accepting the court's decision. On the dialogue theory, the final policy and legislative outcome was the result of an institutional interaction or conversation about human rights between the judiciary, the Executive and the legislature, rather than the view of just one branch of government. However, some critics have taken apparent legislative acquiescence in court decisions as a sign that in those cases the Charter has generated judicial 'monologue' or acts of 'ventriloquism', rather than a dialogue.[17]

The drafters of statutory bills of rights such as the NZ BORA and the UK HRA have taken up the dialogue metaphor to emphasise that, under these statutes, the judiciary is not the final or even the major arbiter of whether particular laws or policies are consistent with human rights guarantees, but a participant (admittedly an influential one) in a public debate over the implementation of human rights in particular contexts.[18] There is, of course, an important difference between the constitutional context of the Canadian debate and the UK, New Zealand and Australian instances. Under statutory bills of rights, the courts do not have the power to declare statutes unconstitutional or repealed; they can do no more than interpret them in a human rights-consistent manner or, if that is not possible, state that they are not able to do so. The issue then goes back to the Executive and the legislature to decide whether, and how, to respond to these findings of the courts.

The NZ BORA, the UK HRA and their Australian counterparts, the *Human Rights Act 2004* (ACT) (ACT HRA) and *Charter of Human Rights and Responsibilities Act 2006* (Vic) (Victorian Charter) effectively tip the balance further in favour of the legislature and enhance the importance of its role in the institutional dialogue. In Canada, once the Supreme Court has held that a statute is inconsistent with the Charter, the legislation will be of no effect. Thus, in order to pursue its policy objectives, the legislature must take positive action by introducing new provisions or by taking advantage of the override provision. However, under the statutory bills of rights noted here, the issuing of a declaration of incompatibility or a formal judicial statement to similar effect does not of itself invalidate the legislation. Accordingly, if the legislature does nothing, its policy choice and the legislation will stand. If it chooses to respond in a positive way to the views of the court, whether because it is persuaded by the reasoning of the court or for some other reason, there is then clear evidence of dialogue or interaction. After all, dialogue often leads to agreement, and it is no necessary indication of a more genuine or higher level dialogue if it ends in disagreement.[19] The situation is slightly different when a court adopts a rights-consistent interpretation which the legislature considers goes beyond the limits of permissible interpretation; in such a case the legislature will need to take positive action to reverse the effect of such an interpretation.[20]

In the case of the statutory bills of rights, various procedures have been devised to increase the opportunities for all branches of government (and civil society more generally) to give their views on the particular human rights issue being considered. The requirement of a compatibility statement when legislation is introduced, the role of scrutiny of bills committees and the response of government to their analyses, the views of the courts and the requirement that the Executive respond to declarations of incompatibility all provide possibilities for informed discussion and debate on the human rights dimensions of proposed policies.[21] These bills of rights recognise that views on the determination of rights disputes will frequently and reasonably differ, and that allowing different voices and interests to be heard will lead to better legislation and decision-making.[22] The supporters of statutory bills of rights maintain that, notwithstanding the attention that might be paid to the views of the judiciary, the role of the democratically elected legislature to fashion its policies is maintained by these models.

Themes in the Australian debate

In this section, we survey the major themes in the often passionate debate about whether Australia should adopt a bill or charter of rights. While some of the claimed advantages and drawbacks of a bill of rights inhere in any of the models that have been proposed, an evaluation of the desirability of a bill of rights depends in part on the form and contents of a proposed instrument. For example, arguments may differ according to whether the proposal is for constitutional entrenchment, whether it allows courts to declare legislation invalid or provide other remedies, and whether it guarantees economic and social rights as well as civil and political rights. Until recently, much of the criticism of bills of rights in the common law world has been directed against the type of constitutionally entrenched document typified by the US Bill of Rights. This has been so notwithstanding the increasing prominence of the legislative dialogue model bill of rights discussed above, which provides a greater role for the legislature in deciding how human rights are to be interpreted and prioritised.

The operation of bills of rights in a number of comparable common law jurisdictions, as well as the early experience under Territory and State human rights legislation in Australia, provide useful evidence to test the claims of both proponents and opponents, and to move the Australian debate beyond its so far rather hackneyed course.

The adequacy of human rights protection in Australia

An important initial issue is how well human rights are already protected in Australia.[23] Clearly, if Australia has a successful system already in place, the impetus for change is lessened. Thus, in 2000, Prime Minister John Howard claimed that in Australia, 'the quality of democracy and the transparency and integrity of our judicial system, the freedom of our press, the freedom people have from fear of political affiliation ... are gold-plated',[24] and Commonwealth Attorney-General Daryl Williams asserted that Australia's protection of human rights was 'second to none'.[25] Neither politician was in favour of a bill of rights. Other opponents agree, contending there are no major human rights issues that need to be addressed through the adoption of a bill of rights.[26] Indeed, some opponents identify the potential for social division through bills of rights in what they see as an unjustifiable focus on the rights of minority or marginalised groups.[27]

Another argument is that a bill of rights is unlikely to have any real effect on complex social issues or have the capacity to solve human rights problems. References to the guarantees of rights provided in the former Soviet Constitution and the Zimbabwean Constitution are often used to emphasise that the existence of a bill of rights is an unreliable indicator of the level of human rights protection in a society.[28] Advocates of a bill of rights respond that it is not a bill of rights in isolation that provides protection, but a bill of rights embedded in the existing system of institutions and protections.[29]

Proponents of bills of rights further argue that the present system for the legal protection of human rights at Commonwealth and State levels in Australia is piecemeal and unsatisfactory. Not only does this mean that it has developed in an *ad hoc* way – and may therefore not cover areas where rights are violated – but it can also be confusing to members of the community.[30] Many proponents further argue that, quite apart from its fragmented nature, the existing system does not address a range of failures to protect the human rights of members of the community, in particular members of disadvantaged and marginalised groups.[31]

On this analysis, the adoption of a bill of rights would be a positive contribution to addressing such issues, either through changing attitudes in public institutions or by providing legal recourse for human rights violations.[32] The four Australian State and Territory non-parliamentary inquiries into bills of rights held from 2002 to 2007 have all concluded that the existing system of human rights protection, although extensive, is inadequate, and that a coherent statement of human rights principles is required.[33] They have identified significant human rights problems that are not adequately addressed by the legal system.[34] The rights of Indigenous people, refugee applicants and prisoners are often used as examples of such gaps, but there are also clear examples of human rights violations in the treatment of children in care and protection systems, and of the elderly and the mentally ill. Although some supporters of bills of rights regard them as a crucial guarantor of individual rights, others acknowledge that human rights laws operate in specific political, social and cultural contexts, and must be supplemented by effective policies, programs and institutions. Bills of rights are thus one piece of a mosaic of human rights protections.

A related argument put forward by proponents is that the adoption of bills of rights – whether at the local or national level – will improve Australia's implementation of the obligations it has accepted under international human rights treaties.[35] Treaties accepted under international law do not directly become part of Australian law and require legislative implementation. The patchwork-style protection of human rights in Australian law, described in chapter 2, includes partial coverage of many of the rights under the treaties to which the nation is party. The many gaps and inconsistencies in present laws mean they do not provide an accessible or uniform coverage.

The effect of bills of rights on Australia's systems of parliamentary democracy

Perhaps the central issue in the Australian debate about bills or charters of rights is their impact on democratic structures and processes. Do such instruments in effect transfer political decisions from a democratically elected legislature to an unelected, unaccountable and unrepresentative judiciary that has no particular expertise for making such decisions? Advocates of this view tend to place primacy on the accountability provided by the electoral process and the institutions of representative government, and have considerable confidence in their ability to ensure the observance of high standards of human rights.[36] Some bills of rights critics, however, accept that the legislature will not always observe human rights principles. They acknowledge that there are drawbacks to majoritarian democracy, especially if you happen to be a member of a disfavoured or relatively powerless minority, but appear nevertheless to argue that the risk of the occasional majoritarian excess is a small price to pay to preserve the primacy of elected institutions in preference to transferring some of that power to the judiciary.[37]

The response often made to the 'democratic' objection to bills of rights is that it is based on a limited understanding of democracy as comprising a 'simple majoritarianism' or 'crude statistical view' of democracy.[38] Other models of democracy posit a system under which majoritarian political processes are combined with respect for the rights of those who may not be in a position to influence political decisions and who may be vulnerable to excesses of the exercise of that power.[39]

The flipside of the concern that a bill of rights will reduce legislative power is the claim that it will politicise the judiciary. It is contended that the open texture of human rights guarantees affords judges considerable scope to interpret them as they wish, thereby introducing a high level of unpredictability and uncertainty into the field of public policy making.[40] Critics further suggest that the nature of the judiciary is such that the courts are likely to interpret a bill of rights in socially regressive ways.[41] Proponents respond to this criticism by arguing that it is based on a misunderstanding of the nature of judicial activity. Courts are inevitably engaged in decision-making that can have broad policy consequences. Judges regularly decide cases in which the relevant principle is expressed in vague and general terms or make decisions on controversial questions of social policy – for example, on Indigenous land rights or 'wrongful life' actions. On this analysis, the interpretation of human rights guarantees is no different in character to the accepted judicial role in statutory interpretation or the development of the common law.[42]

It is difficult for supporters of a bill of rights to dispute the unrepresentative nature of the Australian judiciary. As of June 2008, for example, only six of 50 Federal Court judges were women, with a total of 26 per cent of female judges and magistrates in the Commonwealth jurisdiction; representation of Indigenous Australians and ethnic minorities in the judiciary has generally been much lower still.[43] Some commentators have pointed out that politicians themselves may not as a group be broadly representative of the community insofar as their backgrounds go.[44] Nevertheless, they tend to be more diverse in background than the judiciary, and they are of course accountable to the people through the electoral process – even if the protection of human rights is rarely a significant electoral issue, and despite the fact that important legislative and policy decisions affecting rights are sometimes made without careful scrutiny of rights issues, or for reasons not directly related to the substantive merits of the rights issues raised by a particular proposal.

Another response to the claim that a bill of rights will shift power from the elected representatives of the people to an unelected judiciary is that, while this criticism may have some bite with respect to entrenched bills of rights supervised by a judiciary with the power to invalidate legislation, statutory models that allow the legislature to override human rights guarantees or to take a different view of the scope of the relevant protections than the courts do, preserve legislative power.[45] The New Zealand, UK, ACT and Victorian bills of rights, for example, are legislative instruments that formally have no greater status than any other law. None of these statutes confers on the courts the power to strike down legislation, and it is open to the legislature to expand, dilute or modify the statutory bill of rights simply by following the procedures normally required for the amendment of laws. However, critics have argued that such statutes in fact acquire a status that is more than that of an ordinary piece of legislation, and that it is politically difficult, if not impossible, to repeal them.[46]

The role of the courts under a statutory bill of rights is to interpret legislation in conformity with designated human rights so far as reasonably possible and, where it is not, to make a reasoned finding that the statute is incompatible with human rights. This finding is then brought to the attention of the legislature, which must consider whether it wishes to amend the law in accordance with the views of the court or to adhere to its previous view that there is no impermissible restriction on the enjoyment of a particular right. In this way, as outlined earlier in this chapter, proponents of statutory bills of rights argue that the sovereignty of the legislature is maintained, the courts do not have a monopoly of interpretation of bills of rights, and the result is a constructive dialogue on rights protection between the various arms of government. The courts do not mandate how the Executive and legislature must respond to their views as expressed in a declaration or statement of incompatibility. In legal expert Conor Gearty's words, the only duty on government with respect to judicial rulings on human rights is to 'think twice, not blindly obey'.[47]

Opponents of bills of rights may acknowledge that a statutory charter avoids the worst excesses of a constitutionally entrenched bill of rights. The flexibility of a normal statute and the reserving of final decisions on contested issues to the legislature provide a clear distinction. Nevertheless, concerns have been raised about the interpretation and declaration mechanisms of enforcement in dialogue model bills of rights. Critics such as legal academic James Allan maintain that the mandate given to the courts to interpret legislation consistently with human rights could allow 'Alice in Wonderland' flights of fancy or lead to 'interpretation on steroids', giving judges the power to override clear wording with their own preferences and thus undermining the intention of the legislature.[48]

This concern finds some support in the interpretive approach taken by the courts in the United Kingdom under the UK HRA.[49] In *Ghaidan v Godin-Mendoza*,[50] the House of Lords confirmed that the interpretative obligation in s. 3 of the UK HRA is 'of an unusual and far-reaching character', which may require the court to depart from unambiguous wording and the intent of the legislature in order to give effect to Convention rights.[51] In an earlier case, *R v A (No 2)*,[52] the Judicial Committee of the House of Lords had effectively rewritten 'rape shield' legislation to accord with the right to a fair trial, undermining the intention of the Parliament to give greater protection to victims of sexual assault during court proceedings. However, these decisions reflect the broad scope of the interpretive provision in the UK HRA, and the context of the United Kingdom's binding human rights obligations as a member of the Council of Europe.[53] Other interpretive clauses such as those adopted in the Victorian Charter (s. 32) and the ACT HRA (s. 30) set clearer boundaries to judicial interpretation of legislation, which must be consistent with the purpose of the law.[54]

Bills of rights critics also doubt the willingness of legislatures to override a judicial declaration that legislation is inconsistent with human rights. James Allan cites the failure by the Canadian Government to use the legislative override provision in the Canadian Charter as evidence that the courts have the final say on rights protection. He argues that the dialogue model under the Charter is in fact a monologue.[55] Similarly, he contends that the fact that the UK Government has responded positively to most of the final declarations of compatibility issued under the UK HRA is proof of a *lack* of dialogue on human rights.[56] This reaction by the UK Government to judicial declarations of incompatibility can, however, also be read as a sign that the dialogue is working well: once breaches of human rights have been brought to the attention of the legislature by the courts, the Parliament has acted to remedy them.

An examination of the cases in which legislation has been altered in response to final declarations of incompatibility under the UK HRA suggests that the courts have adopted interpretations of rights that have persuaded Parliament to respond positively through legislative amendment or repeal. For example, a declaration of incompatibility was issued in relation to mental health legislation that required a patient to prove that he did *not* suffer from a mental disorder in order to be released from detention.[57] A Northern Irish law that attracted a declaration of incompatibility, and was repealed as a result, had the effect of criminalising anal intercourse between consenting adults, a 19th century provision repealed decades previously in other parts of the United Kingdom.[58] In other cases, in response to a declaration of incompatibility, legislation has been amended to remove or amend provisions that prevented a deceased father's name from being entered on the birth certificate of his child;[59] to ensure the recognition under matrimonial law of gender reassignment;[60] to amend discriminatory provisions of social security legislation to ensure that certain benefits were paid to widowers as well as to widows;[61] and to repeal provisions permitting the indefinite detention without charge or trial of suspected foreign international terrorists.[62]

Some rights sceptics have acknowledged a distinction between the 'strong' judicial review required by a constitutional bill of rights and the 'weak' judicial review available under a statutory human rights scheme. Legal philosopher Jeremy Waldron, for example, has recognised the democratic compatibility of statutory bills of rights as 'leav[ing] the ultimate decision to the representatives of the people in Parliament, but ... us[ing] courts to bring issues of rights to the attention of the community'.[63] He adds: 'It may not always be easy for legislators to see what issues of rights are embedded in the legislative proposals brought before them; courts can help them see this.'[64] So too legal theorist Jeremy Webber has argued that the most significant aspect of judicial decision-making in the field of human rights, compared to legislative action, is its focus on individual cases: 'the attempt to ensure that the application of general norms is attentive to the detail of particular circumstances; the attempt to ensure that in the practical imposition of social norms, individual people and individual circumstances are given their due'.[65] Webber defends statutory bills of rights as 'combining adjudication's intense focus on the particular case with, at the end of the day, legislative determination of the general normative order of society'.[66]

Proponents of bills of rights argue that such instruments improve the quality of legislative decision-making by ensuring that parliaments focus explicitly on human rights issues when considering new legislation.[67] The formal requirement that a rights-compatibility statement be prepared (and the internal bureaucratic discussion that will normally precede this), the conferral of a rights-scrutiny function on an existing or new legislative committee and the possibility of review by the courts, as well as public engagement in debate about proposed legislation, will allow more effective rights scrutiny.[68] Some of this takes place already in the various Australian parliaments, but it is claimed that a bill of rights will heighten and improve rights scrutiny.[69] While the outcomes will depend not only on the formal procedures, but also on personalities and political context, there is evidence to suggest that these predictions are borne out in practice.

In its 2006 review of the UK HRA, the Department for Constitutional Affairs (DCA) concluded that the Act had had a significant and positive impact on the development of governmental policy. The formal procedures adopted to ensure compatibility, together with outside scrutiny by the Parliamentary Joint Committee on Human Rights, had improved parliamentary accountability, and the Act had led to better policy by requiring explicit consideration of the needs of different communities.[70] The experience in New Zealand has been similar,[71] as has that of the ACT in the first four years of a bill of rights there.[72] Early operation of the Victorian Charter suggests that there will be a similarly beneficial impact in that jurisdiction as well.[73] The effects of the ACT HRA and the Victorian Charter are discussed in more detail in chapters 4 and 5.

The various statutory bills of rights also include elements designed to instil a human rights culture inside government, and to ensure that human rights considerations form an integral part of the legislative and policy-making process. The human rights-compatibility statements for Bills and the requirement for legislative scrutiny committees to consider human rights issues explicitly in their review of draft legislation, discussed above, are the major elements. The process is bolstered by the introduction of procedures that ensure that this substantive review takes place during the development of new policies and legislative proposals, requirements on departments to report regularly on the steps they have taken to give effect to human rights, and by providing for a role for ombudsmen or human rights commissions to provide policy advice, play a monitoring role, or even to consider complaints of violations of human rights.

There is evidence that the aim of modern bills of rights to create a 'human rights dialogue' between the branches of government and the community has been successful in some contexts. In its 2006 review, the DCA pointed out that the UK HRA had caused 'a shift away from inflexible or blanket policies towards those which are capable of adjustment to recognise the circumstances and characteristics of individuals'.[74] In another 2006 study, a non-government organisation, the British Institute of Human Rights, documented the positive role that the UK HRA had played outside the formal legal process. It detailed cases in which use of rights claims outside the court system had led to improved delivery of services and better treatment of individuals by a range of government agencies:

> Too often the *Human Rights Act* is associated with technical legal arguments or perceived to fuel spurious claims by celebrities and criminals. These case studies reveal a very different picture. They show how groups and people themselves are using not only the letter of the law, but also the language and ideas of human rights to challenge poor treatment and negotiate improvements to services provided by public bodies. Giving people the power to use human rights as a check against the state in this way is precisely what the Government envisaged when it passed the Act in 1998.[75]

The development of such a culture, within and outside the bureaucracy, is, however, a gradual process, as other studies of the impact of the UK HRA on public bodies show.[76]

Opponents of bills of rights have registered a concern that bills of rights would impose additional and unwarranted burdens on bureaucracies, since government agencies would have to ensure their policies, programs and actions were consistent with human rights and would have to deal with claims about violations of rights.[77] While the enactment of a significant piece of legislation such as a bill of rights would inevitably create additional work, especially during its initial phase, these concerns appear to be overstated. In many cases, agencies' operations may already be largely in conformity with human rights standards; where they are not, there may be good reasons for insisting on the change.

The effect of a bill of rights on legal systems

Critics of the adoption of bills of rights identify a number of ways that these instruments can distort the legal system. One regularly voiced concern about bills of rights in any form is that they can create an explosion of litigation that clogs up the courts and benefits lawyers more than any other group in society.[78] Every issue, it is said, has the potential to become a 'human rights issue', and lawyers will be able to complicate, delay and exercise control in relation to a wide range of matters. The fear of a 'lawyers' picnic' and a wave of frivolous cases has not, however, been borne out in practice.

The 2006 government review of the UK HRA noted that two per cent of appellate cases raised major issues of human rights, observing:

> The highest density of *HRA* cases is in the House
> of Lords, concentrating as it does on new issues of
> principle. The *HRA* has been substantively considered
> in about one-third of the 354 cases which the House
> decided [since the enactment of the *HRA*] and could be
> said to have substantially affected the result in about
> one-tenth of those cases.[79]

A study that examined the impact of the Act in the Scottish courts between May 1999 and August 2003 found that human rights arguments were raised in just over 0.25 per cent of the total criminal courts' caseload and in 'a tiny fraction' of the total caseload of the Scottish civil and criminal courts over the period of the study.[80] It concluded that 'human rights legislation has had little effect on the volume of business in the courts'[81] and that 'the numbers of cases were not such as to disturb the balance of the court system, and there has been only a small number of successful human rights challenges which required significant policy changes'.[82]

The experience in the first years of the ACT HRA suggests even less impact on the court system.[83] Unlike the UK HRA, the ACT law did not initially confer a right to bring an action based directly on a violation of human rights. However, it allowed human rights issues to be raised in criminal proceedings, judicial review proceedings and other litigation. In the first four years of its operation, there were 66 cases identified in which HRA issues were raised. In most of these cases the point was minor or incidental and the decision turned primarily on other issues. There was substantial argument on human rights issues in a very small number of cases, and only in a handful of those cases was a rights issue central to the decision of the court. As discussed in chapter 4, a right of action against public authorities for human rights breaches which came into force in January 2009 seems unlikely to produce a torrent of litigation.

While it is inevitable that a bill of rights will prompt some frivolous claims, the evidence to date suggests that these will not be a significant part of the courts' workload. The disincentive of costs being awarded against unsuccessful litigants and the courts' power to dismiss unmeritorious claims will limit the extent to which such claims impinge on the time of the courts. Frivolous and vexatious claims are not unknown in the legal system, and courts and tribunals have developed effective means of responding to them. It is also worth noting that most of the examples of outrageous rights claims proffered by critics of rights charters involve unsuccessful claims that were disposed of fairly summarily.[84]

One variation of the fear that bills of rights will generate a litigation explosion is that they could operate as 'rogues' charters', primarily benefiting undeserving criminals who will escape justified punishment by invoking human rights. Experience in jurisdictions with a bill of rights indeed indicates that they tend to be invoked in criminal proceedings very soon after coming into force, but that the ultimate impact on the criminal law has been relatively modest. The DCA review noted that '[i]n general the English criminal law has been found to be consistent with the European Convention on Human Rights – both seek to strike a "fair balance" between the demands of the general interests of the community and the requirements of the protection of the individual's human rights'.[85] Application of human rights principles has sometimes led to the identification of defects in the substantive criminal law, criminal procedural law or the administration of criminal justice.[86] In some instances, initial findings of this type in lower courts are not upheld when the case reaches the apex court; when they are upheld, executive and legislative government can often move fairly rapidly to amend laws in a manner that is consistent with human rights and effective criminal law enforcement.[87] The enactment of a bill of rights can also act as a stimulus to a systematic and principled review of areas of the law and to subsequent improvement and updating that might not otherwise have occurred.[88]

The 'rogues' charter' criticism also rests on the assumption that people charged with a criminal offence do not deserve human rights protection; by implication, those protections should only be available to 'deserving' citizens. While defendants may sometimes escape conviction on grounds that bear no direct relation to their guilt or innocence of the offence charged, this can happen regardless of the presence of a bill of rights. It is also important to observe that some acquittals on procedural grounds arise from legislative directions and judicial efforts to uphold proper law enforcement practices. Adoption of a rights charter does not appear to increase significantly the numbers of acquittals on the basis of so-called 'technicalities'.[89]

It is perhaps unsurprising that the introduction of bills of rights can prompt some anxiety in the community. These instruments are easily misunderstood as a type of 'get out of jail free' card, reflecting the way the US Bill of Rights is sometimes depicted in television dramas. The 2006 review of the UK HRA identified three categories of myths about bills of rights:

> First, there are those which derive from the reporting (and often partial reporting) of the launch of cases but not their ultimate outcomes. These leave the impression in the public mind that a wide range of claims are successful when in fact they are not – and have often effectively been laughed out of court. Secondly, there are the pure urban myths: instances of situations in which someone (often it may not even be clear who) has said that human rights require some bizarre outcome or other, and this is subsequently trotted out as established fact. Finally, there are rumours and impressions which take root through a particular case or decision, and which then provide the backdrop against which all subsequent issues of the type in question are played out.[90]

These myths can exert a powerful influence on the bill of rights debate, and present a real challenge for proponents of rights charters. Public education and the dissemination of accurate information are critical to ensuring that the assessment of the case for a bill of rights is based upon evidence rather than rumours and half-truths.

Will a bill of rights promote the better enjoyment of human rights?

Some critics of the introduction of bills of rights argue that these instruments do not in fact achieve their aim. One aspect of this criticism is that the designation of a particular catalogue of rights will become irrelevant as times and threats to rights change. Future generations will be lumbered with dinosaur-like rights that may indeed be harmful in changed circumstances and it will be difficult to add new rights more responsive to contemporary circumstances to a bill of rights.[91] A notorious example of rights outlasting their historical context and being difficult to amend is the guarantee of the right to bear arms contained in the 2nd Amendment to the US Constitution. These fears arise particularly in the case of entrenched bills of rights, but it is suggested that future amendment may also be a problem with statutory charters because these instruments will quickly achieve *de facto* constitutional status.[92]

The claim of ossification or freezing of rights appears overstated in relation to constitutional bills of rights, and especially in relation to statutory ones. Many of the rights included in bills of rights have a long history, and are responses to commonly recurring threats to human dignity that still persist in the modern state. Their formulation in broad general terms means that they can be interpreted to respond to changing circumstances. In the case of statutory charters, moreover, there is no bar to adding or subtracting rights – indeed, the Australian examples provide explicitly for regular reviews to consider the addition of new categories of rights.[93] The political difficulty of amending particular rights is no different to the political problems in amending any community-supported legislation.

A related concern is that the inclusion of particular rights in a bill of rights can impair the recognition of other rights not included in the charter. As a formal matter, bills of rights frequently provide that the inclusion of certain rights is not intended to suggest that other rights should not continue to be recognised and respected.[94] Nevertheless, the fact that only some rights are included in a charter of rights – in a sense, a community's statement of its priority values and goals – is likely to have the effect of suggesting that other rights are less significant. This appears to be the case especially with economic, social and cultural rights, which are not protected in any systematic way in common law countries. There are various reasons for this, many of them based on inaccurate views of the nature of the obligations relating to these rights, the possibilities for judicial enforcement, and the implications of giving courts a role in their enforcement.[95]

Some opponents of bills of rights worry that the formal protection of rights will contribute to a selfish and egoistic society. They emphasise instead the importance of duties and responsibilities towards others which are a fundamental part of human communities.[96] Some have argued that any statement of rights should be accompanied by a corresponding statement of responsibilities; this thinking is reflected in the title of the Victorian *Charter of Human Rights and Responsibilities*, although the substance of that legislation does not develop the concept of responsibilities. One problem with the language of 'responsibilities' in the human rights context is the implication that only 'responsible' people can claim human rights protection. This could suggest that, for example, prisoners are not able to assert their human rights.

As we noted in chapter 1, human rights are not the only ethical or moral framework appropriate for political life. They offer an internationally recognised statement of the components of human dignity, but they do not allow unbridled assertions of rights. Not only do they recognise the important rights that individuals have to build relationships with others in the personal sphere and in social and political life, but they also recognise the importance of respect for the dignity and interests of others. This can be seen in the language of some rights: for example, art. 19(3) of the ICCPR provides that the exercise of freedom of expression 'carries with it special duties and responsibilities'. Further, many rights are subject to limitations that are justifiable because they promote the rights of others or other aspects of communal welfare.

The literature on bills of rights also contains a more radical critique of the ability of such documents to protect human rights. It sees a focus on civil and political rights and their legal embodiment in a charter of rights as a distraction from the underlying structures of power and exclusion that fundamentally affect the ability of individuals to enjoy a decent life. Rights talk can defuse political issues by allowing them to be transformed into legal issues, as well as allowing governments to pass difficult political issues on to the courts.[97] This critique has its origins in the Marxist attack on 'bourgeois rights', discussed in chapter 1. It has led on the one hand to the promotion of economic, social and cultural rights. On the other hand, it has generated deep scepticism about rights in general, seeing them as a mirage. Claims of legal rights remove essentially political issues from the political arena and divert energies from the political and social action that is needed to bring about fundamental social change. On this analysis, rights can become a tool for the privileged classes to reinforce their status using the power of law and the legitimacy of rights.[98]

As we noted in chapter 1, one response to this critique is to point to the empowering effect that the conferral or affirmation of rights can have on those who are disadvantaged or marginalised. A bill of rights does not have to be the preserve of lawyers and the courts; it can be taken up by civil society as a framework for political and social action. It can also be developed within government as a tool to enhance rights-responsive policy making, and to hold governments politically accountable for their actions.

The major themes in debates about bills of rights have been remarkably consistent over the past four decades. Modern developments in relation to statutory models of bills of rights and the operation of such legislation in jurisdictions such as New Zealand, the United Kingdom, the ACT and Victoria provide us with new perspectives on rights protection, since they appear to respond in significant measure to many of the concerns about bills of rights which are derived from contemplation of entrenched bills of rights. These new models provide empirical evidence with which to test longstanding claims about the impact of different types of bills of rights, and to evaluate the desirability of introducing such instruments in other Australian jurisdictions and at the national level. We consider that the theoretical, political and legal arguments for introducing bills of rights in this country are strong. In the following chapters we trace the development and practice of the bills of rights thus far adopted in Australia to test the claims made by advocates and the criticisms articulated by opponents.

4

The ACT *Human Rights Act 2004*

The enactment of the Australian Capital Territory's *Human Rights Act 2004* (ACT HRA) was a critical step as Australia's first legislative bill of rights. By breaking the political logjam, it added momentum to efforts in other Australian jurisdictions to consider the desirability of a bill of rights, and provided a model that could be adopted and adapted elsewhere. While the ACT HRA preserves parliamentary sovereignty by leaving final decisions about human rights protection to the ACT Legislative Assembly, it establishes a series of mechanisms to ensure that human rights issues are kept on the political agenda.

This chapter first sets out the background to the adoption of the ACT HRA in 2004, then outlines the legislation and describes its effect on the three branches of government. The four first years of the ACT's operation illustrate both the potential and the limits of a dialogue model of human rights protection. Although critics predicted a surge in litigation and an undermining of the elected government by an unaccountable judiciary, the legislation has so far had little impact on the judicial system. Its most profound effects have been on the ACT legislature and Executive, fostering a lively, if sometimes fragile, human rights culture within government.

History

The enactment of the ACT HRA in 2004 built on earlier campaigns to establish a bill of rights in the Territory, which had raised public awareness and understanding of human rights. It also reflected the vision of the Chief Minister of the ACT Labor government, Jon Stanhope, who resurrected the cause. His strong commitment to the ACT HRA overrode considerable resistance within his own party and the Executive, as well as from the Liberal Opposition.

Early moves

At the time of the Territory's move to self-government in 1988, there was public debate about introducing a bill of rights as part of the self-government package. Jack Waterford, a prominent Canberra journalist, advocated a constitution for the ACT, and drafted model legislation that included an interpretive bill of rights, protecting a number of rights including freedom of speech, freedom of association and a free press.[1] However, the *Australian Capital Territory (Self-Government) Act 1988* (Cwlth) eventually negotiated with the Commonwealth did not include a bill of rights.[2]

A more extensive campaign to introduce a bill of rights into the Territory was led by Terry Connolly, Attorney-General in the Follett Labor government. In 1993, Connolly released a detailed issues paper on an ACT bill of rights[3] and sought submissions on the topic.[4] In late 1994, he circulated an exposure draft of a bill of rights. This Bill was remarkable for its inclusion of the right to education, rights particular to Aboriginal Australians, and rights of children, as well as the standard guarantees of civil and political rights. The Labor Party lost office in March 1995 before this project could come to fruition, but Connolly continued the campaign, presenting the Bill from Opposition in May 1995.[5] Although initially it was hoped that a bill of rights might gain a measure of bipartisan support, it was not pursued by the Carnell Liberal government, and eventually lapsed.

Community consultation 2002–03

The bill of rights cause was taken up by Jon Stanhope, who became leader of the ACT Labor Opposition in 1998. Stanhope had served as chief of staff to Commonwealth Attorney-General Michael Lavarch, and in this role had initiated and managed the parliamentary inquiry that resulted in *Half Way to Equal*, a detailed analysis of issues relating to equality for women.[6] During the 2001 election campaign, Stanhope announced that a Labor government would establish a committee to examine a bill of rights for the ACT and to consult with the community. He did not elaborate on the form that a bill of rights might take, other than to express a preference for a legislative charter, and to promise that it would not contain items such as the right to bear arms.[7]

Although the proposal was rejected by the Liberal government,[8] the issue of a bill of rights did not feature prominently in the ACT election debates. Labor went on to claim a decisive victory in October 2001 and, as Chief Minister and Attorney-General of the new government, Stanhope acted promptly upon his election commitment. In December the same year, he outlined the terms of reference for the ACT Bill of Rights Consultative Committee, and announced that the Committee would be chaired by Hilary Charlesworth, Professor of International Law and Human Rights at the Australian National University (and one of the authors of this volume).[9] Further Committee members – Larissa Behrendt, Professor of Law and Indigenous Studies at the University of Technology, Sydney; Penelope Layland, journalist and poet; and Elizabeth Kelly, a senior public servant – were appointed in April 2002.

The Committee's terms of reference were broad and non-prescriptive. It was to consult on whether it was 'appropriate and desirable' to enact an ACT bill of rights, what form such a bill might take, what effect it might have on executive and judicial powers, and what rights should be included.[10] The consultation process took nine months and involved the publication of an issues paper and a pamphlet, the consideration of 145 submissions, meetings (with both the general public and specific community groups), public lectures, seminars and conferences.[11] A unique feature of the consultation process was the use of a 'deliberative poll', in which 250 randomly selected Canberrans participated in a two-day forum that aimed to allow them to reach an informed view about bills of rights.[12] These various forms of consultation all produced similar results, indicating that there was majority in-principle support for an ACT bill of rights (approximately two-thirds of those participating), although this figure was not broken down according to particular methods of consultation.

Consultative Committee Report

The Consultative Committee presented its report to the Chief Minister in May 2003. It recommended that the ACT adopt a bill of rights in the form of a Human Rights Act, a draft of which was appended to the report. The proposed legislation was non-entrenched and aimed to create a 'dialogue' about human rights between the branches of government in the ACT as well as with the community.[13]

The Bill proposed by the Consultative Committee covered most of the rights contained in the International Covenant on Civil and Political Rights 1966 (ICCPR) and the International Covenant on Economic, Social and Cultural Rights 1966 (ICESCR). The draft legislation included in the report attempted to break down the traditional distinction drawn between civil and political rights on the one hand and economic, social and cultural rights on the other by grouping together related rights from both covenants. For example, clause 2 of the schedule to the draft legislation linked together the right to life, the right to an adequate standard of living, and the right to be free from hunger.[14]

The Committee's report drew predictable fire from the

Liberal Opposition. Shadow Attorney-General Bill Stefaniak had consistently opposed a bill of rights on the grounds that existing laws and the common law provided adequate protection for human rights and that a bill of rights would simply produce a 'litigation culture'.[15] More surprising was the reaction from some senior bureaucrats, which ranged from indifference to cynicism to outright hostility. An interdepartmental committee was established to prepare a formal government response to the Committee's report, but it did not succeed in creating cooperation in relation to the initiative across government. Some government departments obtained legal advice that predicted dire budgetary and policy consequences if any form of rights protection were enacted. Within the ACT Labor Party, there were concerns that the Chief Minister's enthusiasm for a bill of rights was electoral folly, as well as anxieties about specific provisions of the legislation.

In this discouraging climate, those responsible for preparing the government's response to the report opted for a cautious approach. This reflected a concern that if the ACT HRA were a political disaster, it might spell the end for bills of rights across Australia for the immediate future. Ultimately, the inclusion of economic, social and cultural rights, the articulation of an express duty on public authorities to comply with the Act, and the provision of a legal remedy for breach of this duty, were considered to be too unpredictable in their impact on government and were excluded from the final form of the legislation.

Drafting the Human Rights Bill required consideration of principles applying across all ACT statute law, including the role of the *Legislation Act 2001* (ACT) as the primary source of the law dealing with legislation in the Territory.[16] At that time it was decided that the interpretive provision in the Human Rights Bill was to be subordinate to s. 139 of the *Legislation Act*, which requires decision-makers to prefer the interpretation of legislation which best achieves the legislative purpose. This issue is discussed further below.

Assembly debate

The Bill finally presented to the Legislative Assembly was a more modest document than that proposed by the Committee, but it nevertheless provoked robust debate. Stefaniak called it 'the most important and potentially most dangerous legislation we have ever seen in this Territory'.[17] Among other objections, he was critical of the failure to refer to the right to own property, the right to safety and security, and the rights of victims of crime.[18] He was also concerned that the Human Rights Bill transferred power from elected politicians to unaccountable judges. Other members of the Opposition described it as a 'can of worms'[19] and predicted that it would allow the circumvention of the parliamentary process by political and legal lobby groups.[20]

Neither the Greens nor Australian Democrats cross-benchers were entirely happy with the Bill either, because they considered it did not go far enough. Both criticised the omission of economic, cultural and social rights.[21] The Greens were also concerned at the absence of environmental rights.[22] The Stanhope government was dependent on the support of at least two of the three cross-benchers to ensure passage of the Bill, and finally agreed to an amendment proposed by Greens representative Kerrie Tucker. This inserted a requirement for review of the Act after 12 months to consider the inclusion of environmental rights and other economic, social and cultural rights.[23]

Passage of the ACT HRA in the Legislative Assembly prompted the Shadow Attorney-General to introduce a Charter of Responsibilities Bill in order to temper the 'excesses' and selfishness he associated with the Act.[24] The responsibilities covered by the Bill included the responsibility to be honest (cl.5), the responsibility not to misuse 'economic and political power ... as instruments of domination' (cl. 18(1)), the responsibility to confess any breach of the law and to accept appropriate punishment (cl. 17), and a judicial responsibility to take 'community expectations into account when sentencing offenders in criminal matters and in giving judgments in civil claims affecting the community generally' (cl. 10(5)). The Bill was not supported by the government or the cross-benchers and was defeated in the Legislative Assembly.

At the time of the passage of the Human Rights Bill through the Legislative Assembly in March 2004, the prospect of Commonwealth intervention to override the legislation was raised.[25] Prime Minister John Howard had expressed concern in a letter to the Chief Minister that the ACT HRA was a dangerous precedent and that it unnecessarily replicated existing human rights mechanisms.[26] He later described the Act as 'ridiculous' in a radio interview,[27] leading to keen speculation within the ACT that he might intervene to invalidate it. In the event, however, no formal steps were taken to interfere with the legislation.

The *Human Rights Act 2004 (ACT)*

The ACT HRA is a non-entrenched law, which aims to promote respect for human rights in legislation and policy through stimulating a 'dialogue' between the Executive, the legislature and the courts.[28] The legislation:

- includes an obligation on decision-makers to interpret Territory laws (including regulations and other statutory instruments, but not the common law) to be consistent as far as possible with human rights (s. 30);
- confers on the ACT Supreme Court jurisdiction to issue a declaration of incompatibility in cases where legislation cannot be interpreted to be consistent with human rights (s. 32); the declaration does not affect the validity of the legislation in question (s. 39), but the Attorney-General is required to report the government's response to the declaration to the Legislative Assembly (s. 33);
- imposes a duty on the Attorney-General to present a written statement on the human rights-compatibility of each government bill presented to the Legislative Assembly (s. 37);

- provides for pre-enactment scrutiny of all legislation for consistency with human rights by the relevant Standing Committee of the Legislative Assembly (s. 38); this committee presents a report to the Legislative Assembly, to which the government must then respond;
- creates the office of Human Rights Commissioner, which has among other functions that of reviewing the effect of laws to ensure compliance with the ACT HRA and of advising the Attorney-General on the operation of the Act (s. 41);
- requires government departments to report on their implementation of the ACT HRA in their annual reports (sch. 2); and
- provides for reviews of the operation of the ACT HRA to take place after one year (now completed), and five years after the Act comes into force (ss. 43, 44).

From 1 January 2009, as the result of amendments enacted in 2008, the ACT HRA imposes a direct duty on public authorities to comply with human rights in decision making, and provides a direct right of action in the Supreme Court where this obligation is breached (new Part 5A).

Rights protected by the ACT HRA

The human rights protected by the ACT HRA are drawn from the ICCPR. They include:
- rights to recognition and equality before the law (s. 8);
- the right to life (s. 9);
- the right to be free from torture and cruel, inhuman or degrading treatment and involuntary medical treatment or experimentation (s. 10);
- protection of the family and children (s. 11);
- the right to privacy and protection of reputation (s. 12);
- the right to freedom of movement (s. 13);
- the right to freedom of thought, conscience, religion and belief (s. 14);

- the right of peaceful assembly and freedom of association (s. 15);
- the right to freedom of expression (s. 16) and the right to take part in public life (s. 17);
- the right to liberty and security of the person (s. 18) and the right to humane and dignified treatment when deprived of liberty (s. 19);
- the rights of children in the criminal process (s. 20);
- the right to a fair trial (s. 21) and due process rights in criminal proceedings (s. 22);
- the right to be compensated for wrongful conviction (s. 23);
- the right not to be punished more than once for the same offence (s. 24);
- the right not to be held guilty under retrospective criminal laws (s. 25);
- the right to be free from slavery or forced labour (s. 26); and
- the rights of minorities to enjoy their own culture, religion and language (s. 27).

Article 1 of the ICCPR, the right of peoples to self-determination, was not included on the ground that it is a group, rather than an individual right.[29] Other ICCPR provisions omitted from the ACT HRA include the prohibition on propaganda for war and national, racial or religious hatred,[30] and the right to form trade unions.[31]

Rights under the ICESCR were not included in the ACT HRA when it was passed in 2004. The first review in 2006 reconsidered this issue, but did not recommend the immediate inclusion of economic, social and cultural rights. It proposed instead that the government explore support for specific rights such as housing and education and that these issues be given further consideration in the five-year review. The review did not recommend providing additional protection for environmental rights.[32]

Under s. 6 of the ACT HRA, '[o]nly individuals have human rights'. While the intention is clear that corporations should not be able to rely on the Act on the basis that they do not possess human rights, the provision nevertheless gives rise to some complex issues. For example, corporations might indirectly assert their rights through individuals such as their owners or shareholders invoking their own individual rights. Furthermore, in a case in which the interpretation of a statute is at issue, it is likely that corporations might have standing to argue that the accepted interpretation of a statute needs to be modified because it violates on its face the human rights of others.[33]

Limitations on rights

Rights under the ACT HRA are not absolute. Rather than replicating the specific limits on each right set out in the ICCPR, s. 28 of the Act imposes a general qualification on all the rights, namely that:

> Human rights may be subject only to reasonable limits
> set by Territory laws that can be demonstrably justified
> in a free and democratic society.[34]

This section borrows the language of the Canadian Charter of Rights and Freedoms, and imports the concept that any limitations on rights must be proportionate to the objective sought to be achieved by the legislation. Section 28 was supplemented in 2008 by the insertion of a list of factors that should be taken into account when deciding whether an infringement of a right is justified.[35] Section 28(2) now provides:

> In deciding whether a limit is reasonable, all relevant
> factors must be considered, including the following:
> (a) the nature of the right affected;
> (b) the importance of the purpose of the limitation;
> (c) the nature and extent of the limitation;

    (d) the relationship between the limitation and its
        purpose;

    (e) any less restrictive means reasonably available to
        achieve the purpose the limitation seeks to achieve.

It is notable that a limitation under s. 28 may only be imposed by a 'Territory law', which is defined to mean an Act or a statutory instrument. This appears to imply that government policies and decisions of public authorities cannot impose any limitations on human rights, proportionate or otherwise, unless the limitations are explicitly contemplated by an authorising Act, or the policies have the status of statutory instruments (documents made under power conferred by an Act or another statutory instrument).[36] It is not clear whether this distinction has been recognised in practice, or its implications fully explored.[37]

The interpretive provision

At the heart of the ACT HRA is the obligation imposed on courts and other decision-makers to interpret all ACT legislation to be compatible with the specified human rights (s. 30). The original structure of the obligation contained in s. 30(1) was convoluted, as its direction to prefer, as far as possible, an interpretation of legislation that was consistent with human rights, was explicitly subject to a countermanding provision of the *Legislation Act*. Section 139 of the *Legislation Act* mandates that the interpretation of an Act that would best achieve the purpose of that Act is to be preferred to any other interpretation. These apparently contradictory directions as to which interpretation should be preferred by decision-makers were never directly addressed by the courts, despite the numerous cases in which the ACT HRA was cited.

In its report on the 12-month review of the ACT HRA, the Department of Justice and Community Safety recommended that 's. 30 ... be amended to clarify that a human rights consistent interpretation must prevail unless this would defeat the purpose of the legislation'.[38] This recommendation was taken up by the ACT Government in 2008. The amended s. 30 now provides:

> So far as it is possible to do so consistently with its
> purpose, a Territory law must be interpreted in a way
> that is compatible with human rights.

This wording is consistent with the equivalent provision (s. 32) of the *Charter of Human Rights and Responsibilities Act 2006* (Vic) (Victorian Charter).[39] However, it is significantly different from the interpretation provision in s. 3 of the Human Rights Act 1998 (UK) (UK HRA), which is not constrained by any reference to the purpose of the legislation.

The Explanatory Statement to the amendment notes that the new provision:

> clarifies the interaction between the interpretive rule
> and the purposive rule .... This means that unless the
> law is intended to operate in a way that is inconsistent
> with the right in question, the interpretation that is most
> consistent with human rights must prevail.[40]

The effect of the new s. 30 has not yet been considered in any detail by the ACT courts, and there is no indication of the methodology that might be adopted in applying the new interpretive approach. The Explanatory Statement appears to suggest that human rights should be the central focus and starting point of the interpretation process, which would involve identifying possible meanings of a law to determine which is most consistent with human rights. This interpretation should then be preferred, provided that it accords with the purpose of the law as a whole. This methodology would broadly reflect the approach of the Court of Appeal of New Zealand in *Moonen v Film and Literature Board of Review*.[41] An alternative approach, taken by the Supreme Court of New Zealand in the more recent case of *Hansen v The Queen*,[42] takes the opposite starting-point, using ordinary principles of interpretation to determine the meaning of the law, and only considering alternative meanings if the ordinary meaning imposes an unjustifiable limitation on human rights.[43] In our view, the *Moonen* approach has the advantage of placing human rights at the centre of the interpretive process, rather than bringing them into play only if a limitation on a right is unreasonable. The *Hansen* approach seems to start from the assumption that a legislative provision is *not* intended to be consistent with human rights, and focuses on limitations. This approach is at odds with the well-established presumption of statutory interpretation that the legislature does not intended to encroach on fundamental rights unless it makes such an intention clear.[44] It is also inconsistent with international approaches to interpretation of rights and limitations on rights, which construe rights generously and limitations narrowly.[45]

Duty on public authorities and direct right of action

While the ACT HRA did not initially create a new cause of action based directly on the violation of human rights, it was nevertheless possible to raise alleged violations of the Act before the courts. The Act could be invoked in criminal proceedings and, indeed, in civil proceedings where the issue of the interpretation of a Territory law arose. Theoretically, it could also be used as the basis of an action, for example, a violation of the Act or a failure to take it into account could be relied on in proceedings for judicial review of the actions of public authorities. However, this possibility was not tested during the Act's first four years.

Following the review of the ACT HRA after its first year of operation, and its limited use in the courts, the government amended the law to improve accountability for complying with human rights. The *Human Rights Amendment Act 2008* (ACT) introduced, with effect from 1 January 2009, an explicit obligation on public authorities to comply with the Act, and created a direct right of action for breach of this duty.[46] Although

influenced by a similar provision in the Victorian Charter
(s. 39), the free-standing right of action under the new s. 40C of
the ACT HRA is more generous and straightforward. While the
Victorian Charter requires a plaintiff to establish a case under
an existing cause of action, under the ACT HRA provision,
a victim of a breach of human rights obligations by a public
authority may directly institute proceedings for that breach in
the Supreme Court, as well as relying on these obligations in
other legal proceedings. The Supreme Court is empowered to
grant any relief it considers appropriate, except damages.

The Act's provisions mirror those in the Victorian Charter in defining public authorities through the identification of
specific 'core' public entities, in addition to a functional test
that captures other entities carrying out government functions.
The Act also includes an innovative 'opt in' provision which
provides that an entity that is not a public authority may ask
the Minister to declare that the entity is subject to the obligations of a public authority under this part, a request to which
the Minister is obliged to accede.[47] The stated purpose of this
provision is to encourage the private sector to subject itself to
explicit human rights obligations under the Act,[48] but it could
also be used by other entities whose standing might otherwise be
unclear, to clarify their status as public authorities.

The ACT HRA in operation

The coming into force of the ACT HRA on 1 July 2004 did not
lead to the dire consequences predicted by some of its critics,
such as an increase in unmeritorious litigation. Some supporters
may have hoped for a more energetic invocation of the Act in
the courts, and its low public visibility has led to charges that
the legislation is mere symbolism or even a hoax.[49] But the real
story is more complex, and lies primarily in the impact of the
legislation on the policy-making and legislative processes rather
than in the courts.

The Executive

The most significant effect of the ACT HRA has been on the generation of government and legislative policy. A small Human Rights Unit was established in the Department of Justice and Community Safety to monitor and support the implementation of the Act within government. The Unit has published several documents to assist government departments in applying the Act, including a Plain English Guide to the Act and guidelines on the development of legislation and policy in light of the Act.[50] The three lawyers in the Unit are responsible for advising Cabinet and all other government departments about the human rights implications of new policy proposals and conducting the compatibility assessments of all government Bills required by s. 37 of the Act. The Unit has been involved in the drafting of major legislation, such as the ACT's counter-terrorism laws, and was responsible for the first review of the ACT HRA.

Statements of compatibility

Under s. 37 of the ACT HRA, the statements of compatibility issued by the Attorney-General are not specifically required to include reasons for the Attorney-General's opinion. While there have been ongoing calls for the compatibility statements to contain reasons, so as to serve an educative role for the Assembly,[51] in general the statements issued by the Attorney-General have not given the reasons for an assertion of human rights compatibility. Exceptions were made for the Mental Health (Treatment and Care) Amendment Bill 2005 (ACT), which annexed a detailed statement of reasons to the compatibility statement, and the Terrorism (Extraordinary Temporary Powers) Bill 2006 (ACT), discussed below, for which barrister Kate Eastman's advice on compatibility was tabled separately in the Assembly.[52] The general policy of the government has been to require that human rights issues be addressed in the Explanatory Statements, which are prepared by the department responsible for the Bill. This is partly an issue of resources, but the Human Rights Unit also considers that there are benefits to the quality of the human rights dialogue from sharing the responsibility for human rights compliance across government, and requiring each department to analyse and justify its legislation in human rights terms.

The Scrutiny of Bills Committee of the ACT Legislative Assembly[53] has confirmed the importance of the Explanatory Statements:

> The point of this exercise is not simply to inform the Committee, the Assembly, the legal profession and the courts. An Explanatory Statement has the potential to be the vehicle for discourse between the promoter of the Bill and the general public, and thus enhance the growth of a human rights culture in the ACT. The work involved in writing an Explanatory Statement is tedious and difficult, but the outcome is of great value.[54]

The first review of the ACT HRA recommended in 2006 that:

> Within the Executive, the Government should continue to encourage Agencies to make greater use of the Explanatory Statements to make the case for compatibility. But, where a bill raises significant human rights issues, the compatibility statement should provide a 'summary of reasons', focusing on the human rights principles and drawing on the case established by the sponsoring agency.[55]

This recommendation has not been fully implemented. Reasons have not been included in any statement of compatibility since the release of the review, although some Bills, such as the Corrections Management Bill 2006 (ACT) and the Children and Young People Bill 2008 (ACT), raised significant human rights issues, and detailed reasons were included in the Explanatory Statements in these cases.

Impact on policy and legislation

Although the content of government deliberations is not reflected in the statements of compatibility, the obligation to certify whether each new bill is compatible with human rights, and the potential for further scrutiny of these pronouncements by the legislature and the courts, places a significant responsibility on the Executive to carefully consider human rights in the shaping of all new legislation. The Human Rights Unit ultimately advises the Attorney-General whether a statement of compatibility should be issued in respect of a bill, but the task of identifying and addressing human rights issues is the responsibility of the agency developing the bill, with the guidance of the Human Rights Unit. As Attorney-General Simon Corbell has noted:

> The approach of the Human Rights Unit is to define the questions for agencies to ask themselves, send them away to explore those questions, and return to participate in a conversation, rather than receive the definitive answer to their human rights issue. Each interaction is a tutorial on the particular human right engaged, rather than a conference with a client at which advice is provided. This reflects the Government's focus on building a human rights culture within the public sector.[56]

One example of how the ACT HRA has influenced the policy-making and legislative process is the development of the *Children and Young People Act 2008* (ACT). This is a comprehensive updating and codifying statute that is intended to be the primary law in the ACT providing for the protection, care and wellbeing of children and young people.[57] The government released an exposure draft of the legislation and the Human Rights Commissioner and the Children and Young People's Commissioner made comments on it. Human rights issues were raised by practices such as therapeutic protection orders, pre-natal reporting of children at risk, strip-searching of detained children, and behaviour management schemes proposed for the youth detention centre. These human rights issues were considered extensively by policy officers involved in the preparation of the legislation, with assistance from the Human Rights Unit. This is reflected in the lengthy Explanatory Statement presented with the Bill, which refers not only to the provisions of the ACT HRA, but also to an array of relevant international standards, including the Convention on the Rights of the Child and United Nations principles relating to juvenile justice. It also draws on the audit reports of the ACT Human Rights Commissioner, discussed below.[58]

Other issues that have been considered from a human rights perspective within the ACT Executive have included sentencing laws, emergency electro-convulsive therapy legislation, the exclusion from public employment of a person with a criminal record, the setting-up of roadblocks, the prevention of prisoners from voting, the use of children for tobacco test purchases, promotional messages for blood donation on car registration stickers, the wearing of headscarves in ACT schools, and whether there are circumstances that could justify the reversal of the onus of proof in criminal cases.[59] An independent audit of ACT health legislation has been the basis of a range of legislative amendments, although the report has not been made public.[60] The audits of the Quamby Youth Detention Centre and other corrections facilities by the Human Rights Commissioner, discussed below, led to immediate reform as well as longer term plans for improvements. The newly completed Alexander Maconochie Centre is the first prison in Australia specifically designed to meet human rights standards.[61]

Changing the culture of government

One of the objectives of the ACT HRA was to 'encourage the development of a human rights-respecting culture in ACT public life and in the community generally'.[62] While the compatibility obligation has played an important role in fostering awareness of human rights, interviews with public servants suggest wide variations in the levels of knowledge about and use of the Act within the ACT Executive.[63] Senior executives and policy officers responsible for the preparation of draft legislation are likely to have been involved in the compatibility assessment process or in dialogues with the Scrutiny Committee, and generally have the greatest appreciation of the Act, but there is more limited awareness among frontline decision-makers. Although the interpretive provision in s. 30 applies not just to the courts, but to anyone interpreting Territory laws, some government officers who administer legislation do not appreciate the requirements of this provision. The need to raise awareness about the relevance of human rights to all areas of government is also reflected in the statements on the implementation of the Act in the departmental annual reports published since its commencement.[64] While a few departments have provided detailed commentary on their human rights activities, many others have given only perfunctory accounts. Revised guidelines have been issued for human rights reporting which will require more detailed information to be compiled in future annual reports.[65]

It will take time, of course, for a human rights culture to permeate all levels of government, but it will also require an ongoing commitment of resources for human rights training and the dissemination of information. The direct obligation on public authorities to comply with human rights, in effect from 1 January 2009, is likely to increase the perceived relevance of human rights considerations for a broader range of public officials, and to deepen the fledgling culture of human rights developing in the Territory.

The Human Rights Commissioner

The ACT Human Rights Commissioner, Dr Helen Watchirs, has played an important role in implementing the ACT HRA. The functions of the Commissioner include providing education about human rights and the Act, and advising the Attorney-General on anything relevant to the operation of the legislation.[66] The Commissioner has conducted regular community forums, and a range of training and education sessions on the ACT HRA for schools, the community, legal practitioners and government officers. Chief Minister and former Attorney-General Jon Stanhope has sought the advice of the Human Rights Commissioner on a range of issues, including the Commonwealth and ACT terrorism laws and the Commonwealth Government's 2007 intervention in Aboriginal communities in the Northern Territory.[67] The Commissioner has also made submissions to government on the human rights implications of proposed legislation.[68] In particular, the Commissioner's advice that a proposed law permitting the use of electro-convulsive therapy in emergency situations breached human rights led to some significant amendments to the Bill.

Under s. 36 of the ACT HRA, the Commissioner is given standing to intervene in proceedings involving the application of the Act, with the leave of the court. The Commissioner exercised this power in the case of *SI bhnf CC v KS bhnf IS*,[69] discussed below, filing comprehensive legal arguments that were adopted by the applicant in that case. The Commissioner has also intervened in some Mental Health Tribunal cases and in a discrimination claim brought against the *Canberra Times*.[70] Perhaps most significantly, s. 41 of the Act provides that the Commissioner has the power to review the effect of Territory laws on human rights, and to report on the reviews to the Attorney-General. This review power extends to laws that were in existence prior to the introduction of the Act, and includes the common law. Dr Watchirs has used this power to conduct two major human rights audits, one of the Quamby Youth Detention Centre[71] and the second of other ACT corrections facilities, including the Belconnen Remand Centre and the Symonston Temporary Remand Centre.[72] The Quamby audit made 52 recommendations for reform. The government agreed to implement 25 of the recommendations and agreed in principle with the remainder.[73] The corrections facilities audit, published in 2008, identified human rights concerns such as the treatment of detainees with mental illness, lack of activities for detainees and overcrowding, which had led to discrimination against female detainees, who were being moved back and forth (and thus subjected to additional strip-searches and sometimes missing meals) to accommodate prisoners serving weekend detention. The government accepted all but four of this audit's 98 recommendations, noting that many had already been planned for implementation in the new prison.[74]

The ACT HRA does not confer jurisdiction on the Human Rights Commissioner to receive and investigate complaints alleging violations of the Act. Nor, unlike the Victorian Charter, does the ACT HRA confer any specific role on the ACT Ombudsman.[75] However, just as violations of the Act or a failure to take it into account in relevant circumstances could be challenged in judicial review proceedings using standard grounds of review, the ACT Ombudsman has jurisdiction to consider such complaints if they relate to a 'matter of administration' falling within the *Ombudsman Act 1989* (ACT).[76]

The legislature

The ACT HRA has been effective in stimulating dialogue on human rights issues within the Legislative Assembly. Since the inception of self-government in the ACT, there has been a history of minority governments; indeed the Stanhope Labor government was dependent on the support of the cross-bench in its first term, when it passed the ACT HRA. However, Labor was re-elected in October 2004 with a majority – nine of the 17 members of the unicameral Assembly. In this context, without the usual checks and balances of a cross-bench, the ACT HRA has taken on increased importance as a tool to encourage government accountability. Although the Liberal Opposition remains sceptical about the Act, labelling it 'political self-indulgence', and has threatened to repeal it if elected,[77] its members, as well as the single member of the ACT Greens, are increasingly relying on it to hold the government to its own human rights standards. This has occurred in the context of breaches of the Act at Quamby Youth Detention Centre,[78] government intervention in the bushfire coronial inquest,[79] support for compulsory student unionism,[80] treatment of public housing tenants,[81] reducing access to administrative review,[82] imposing penalties for removing trees,[83] criticising opponents of its civic development plan,[84] and prematurely closing parliamentary debates.[85]

The ability of the legislature to participate in a dialogue with the Executive on human rights issues depends in part upon the information available to the Assembly. In some cases, such as the development of anti-terrorism laws, discussed below, the Executive has been admirably transparent, issuing an exposure draft of the proposed legislation, publishing reasons for the compatibility statement and making all advices received by the Chief Minister publicly available online. However, in other cases, both the Opposition and the ACT Greens have raised concerns about the government being unnecessarily secretive, or hiding behind the veil of Cabinet confidentiality. Greens Member Dr Deb Foskey has long campaigned for reasons to be provided for all compatibility statements.[86]

Issues that have produced serious human rights debate since the commencement of the ACT HRA include:

- the framing of offences against pregnant women, and whether the right to life under the Act prevents appropriate protection of the unborn foetus;[87]
- the use of privative clauses and call-in powers which are intended to prevent litigation;[88]
- the use of strict liability offences, and the appropriate level

of justification to be provided by the government;[89]
- lowering the compulsory voting age in the ACT to 16, in accordance with the right to equality and the rights of children;[90]
- retrospective provisions in planning legislation;[91]
- amendments to the *Freedom of Information Act 1989* (ACT), and the perception that the government lacks transparency;[92]
- a proposed needle-exchange program in the new prison;[93] and
- detention powers proposed for the Health Professions Tribunal.[94]

Perhaps the best example of the effect of the ACT HRA on ACT legislation is the cooperative counter-terrorism regime proposed by the Commonwealth Government in the wake of the London bombings in 2005.[95] Although the ACT Government had committed to introducing parallel anti-terrorism laws, it was highly critical of the Commonwealth's *Anti-Terrorism Act (No 2) 2005*, maintaining that many provisions of this Act were in breach of the right to liberty under the ICCPR. The ACT Executive prepared legislation that it considered human rights-compliant, referring an exposure draft Bill to the Standing Committee on Legal Affairs. The ACT's Terrorism (Extraordinary Temporary Powers) Bill 2006 differed in many aspects from the Commonwealth regime, including its provisions for judicial oversight of preventative detention orders, the exclusion of children from the preventative detention regime, and the omission of draconian penalties for disclosing the fact of detention. The Bill was tabled with an advice on human rights compliance by Sydney barrister Kate Eastman.

The Opposition criticised the restrictions imposed by the ACT HRA in addressing the threat posed by terrorism, but also considered that the government took too narrow a view of the Act. It argued that community interests should be given more weight under s. 28, which permits legislation to restrict the enjoyment of human rights, provided that the limitations are demonstrably justified in a free and democratic society.[96] However, others in the Assembly, including the Greens and Labor MLA Wayne Berry, expressed concerns that the Bill went too far in its incursions on the right to liberty and security of a person without sufficient justification.[97] The 2005 counter-terrorism regime was one area in which the ACT was able to have some influence over the debate at national level, with the Chief Minister releasing both the draft Commonwealth laws and his advice about the human rights compatibility on his website, galvanising opposition to the national laws.[98]

Scrutiny Committee

The ACT HRA has significantly enhanced the role of the Standing Committee on Legal Affairs, performing the duties of a Scrutiny of Bills and Subordinate Legislation Committee (the Scrutiny Committee). The bipartisan Committee already had a human rights focus prior to the enactment of the ACT HRA, but this was formalised under s. 38 of the Act, which requires the Committee to report to the Assembly on the human rights issues raised in all new bills. Unlike statements of compatibility, which only apply to government bills, the scrutiny process covers all legislation presented to the legislature. However, neither the statements of compatibility nor the scrutiny reports address the human rights implications of amendments made on the floor of the Legislative Assembly.

The scrutiny process has contributed significantly to the development of a human rights dialogue in the ACT. By 30 June 2008 the Scrutiny Committee had issued 59 reports from the time the Act came into force,[99] making thorough and detailed comments on a wide range of issues raised by bills and subordinate legislation under the Act.[100] The responses of the government to the Scrutiny Reports suggest that serious consideration is being given to the views of the Committee. The government has amended some legislative proposals in light of criticisms in the Committee's reports, for example by limiting overly broad powers given to the Environmental Protection Authority under the Water Resources Bill 2007 (ACT) and restricting the powers given to the Health Professions Tribunal to issue warrants of detention under the Health Legislation Amendment Bill (No 2) 2006 (ACT).[101]

More often, however, the government has provided additional justification in response to the Committee's concerns, but has defended its views on compatibility. There may be a tendency for some government agencies to view the statement of compatibility as a sufficient answer to issues raised by the Scrutiny Committee, which limits the potential for fruitful dialogue. For example, in his response to the Committee's concerns over provisions of the Domestic Animals Amendment Bill 2007 (ACT), Minister John Hargreaves noted that:

> The provisions of the Bill were drafted after discussion with Parliamentary Counsel's Office and in consultation with the Human Rights Unit ... A Human Rights Compatibility Statement has been provided for the Bill in its entirety. Consequently, I am confident that the strict liability offences created and the additional defences provided adequately accommodate the requirements of the *HRA*.[102]

The inclusion of, and justification for, strict liability offences have been ongoing themes in the Scrutiny Committee reports. Such provisions do not require the prosecution to prove a fault element for the offence (or part of the offence), and have the potential to infringe the presumption of innocence and the right to liberty and security of a person, particularly if the offence carries a penalty of imprisonment. The Committee has commented at length on these matters, and has frequently noted the inadequacy of some Explanatory Statements in addressing the issues.[103] In 2005, the Chief Minister acknowledged that an impasse had been reached between the views of the government and the Committee, and agreed to refer the issue to the ACT Standing Committee on Legal Affairs (essentially the same Committee) for inquiry.[104] The Committee released its report in February 2008, recommending a comprehensive audit of ACT legislation to determine the prevalence of strict liability offences and their appropriateness in each case.[105]

As a bipartisan committee, the Scrutiny Committee does not comment on the policy aspects of the legislation it scrutinises.[106] In accordance with this approach, the Committee has not generally taken a conclusive view on whether particular restrictions on rights can be justified under the limitation provision in s. 28 of the Act, and has instead left these questions to be considered by the Assembly. However, the Committee has increasingly provided guidance on the methodology for applying s. 28,[107] and has occasionally expressed strong opinions about whether particular limitations might be considered disproportionate.[108]

Other committees

The ACT HRA has also been considered in inquiries of other committees of the Legislative Assembly. One striking example is in the report of the Standing Committee on Planning and Environment into a proposed commercial development in the Canberra suburb of Kingston.[109] The Committee examined whether the development would infringe the right to privacy of nearby residents, and the right of protection of the family, devoting several pages to a detailed analysis of judgments of the UK courts and the European Court of Human Rights where these issues had been considered. The Committee ultimately concluded that the development would not infringe these rights, but recommended that the ACT Planning and Land Authority expressly address the relevance of the ACT HRA to the discharge of its statutory and non-statutory responsibilities.

The courts and tribunals

The ACT HRA has been used cautiously by both the ACT judiciary and legal profession. As at 30 June 2008, the Act had been referred to in some 66 cases. The majority of these (42 cases) have been in the Supreme Court, with the remainder divided between the Court of Appeal (nine cases), Magistrates Court (four cases), Administrative Appeals Tribunal (five cases), Residential Tenancies Tribunal (four cases) and the Children's Court (one case). A further case was heard by the Discrimination Tribunal in mid-2006, but the judgment remains reserved.[110] Leave to appeal to the High Court was sought but refused in the case of *Griffin v The Queen*.[111]

Some 60 per cent of these cases concern the criminal law, covering issues such as bail, search warrants, admissibility of evidence, treatment of persons in custody, the particular rights of children in the criminal process, the right to trial without undue delay, and sentencing issues, including circle sentencing, a community-based sentencing option for Indigenous offenders. The Act has also been referred to in variety of civil matters, including those involving protection orders, adoption, care matters, defamation, discrimination, personal injury, mental health proceedings and public housing, as well as fencing of yards, poker machine licensing and leasing disputes. However, many of these cases involve only a very superficial consideration of the Act, and in most cases it has been used to bolster a conclusion reached on other grounds. As of mid-2008, no declarations of incompatibility had been made by the Supreme Court.

Interpretation of legislation

As noted above, the original interpretive provision in the ACT HRA was a complex one, which was never the subject of detailed analysis by the ACT courts or tribunals. Nevertheless, competing approaches emerged as to whether ambiguity was required before the interpretive principle could be brought into play. A number of tribunal decisions took a narrow view, refusing to consider the application of the Act unless there was a clear ambiguity in the legislation to be interpreted, even though the original wording of s. 30 defined the task of interpretation to include 'confirming or displacing the apparent meaning of the law'.[112] The courts generally appeared to take a broader view of the interpretive mandate.[113] The narrow approach of the Administrative Appeals Tribunal was explicitly overruled by the Supreme Court in *Commissioner for Housing in the ACT v Y*.[114] In that case, a single mother of two young children had been refused public housing after the income threshold for eligibility was lowered while she was on the waiting list. A substantial portion of her income was committed to leasing a car which she needed to transport her children to school and childcare, and she could not afford to rent in the private market. Chief Justice Higgins found that the Commissioner should have interpreted an exemption provision more broadly, in accordance with human rights, and should have given the applicant the benefit of this exemption in assessing her income, overturning the restrictive approach taken by the Tribunal in an earlier case.[115]

In a case relating to the requirement under the *Legislation Act* to interpret legislation consistently with its purpose, the ACT Court of Appeal noted that both this provision and the interpretive provision in s. 30 of the Act shared a similar form to the interpretive clause of the UK Human Rights Act 1998 (UK HRA).[116] In this context, the Court endorsed the views of Lord Nicholls in *Ghaidan v Godin-Mendoza*,[117] that such a provision 'may require a court to depart from the unambiguous meaning the legislation would otherwise bear'.[118] However, as discussed below, this reasoning may not be readily applicable to the new wording of s. 30 of the ACT HRA, which is constrained by reference to the purpose of the legislation being interpreted.[119]

Another case that raised the issue of the scope of the interpretive mandate (prior to the 2008 amendment) and its interaction with the power to issue a declaration of incompatibility, was *SI bhnf CC v KS bhnf IS*.[120] This case concerned a protection order sought by one child against another child at the same Canberra high school. It involved consideration of a new provision in the *Domestic Violence and Protection Orders Act 2001* (ACT) that required the respondent to return a notice seven days prior to the hearing, failing which an interim protection order would become final automatically. The ACT Attorney-General and the Human Rights Commissioner both intervened in this case and made detailed submissions (urging opposite conclusions) about the compatibility of this provision with the right to a fair trial. A declaration of incompatibility was one outcome sought by the respondent child, and this found some support in the submissions of the Human Rights Commissioner, but the possibility of a declaration was not considered by Chief Justice Higgins. Instead, the Chief Justice reinterpreted the statute, in essence rewriting the fairly clear words of the provision, to give the magistrate discretion to hear the matter where the notice requirement had not been complied with. Although this outcome suggests a broad and robust approach to the interpretive power, the utility of the decision as a precedent is undermined by its lack of explicit reasoning, and the fact that the Chief Justice also relied upon the doctrine of separation of powers, and even the Magna Carta, to justify the result.[121]

From 18 March 2008, the interpretive task of the courts under the new s. 30 is similar, though not identical. This provision maintains the condition that any human rights-consistent interpretation must be consistent with the 'purpose' of the statute, a phrase that does not appear in the corresponding interpretive provision in the UK HRA.[122] The key difference is that under the new s. 30 a human rights-consistent interpretation of a law must prevail, unless it is inconsistent with the purpose of the law. The new provision had not been directly considered by the ACT courts by mid-2008, although Justice Refshauge of the ACT Supreme Court has noted the effect of the amendment has been to 'strengthen the requirement for consistency with human rights'.[123]

Specific issues addressed by the courts

The courts have expressed their views on a number of important issues relating to the application of the ACT HRA, though often only in passing or in comments that do not form an essential part of the decision's reasoning. For example, the Supreme Court has argued that its own powers, being conferred by statute, must be construed and exercised in accordance with the Act. Under s. 20 of the *Supreme Court Act 1933* (ACT), the Supreme Court has 'all original and appellate jurisdiction that is necessary to administer justice in the Territory' and any 'jurisdiction conferred by a Commonwealth Act or a law of the Territory'. The Court has affirmed the relevance of the ACT HRA to its power to grant stays of proceedings in criminal cases or to decide whether to take coercive measures to compel a witness to testify.[124] It has similarly noted the relevance of the Act when exercising specific discretions conferred on it by other statutes, for example its power to grant bail under the *Bail Act 1992* (ACT),[125] its power to authorise adoption and dispense with parental consent under the *Adoption Act 1993* (ACT),[126] its power to strike out applications under the *Court Procedures Rules 2006* (ACT),[127] or its discretion to permit a personal injury action to proceed even though the applicant had failed to give the respondent notice of her intention to bring proceedings within the prescribed time.[128] The Court has not considered whether it is obliged to take the ACT HRA into account in stating or developing the common law in the exercise of its statutory jurisdiction.

A range of other ACT HRA-related issues have come before the courts. For example, the Supreme Court has held that the power of the Director of Public Prosecutions to discontinue a prosecution by entering a *nolle prosequi* under the *Director of Public Prosecutions Act 1990* (ACT) must be read in light of the rights in criminal proceedings and the right to a fair trial of the ACT HRA.[129] It has suggested that while 'there is nothing in the [ACT HRA] which prevents the legislature from enacting offences of strict liability',[130] the right to liberty and security of person and protection against arbitrary arrest and detention in s. 18(1) 'would be inconsistent with disproportionate punishments or the imposition of punishment for conduct for which the actor is not, on any rational view, responsible'.[131] Another case has held that a civil servant acting as a coroner may breach the right to a hearing by an independent tribunal.[132] The courts have also decided that the provision in the *Magistrates Court Act 1930* (ACT) permitting an appeal by the prosecution upon the ground that 'the decision ... should not in law have been made' is consistent with the right not to be tried for an offence for which one has 'already been finally convicted or acquitted according to law'.[133] The courts have also decided that the ACT HRA affects police powers when the Australian Federal Police (AFP) are applying for and executing warrants under ACT law, even though the Act does not directly bind the AFP.[134]

The remedial power of the courts in cases involving violations of the Act has not attracted much attention. Prior to the direct right of action and remedy provision coming into effect in 2009, the courts have relied on their inherent powers to rectify some breaches of human rights.[135] Thus, the Supreme Court has held that in the case of unreasonable delay in bringing a person to trial contrary to the Act, a stay may be appropriate. In two cases, conditional stays were granted, which were to become permanent if the prosecution did not pay the defendants costs for the delay in bringing on the trial.[136] In a case in the Children's Court, a permanent stay of proceedings was granted because of unjustified delay in bringing a prosecution against a minister.[137]

A recurring issue with bills of rights in other jurisdictions has been the extent to which the rights contained in such instruments go beyond the rights already enjoyed under statutory provisions or the common law.[138] The ACT courts have recognised that, while many of the protections contained in the ACT HRA are already guaranteed by existing laws, the Act extends those protections in some areas. One example is the guarantee of a right to a fair hearing under s. 21 of the Act. The Court of

Appeal in *R v Griffin*[139] noted that s. 21:

> now is the source, under Territory law, of the right to a
> fair trial. The difference may be one of emphasis rather
> than of substance. It does, however, mean that there is
> now a positive right to a fair trial rather than the right
> not to be tried unfairly as the common law provides.
> It may be that would make a difference in some cases,
> though in this case it seems to us to lead to the same
> result.[140]

Use of international human rights law

Section 31 of the ACT HRA allows 'international law, and the
judgments of foreign and international courts and tribunals,
relevant to a human right' to be used in interpreting rights under
the Act. A good example of recourse to such jurisprudence is
the Supreme Court decision in *R v Upton*.[141] In considering an
application for a stay of criminal proceedings because of considerable delay in the prosecution, Justice Connolly noted that the
common law allowed a stay to be granted in certain cases. The
source of this power was the broad grant of jurisdiction in s.
20 of the *Supreme Court Act 1933* (ACT). If this provision was
interpreted to be consistent with the right to trial without unreasonable delay in the ACT HRA, it might confer a greater power
on the Court than it enjoyed under the common law. Justice
Connolly examined cases decided under the UK HRA and the
Bill of Rights Act 1990 (NZ) on the right to be tried without
delay, and relied on the principles they had expounded to grant
a conditional stay of proceedings.[142] The ACT Court of Appeal
has also drawn on comparative jurisprudence, as well as the
views of the UN Human Rights Committee.[143]

Role of the legal profession

A striking feature of the first four years of the operation of the ACT HRA has been the relatively low level of interest on the part of the legal profession. While there have been some cases where lawyers have put forward detailed submissions drawing on the Act, there is still reticence among the ACT legal profession to invoke it. The Human Rights Commission has run a number of general training sessions, but there has been little funding for education programs in the ACT compared, for example, to those preceding the introduction of the UK HRA and the Victorian Charter.

The ACT legal profession has also generally tended to dismiss the value of a bill of rights that contains no explicit right of action. A leading Hong Kong and New Zealand barrister, Gerard McCoy QC, has speculated that this might be the result of either 'forensic somnolence or intellectual recumbency',[144] but it is more likely a product of the small size and strongly practical focus of the Canberra legal community and its unfamiliarity with international human rights law and standards. The limited use of the ACT HRA mirrors the early New Zealand experience, where it took almost five years for the Bill of Rights Act to be used regularly. The earlier take-up of the UK HRA may be explicable by UK lawyers' experience with human rights litigation under the European Convention on Human Rights and the fact that the UK law provided an explicit right of action against public authorities from the start. Invocation of the UK HRA is now almost a necessary step on the way to the European Court of Human Rights, due to the requirement under the European Convention that local remedies be exhausted.[145]

The existence of a direct right of action under the ACT HRA, introduced in 2008 and in force from 2009, might significantly increase the appeal of the Act to the legal profession. The Attorney-General has predicted:

> In time, the government looks forward to the growth in
> the number of cases and the depth of argument on the

> issues. In due course, we may see the trickle of human
> rights case law turn into a stream. This stream will be
> the evidence of the growing awareness of human rights
> in this jurisdiction and the strength of the underlying
> legal principles.[146]

Nevertheless, it is likely that the exclusion of damages as an available remedy under the new amendments will continue to restrain the development of human rights litigation in the Territory.

What difference has Australia's first bill of rights made to the protection of human rights in the Territory? Since its enactment in 2004, the ACT HRA has not attracted significant public attention, and its workings have not always been apparent to the broader community. Parts of the bureaucracy are still to become familiar with the legislation and the implications of protecting human rights. Nevertheless, the Act has operated in subtle ways to enhance the standing of human rights in the ACT.

One of the clearest effects of the Act has been to improve the quality of law-making in the Territory, to ensure that human rights concerns are given due consideration in the framing of new legislation and policy, and that rights are not sacrificed in the pursuit of other community objectives. The development of new laws by the Executive has clearly been shaped by the requirement to issue a statement of compatibility for each new bill, and the approach of government has been influenced by a robust dialogue with the legislature, the Scrutiny Committee and the Human Rights Commissioner. These improved laws may have tangible benefits over the longer term, particularly in the form of additional safeguards for vulnerable individuals in the community, including children in the care and protection system, those in the criminal justice and corrections system, the mentally ill, and others dependent upon government services. Although human rights case law has not yet developed to a sophisticated level in the ACT, at times the courts have also played a valuable role in considering the human rights implications of legislation and procedure, and in moderating the effect of bureaucratic decisions that have unfairly affected the rights of individuals.

The ACT HRA has not remained a static document, and a number of provisions have already been improved in response to the lessons learned in these early years. The amendments to the Act that come into effect in 2009 will have a more far-reaching effect on the relationship between the government and the community, with all public servants and agencies required to directly apply human rights principles in their actions and decision-making. These provisions will also give greater prominence to the courts in overseeing the implementation of human rights principles by public authorities.

Another significant impact of the Act has been on the debate about bills of rights in other States and Territories, and at a national level. The enactment of the ACT HRA served as a catalyst for a public consultation on human rights protection in Victoria, which in turn led to the enactment of the Victorian Charter. This development is explored in chapter 5.

5

The Victorian *Charter*
of Human Rights and
Responsibilities 2006

On 25 July 2006, just over two years after the introduction of the ACT *Human Rights Act 2004* (ACT HRA), the Victorian *Charter of Human Rights and Responsibilities Act 2006* (Victorian Charter) passed into law. The Victorian Charter was developed following a wide-ranging community consultation conducted by an independent committee that had drawn lessons from the ACT experience. The resulting Charter is a non-entrenched Act of Parliament sharing most of the features of the ACT HRA, but with some interesting variations that in turn have been a catalyst for further development in the ACT. The Victorian Charter has been progressively implemented, with parliamentary scrutiny and compatibility processes coming into effect on 1 January 2007, and provisions relating to public authorities and the courts commencing on 1 January 2008.[1] This chapter describes the background to the adoption of the Charter, explores the key features of this legislation, then considers its impact on the Victorian government, legislature and the courts in its early years.

History

Previous attempts to develop a Victorian bill of rights

The issue of a Victorian bill of rights was considered in the 1970s as part of a brief debate over the consolidation of the Victorian Constitution into the *Constitution Act 1975* (Vic),[2] and was referred to the Statute Law Revision Committee for consideration after the new Constitution was proclaimed.[3] The Committee conducted a perfunctory inquiry and issued a slim report in 1979, in which it concluded that there were already sufficient safeguards for human rights in the State, and that the case for a bill of rights had not been made out.[4]

The issue was revived in 1983 with Commonwealth Attorney-General Gareth Evans' proposal for a national bill of rights and the subsequent referral of an inquiry to the Senate Standing Committee on Constitutional and Legal Affairs in April 1985.[5] In May 1985, Victorian Attorney-General Jim Kennan asked the Legal and Constitutional Committee of the Victorian Parliament to inquire into 'the desirability of Parliament enacting legislation which defines and protects human rights in Victoria'.[6] The Committee conducted a public consultation, releasing three discussion papers. It sought submissions and conducted hearings in rural Victoria and Melbourne, and within Melbourne's major prisons.[7] The Committee found much evidence to suggest that human rights were not adequately protected in the State.[8] The controversy generated by the Bowen Bill (1985) (see chapter 2) at the Commonwealth level, however, effectively ruled out an enforceable bill of rights as a viable political option for Victoria.[9] The Victorian Legal and Constitutional Committee instead recommended that an unenforceable 'Victorian Declaration of Rights and Freedoms' (comprising civil and political rights) be added to the State Constitution, coupled with a human rights scrutiny of bills function to be assigned to a parliamentary committee.[10]

The Labor government of Premier John Cain reacted strongly

to criticisms of its human rights record in the Committee's report. The Premier went as far as to condemn the report as 'one of the worst pieces of rubbish' he had seen from a committee, although he later withdrew this remark.[11] In 1988, the Victorian Labor government introduced the Constitution (Declaration of Rights and Freedoms) Bill, which conspicuously omitted the recommended scrutiny of bills function. In the end, the Bill was not pursued by the government, and was allowed to lapse.[12] In 1992, after a change of government in the State, the Scrutiny of Acts and Regulations Committee (SARC) was established, with general scrutiny powers, but no specific declaration of rights was added to the Constitution.

The Justice Statement 2004

Like the ACT HRA, the Victorian Charter was the product of individual political commitment and determination, rather than a broad-based party initiative. Victorian Attorney-General Rob Hulls had witnessed first-hand the human rights issues faced by Indigenous Australians when he had worked as a defence lawyer in Mount Isa,[13] and had served as chief of staff to Jim Kennan, proponent of the ill-fated 1985 bill of rights inquiry.

In the Attorney-General's Justice Statement, *New Directions for the Victorian Justice System 2004–2014*, issued in May 2004, Hulls promised to establish a process of discussion and consultation with the Victorian community on how human rights and obligations could best be promoted and protected in the State, including the examination of options such as a charter of human rights and responsibilities.[14] The Justice Statement included an overview of the possible models of a human rights charter, and the advantages and disadvantages of adopting human rights legislation, without expressing a governmental view or preference.[15]

The Consultation Committee

On 17 April 2005, Attorney-General Hulls announced the appointment of the Human Rights Consultation Committee that would lead this discussion.[16] The Committee was to be chaired by constitutional lawyer Professor George Williams of the University of New South Wales. The other members were Rhonda Galbally AO, a disability advocate, Professor Haddon Storey QC, a former Liberal politician and State Attorney-General, and Andrew Gaze, a high-profile basketball player and former Olympic team captain. A Human Rights Unit was established within the Department of Justice to support the work of the Committee, which was to be provided with specialist legal counsel by the Victorian Solicitor-General, Pamela Tate SC.

In contrast to the broad terms of reference given to the ACT Bill of Rights Consultative Committee, in May 2005 the Victorian Government issued a detailed and prescriptive 'Statement of Intent' for the consultation process, setting out the government's view of the scope of issues that should form the basis of the Committee's work and be the subject of public submissions.[17] The Statement specified the particular form and content of a bill of rights preferred by the government. The favoured model was a non-entrenched legislative charter virtually indistinguishable from the ACT HRA, one that would not give the courts power to invalidate legislation, but that would allow judges to play a role through interpretation and 'mechanisms that promote dialogue' about human rights. The creation of new individual causes of action based on human rights breaches was ruled out.[18] The Statement of Intent also excluded economic, social and cultural rights from any charter, as it considered that these would 'raise difficult issues of resource allocation' better left to Parliament for scrutiny and debate.[19] Within these significant constraints, the Committee was asked to make recommendations on a suitable framework for human rights in Victoria, based on the views of the community, to be obtained through written submissions and public consultations.

The detailed prescriptions in the Statement of Intent elicited some criticism, particularly from the community sector, that the government had prejudged critical issues prior to public consultation. The Chair of the Committee, George Williams, however, has argued that the Statement of Intent was valuable in signifying the government's endorsement of a bill of rights and the political will to implement such a model if the Committee found it had public support.[20]

The community consultation was formally launched by the Attorney-General on 1 June 2005. At that time, the Committee released a discussion paper with a range of brochures and summary versions of the paper in English and community languages.[21] The consultation process adopted was influenced by the community-based consultation conducted by the ACT Committee, but adapted to a much larger scale. Rather than holding public 'town hall' style meetings, which had had mixed success in attracting attendance in Canberra, the Committee met with small groups and community associations throughout Victoria. These consultations targeted potential opponents of bills of rights, and those who knew little about them, rather than preaching to the converted.[22] The Committee also used 'devolved consultation', working with the Victorian Council of Social Services, the Federation of Community Legal Centres (Vic), the PILCH Homeless Persons Clinic and the Youth Affairs Council to engage with disadvantaged groups which would otherwise have been difficult to reach through the public consultation.[23]

The ACT experience had shown the importance of engaging with the public service bureaucracy throughout the consultation, rather than assuming support from the Executive for a bill of rights initiative. The Victorian Committee thus conducted a parallel process of consultation within government. An interdepartmental committee was established to shadow the consultation process and to have input before ideas were crystallised in the Committee's report.[24]

The consultation process led to an exceptional response from the community. Despite the very tight timetable, the Committee received 2524 written submissions.[25] Of these, 84 per cent supported change to protect human rights in Victoria, and an overwhelming majority were in favour of a charter or other formal instrument.[26] A substantial proportion (41 per cent) of submissions specifically supported the inclusion of economic, social and cultural rights.[27] The importance of responsibilities as a counterpart to human rights also emerged as a strong theme from the community consultation.[28]

Consultation Committee Report

The Committee delivered its report, entitled *Rights, Responsibilities and Respect*, on 30 November 2005. It contained 35 recommendations, proposing a legislative charter of rights which fell largely within the parameters set by the Victorian Government in its Statement of Intent. The report annexed a draft 'Charter of Human Rights and Responsibilities' in the form of a non-entrenched Act of Parliament.[29] The Committee recommended that this charter be limited to rights drawn from the International Covenant on Civil and Political Rights 1966 (ICCPR),[30] with the language modernised for the Victorian context.[31] The Committee did not favour the inclusion of economic, social and cultural rights, but recommended that this be reconsidered in future reviews.[32] No specific responsibilities were to be added to the list of human rights, but it was recommended that the Preamble should recognise that 'human rights come with responsibilities and must be exercised in a way that respects the human rights of others'.[33]

The Charter of Human Rights and Responsibilities Bill 2005

Attorney-General Hulls announced three weeks later that the government would enact a charter in line with the report's central recommendations.[34] After five months of negotiation and fine-tuning, the Charter of Human Rights and Responsibilities Bill was introduced into the Victorian Parliament on 2 May 2006. The Bill substantially replicated the draft Charter annexed to the Consultation Committee's report, but with some key differences. The 'declaration of incompatibility' in the draft

Charter was recast in the Bill as a 'declaration of inconsistent interpretation',[35] emphasising that the opinion of the Supreme Court should not be regarded as the final word in a human rights dialogue.[36] In the final Bill, the consequences of such a declaration would also be less immediate: the Minister would have up to six months to publish the declaration, rather than the ten days recommended by the Committee, and the role of the Scrutiny Committee in responding to declarations was removed.[37] A provision giving standing to third parties to intervene in human rights cases was also omitted.[38] The Committee had recommended that the Charter include an override provision, giving the Parliament power to exempt specified laws from the operation of the Charter. In the draft, this provision only applied to new legislation, but was extended in the Bill to allow Parliament to pass an override declaration in relation to an existing Act.[39]

Following intense lobbying from religious groups, the government moved a last-minute amendment to the Bill on 15 June 2006, which gave specific protection to religious bodies carrying out public functions where such bodies are 'acting in conformity with the religious doctrines, beliefs or principles in accordance with which [they] operate'.[40] The amended Bill was passed by the Legislative Assembly that afternoon, and by the Legislative Council on 20 July 2006. It received royal assent on 25 July 2006.

The Victorian Charter

The Victorian Charter came into force on 1 January 2007, with the exception of Divisions 3 and 4 of Part 3, relating to the interpretation of laws, declarations of inconsistent interpretation and the new obligations on public authorities, which did not commence until 1 January 2008. Although some significant changes were made in its transition from the Consultation Committee's proposals to the Act as passed, the Victorian

Charter largely reflects the work and recommendations of the Consultation Committee. It also shares most of the features of the ACT HRA, with some notable modifications.

Rights protected by the Victorian Charter

The rights protected by the Victorian Charter are drawn from the ICCPR:

- the right to recognition and equality before the law (s. 8);
- the right to life (s. 9);
- protection from torture and cruel, inhuman and degrading treatment (s. 10);
- freedom from forced work (s. 11);
- freedom of movement (s. 12);
- protection of privacy and reputation (s. 13);
- freedom of thought, conscience, religion and belief (s. 14);
- freedom of expression (s. 15);
- free assembly and association (s. 16);
- protection of families and children (s. 17);
- the right to participate in political and public life (s. 18);
- cultural rights (s. 19);
- the right to liberty and security of person (s. 21);[41]
- the right to humane treatment when deprived of liberty (s. 22);
- rights of children in the criminal process (s. 23);
- the right to a fair hearing (s. 24) and rights in criminal proceedings (s. 25);
- the right not to be punished more than once for the same offence (s. 26); and
- a prohibition against retrospective criminal laws (s. 26).

The cultural rights guaranteed under s. 19 of the Victorian Charter go further than the minority rights provision in the ACT HRA (s. 27). Section 19 affirms the rights of members of all cultural, religious, racial or linguistic communities to exercise various rights related to membership in those communities. It further recognises the distinct cultural rights of Aborigines to maintain kinship ties, and their spiritual, material and economic relationship with the land, waters and other resources with which they have a traditional connection. Section 20, which protects people from being deprived of property other than in accordance with law, is also a distinguishing feature of the Victorian Charter.

Unlike the ACT HRA, the right to life in the Victorian Charter does not include an express limitation that the right commences from birth. However, s. 48 provides that the Charter does not affect any law applicable to abortion or child destruction, whether passed before or after the Charter.[42] While this change may have been calculated to avoid controversy over a more obvious limitation on the right to life, it has led to speculation as to the scope of the right, for example in relation to laws dealing with scientific research on *in-vitro* fertilisation and cloned embryos, which do not fall squarely within the class of laws exempted.[43] This provision may have the consequence of excluding abortion and child destruction laws from the application of other human rights in the Charter, so that, for example, a law that compelled intellectually disabled women to undergo abortions could not be challenged under the Charter even though it might breach numerous other rights.

The rights in the Victorian Charter are enjoyed only by human persons, not corporations. They are subject to a general limitation in s. 7, which provides that a human right may be subject under law only to such reasonable limits as can be demonstrably justified in a free and democratic society based on human dignity, equality and freedom. The section goes on to specify the relevant factors that must be taken into account in determining whether a limitation is reasonable; these are essentially the same, non-exhaustive factors that also now appear in s. 28 of the ACT HRA.[44]

Some Charter rights are subject to additional limitations not found in the ACT HRA. For example, the right to a fair hearing in s. 24 of the Charter provides that journalists and the general public may be excluded from court proceedings where permitted by another law.[45] The right to legal representation in s. 25 is also specifically limited by eligibility criteria for legal aid. The right to examine witnesses for and against one is guaranteed in s. 25(2)(g) 'unless otherwise provided by law'.[46] The right to vote and be elected and the right of access to public service employment and public offices is limited to 'eligible' persons, and the right to freedom of expression may be subject to additional restrictions apart from those in s. 7.

The guarantees against discrimination in the Victorian Charter are tied to the concept of discrimination in the *Equal Opportunity Act 1995* (Vic).[47] This has three consequences: first, the Charter's protection against discrimination will vary as the coverage of the *Equal Opportunity Act* changes. Second, the protection afforded under Victorian law by the combined effect of the Charter and the *Equal Opportunity Act* is less extensive than is required under the ICCPR, art. 26 of which contains an open-ended list of statuses on the basis of which discrimination is not permissible. Third, the Equal Opportunity and Human Rights Commission's complaint jurisdiction will in effect apply to claims of discrimination under the Charter, though these will need to be couched in terms of the *Equal Opportunity Act*.

Overview of the enforcement provisions of the Victorian Charter

The Victorian Charter contains a number of mechanisms for the implementation and enforcement of its rights guarantees:

- any Member of Parliament (including an Opposition Member) who introduces a new Bill must prepare a compatibility statement. Unlike the ACT HRA, the Charter requires reasons to be stated for the determination of compatibility or incompatibility (s. 28);
- the SARC must consider and report to Parliament on the compatibility of new bills and subordinate legislation with human rights (s. 30);

- Parliament may exempt an Act (or part of an Act) from the operation of the Charter for a period of five years (with provision for renewal (s. 31)), by enacting an override declaration. This override provision is similar to that in the Canadian Charter of Rights and Freedoms 1982 (albeit in a very different context), and has no counterpart in the ACT HRA. Such a declaration is meant to be used only in 'exceptional circumstances', and these must be explained to the Parliament by the proponent of the override Bill (ss. 31(3), (4));
- all statutory provisions must be interpreted, by the courts and any other decision-maker, in a way that is compatible with human rights, so far as is possible to do so consistently with their purpose. International and comparative human rights jurisprudence may be considered in the process of interpretation (s. 32);[48]
- where the Supreme Court forms an opinion that a statutory provision cannot be interpreted consistently with a human right, it may make a declaration of inconsistent interpretation (s. 36). The Minister administering the relevant statutory provision has six months in which to table the declaration of inconsistent interpretation and a written response in Parliament (s. 37);
- it is unlawful for a public authority to act in a way that is incompatible with a human right or to fail to give proper consideration to a relevant human right in decision making, except where the public authority is constrained by law, and could not reasonably have acted or decided differently (s. 38).[49] The Charter provides a limited remedy for breach of this obligation (s. 39);[50]
- the Victorian Equal Opportunity and Human Rights Commission (VEOHRC)[51] may intervene in proceedings involving Charter issues (s. 40). The Commission plays an educative and advisory role, and can conduct human rights reviews where requested by the Attorney-General or a public

authority (s. 41), but is not given power to carry out audits on its own initiative such as those undertaken by the ACT Human Rights Commissioner. Nor is it given the function of receiving individual complaints of violations of the Charter by public authorities; and

- the Victorian Ombudsman has the power to inquire into or investigate whether any administrative action is incompatible with a human right set out in the Charter.[52]

The Victorian Charter is to be reviewed in 2011 and 2015. The first review must consider whether additional human rights, including economic, social and cultural rights, should be included in the Charter. It must also consider whether further provision should be made for remedies for breach of the Charter rights by public authorities (s 44).

Application of the Victorian Charter

Unlike the ACT HRA, which is silent on the issue of to whom it applies, the Victorian Charter is explicitly stated to apply to the Parliament, to courts and tribunals and to public authorities, each to a specified extent. This provision notes (in s. 6(2)(b)) that the Charter applies to courts and tribunals in relation to their 'functions' under Part 2 of the Charter, that is, the list of substantive human rights, *as well as their other specific duties.* Some commentators have taken this to mean that the courts and tribunals are directly bound by the Charter's human rights guarantees relating to court proceedings, such as the right to a fair trial or the presumption of innocence,[53] or that the courts and tribunals may be required to give effect to human rights more generally in interpreting and applying the common law.[54] It appears that this was not a result explicitly contemplated by the government or the Consultation Committee.[55] The precise meaning and implications of s. 6(2)(b) have yet to be resolved by the courts.[56]

Obligations on public authorities

The direct duty imposed on public authorities was an innovative feature of the Victorian Charter, although a similar provision has now been introduced in the ACT HRA.[57] Section 38(1) of the Charter, which came into effect on 1 January 2008, provides that:

> It is unlawful for a public authority to act in a way
> that is incompatible with a human right or, in making
> a decision, to fail to give proper consideration to a
> relevant human right.[58]

This does not apply where as a result of a law (including a Commonwealth, State or other law), the public authority could not reasonably have acted differently or made a different decision,[59] and applies only to public, not private, actions.[60] Under a specific exemption for religious bodies, a public authority (including a religious body) is not required to act or make a decision that has the effect of impeding or preventing a religious body from acting in conformity with its religious doctrines, beliefs or principles.[61]

The duty imposed under this provision is significant, particularly in its clear prohibition on public authorities acting in a way which is incompatible with a human right. This duty has not yet been the subject of detailed analysis by Victorian courts or tribunals. One contentious issue is whether public authorities may rely on the justifiable limits provision in s. 7(2) of the Charter, or whether (as a literal reading of ss. 7(2) and (3) suggest), even proportionate limitations on human rights may only be imposed under laws.[62]

The definition of 'public authority' in s. 4 of the Charter conclusively identifies a range of entities as public authorities, including government Ministers, public officials, Victoria Police, local councils, councillors and staff, and, when acting in an administrative capacity, courts and tribunals. Other entities may be added or excluded through regulations.[63]

The specific exemption of the courts and tribunals from the obligations of public authorities when acting in their judicial capacity was the result of constitutional concerns.[64] However, as legal academic Jeremy Gans has warned, this exclusion might considerably weaken the enforcement of key human rights under the Charter:

> the resulting legal effect of the Charter on the conduct of court proceedings would be, at best, a pastiche of weak restraints, waxing and waning as courts drift between their administrative and non-administrative capacities, proceedings pass in and out of the purview of suitably malleable statutory provisions and public authorities enter and leave the courtroom.[65]

In addition to the specified public authorities, the definition extends to statutory authorities that have functions of a public nature and other entities whose functions are or include functions of a public nature, when exercising those functions on behalf of the State or a public authority (whether under contract or otherwise). This open-ended definition recognises the increasing tendency of governments to outsource their traditional functions to private entities, and seeks to ensure that a government agency cannot in this way 'contract out' of its human rights obligations. This approach follows the lead of the Human Rights Act 1998 (UK), but includes an explicit list of criteria to be considered in applying the test of functionality, in an attempt to avoid the unduly narrow approach that has been taken by the courts in that jurisdiction.[66] Nevertheless, as legal academics Simon Evans and Carolyn Evans have noted, the key Charter criterion of a public authority having a function connected to or identified with a 'function of government' is not an objective one, and its meaning may need to be determined by the courts.[67]

Remedies for breach of human rights obligations

Although the Victorian Charter imposes a robust duty on public authorities to comply with human rights, the remedies available under the Charter for a breach of these duties are limited.[68] This reflects the constraints of the Statement of Intent on the Victorian human rights consultation, which declared that 'the Government does not wish to create new individual causes of action based on human rights breaches'.[69] Section 39 relevantly provides:

> (1) If, otherwise than because of this Charter, a person may seek any relief or remedy in respect of an act or decision of a public authority on the ground that the act or decision was unlawful, that person may seek that relief or remedy on a ground of unlawfulness arising because of this Charter.
>
> ...
>
> (3) A person is not entitled to be awarded any damages because of a breach of this Charter.

The remedy provision in the Charter has been the focus of much speculation, and competing interpretations have been suggested regarding the interaction of the pre-existing cause of action and the ground of unlawfulness under the provision.[70] It would be unfortunate if a remedy for a breach of the Charter by a public authority were to depend on an artificial process requiring plaintiffs to identify and develop a case under an existing ground of review, for which a Charter ground would later be substituted. Such a construction would be inconsistent with the Charter's objectives, as it might arbitrarily deny redress to some plaintiffs who had a strong case under the Charter, but not an additional claim under existing administrative law grounds. It remains to be seen which approach will be favoured by the courts.[71]

The Victorian Charter in operation

The progressive implementation of the Victorian Charter reduced its visibility in the early stages, as the first raft of provisions to become operative related primarily to the certification and scrutiny of legislation in Parliament. Indeed, some commentators appear to have missed its commencement on 1 January 2007, reporting it as a new development for 2008.[72] However, the introduction of the Charter was marked by considerable preparatory activity in the public sector, the foreshadowing of Charter issues in the courts, and the opening remarks in a fledgling human rights dialogue between the Executive and the Parliament.

The Executive

As in the ACT, the greatest impact of the Victorian Charter in its first years has been felt by the Executive. The requirement to assess all new legislative proposals for consistency with human rights and to issue reasoned statements of compatibility under s. 28 has had a significant effect on government practice. Government agencies and public servants are also subject to the obligations of public authorities, which came into effect on 1 January 2008.

Statements of compatibility

The VEOHRC register recorded 88 statements of compatibility tabled in 2007, 85 of which were prepared by the government.[73] The scrutiny process followed by the government is more readily apparent in Victoria than in the ACT, as the Victorian Charter requires that compatibility statements include reasons for the determination of compatibility, in contrast to the minimalist statements provided for in the ACT HRA. Each of the statements of compatibility tabled thus far have found the respective Bill to be compatible with the Charter, many noting that there was a restriction on a guaranteed right but arguing that it was a justifiable limitation. By 30 June 2008, there had been no use of the override provision in the Charter.

While the statement of compatibility is made by the Member of Parliament responsible for the bill, in practice the preparation of statements for government bills falls to the departmental officer responsible for developing the legislative proposal.[74] The Human Rights Unit in the Department of Justice nevertheless played a supervisory role in the early days of the Charter. The Government Solicitor's Office also convenes a practice group and provides legal advice and assistance to other government departments on Charter matters. However, the government has not adopted the New Zealand practice of releasing legal advice on Charter consistency issues.[75]

Guidelines and a template have been adopted for government statements of compatibility, which require an overview of the purpose of the bill, a statement regarding each Charter right that is engaged by the bill, the provisions that engage it, and whether the right is limited. Where a right is limited, the template requires analysis of whether the limitation can be justified as 'reasonable' and 'demonstrably justified in a free and democratic society based on human dignity, equality and freedom' under s. 7(2) of the Charter.[76]

While government statements of compatibility have generally adhered to the template format, and most are well reasoned, the depth of the analysis varies. For example, the statement of compatibility for the contentious Infertility Treatment Amendment Bill 2007 (Vic) was very brief, and stated baldly that 'the Bill has no human rights impacts'. The Bill was introduced by the Minister for Health, and modified the existing regulatory framework to allow limited therapeutic cloning of embryos for research under a national framework. By contrast, the statement of compatibility for the Crimes (Decriminalisation of Abortion) Bill 2007 (Vic), introduced as a Private Member's Bill by Labor backbencher Candy Broad, provided more explicit reasoning, even though this Bill more clearly fell within the exemption for laws dealing with abortion or child destruction in s. 48 of the Charter. Many statements of compatibility are very thorough indeed.

Some, such as those for the Road Legislation Further Amendment Bill 2007 (Vic) and the Confiscation Amendment Bill 2007 (Vic), also discuss comparative and international jurisprudence.

The reasoned statements of compatibility play an important role in the human rights dialogue under the Victorian Charter, and provide much greater transparency and consistency than the more variable human rights content in the ACT Explanatory Statements. Some Charter critics have seized upon the limitations on human rights revealed in many of the compatibility statements to predict a 'flood' of litigation based upon Charter 'breaches'.[77] These concerns appear overstated, as they do not take account of s. 7(2) of the Charter, which allows rights to be limited where reasonable and demonstrably justified according to stated criteria.

Nevertheless, in some cases the Victorian Government has taken a very broad view of the justified limits provision in s. 7(2), concluding that some apparently draconian and discriminatory provisions are compatible with the Charter. Examples include liquor control provisions allowing offenders to be excluded from a designated area for up to 12 months, where the size of a designated area is determined by the Director of Liquor Licensing,[78] and provisions prohibiting people under 18 years old from purchasing cans of spray paint and banning all persons from carrying spray cans on public transport without lawful excuse.[79] Indeed, the compatibility statement for the Graffiti Prevention Bill 2007 (Vic) prompted an Opposition member to query the point of having a Charter 'when on almost every occasion the Minister providing the statement to the Parliament will go through the areas where the Bill transgresses human rights and then conclude that the human rights transgression is reasonable under the circumstances'.[80]

The Victorian Charter also requires 'human rights certificates' to be prepared in relation to subordinate legislation,[81] another feature that has no equivalent in the ACT HRA. Unlike the statements of compatibility, human rights certificates are not publicly available. More information about these certificates and their effect will be included in the Regulation Review published annually by the SARC.

Impact of the direct obligations on public authorities

The early signs are that government bodies and officials have taken their obligations under the Charter seriously, and have devoted considerable resources to preparation for its application to public authorities in the fields of public policy making and legislative development (including the review of existing legislation), as well as in service delivery and at the local government level.[82] The direct obligation of public authorities in Victoria to comply with human rights has given impetus to training programs and preparatory work within the public service. In the 2006/07 Budget, the Victorian Government allocated $6.5 million over four years to support the introduction of the Charter. This included funding for community education to be provided by the VEOHRC, and training for key government agencies including Victoria Police, Corrections Victoria and the Department of Human Services.[83]

Initial training programs conducted by the Human Rights Unit in the Department of Justice targeted legal and legislative policy officers, with more than 500 government legal staff attending a one-day course on the Charter rights and statement of compatibility requirements.[84] Other training sessions have been aimed at prosecutors and criminal law practitioners and the judiciary has received specialised training. Within Victoria Police, a Human Rights Project team has conducted introductory seminars with more than 400 employees.[85] Many government departments and agencies have also commenced reviews of their legislation and policies for human rights compliance.[86]

The Victorian Equal Opportunity and Human Rights Commission

On 1 January 2007, the re-named VEOHRC (formerly the Victorian Equal Opportunity Commission) took on new responsibilities for human rights reporting and training. The VEOHRC is now required to report annually on the operation of the Victorian Charter, its interaction with other statutory provisions and the common law, and on any declarations of inconsistent interpretation and override declarations. In its Charter report for 2007, the Commission focused on the preparations being made by government agencies and other public authorities for the commencement of their Charter obligations.[87] While generally positive about the achievements of the first year, the Commission took a robust and critical view of the measures that had been taken by individual agencies.[88]

The VEOHRC's powers to intervene in cases raising Charter issues commenced on 1 January 2008, and the Commission has developed guidelines on the exercise of this power.[89] The Commission attempted to intervene in the case of *Kortel v Mirik*,[90] a case where respondents to compensation proceedings arising out of serious criminal convictions had been refused representation by Victoria Legal Aid. The Commission sought to argue that the Supreme Court had a positive duty to ensure a fair hearing under s. 6(2)(b) of the Charter. The Court refused to allow the intervention, as the defendants had been granted legal aid by the time the matter came to hearing, and the Court found that the Charter issue had thus been resolved.

The Ombudsman

The Victorian Charter conferred powers on the Ombudsman to investigate alleged violations of the Charter. As the explicit obligation on public authorities to comply with the Charter had not yet commenced, the Ombudsman devoted his activities in 2007 to preparatory measures establishing the procedures and data collection systems in his own office.[91] The Ombudsman's report for 2007 provides no details of whether complainants had begun to invoke the Charter in their complaints. Many of the complaints that fall within the Ombudsman's historical jurisdiction have human rights dimensions and one would expect that Charter grounds will be added to complaints in the future.

The legislature

The Charter provisions relating to statements of compatibility, override declarations and human rights scrutiny by the SARC, a joint investigatory committee of both Houses of the Victorian Parliament, came into effect on 1 January 2007.

Debate in Parliament

The impact of the Charter on parliamentary debate in Victoria has so far been modest, and has been largely confined to the reiteration of issues raised by the SARC, or comments on the adequacy of compatibility statements and general views on the Charter compatibility process. Government members have not often cited the Charter, apart from reciting the conclusions contained in the statements of compatibility in second reading speeches.

The Opposition made much of the shortcomings of the statement of compatibility for the Infertility Treatment Amendment Bill 2007 (Vic) prepared by the Minister for Health, and has sometimes suggested that the government is not taking the compatibility process seriously.[92] At other times, however, members of the Opposition have been critical of what they perceive as overly lengthy statements of compatibility.[93] There have also been substantive issues discussed in debates. Shadow Attorney-General Robert Clark noted his concerns that the protection of a limited class of human rights in the Charter 'leaves aside a whole lot of other rights that are equally important to the proper functioning of our democratic system under the rule of law', leading to a 'lopsided emphasis [and] serious institutional problems'.[94] Clark raised this issue in relation to provisions amending the *Coroners Act 1985* (Vic) to regulate public access to coroners' reports. The statement of compatibility had considered the impact of these amendments on the right to privacy and the right to free speech.[95] Clark argued that this reasoning was 'convoluted' because it did not refer to the principle that judicial proceedings should take place in open court.[96] Clark assumed that this right was not protected in the Charter because it was not discussed in the compatibility statement, but in fact there is some protection for public and transparent court and tribunal proceedings under the right to a fair hearing in s. 24.

Scrutiny of Acts and Regulations Committee

Under s. 30 of the Charter, the SARC must consider any Bill introduced into Parliament and report to Parliament as to whether it is incompatible with human rights. The SARC is also required to review all statutory rules, and report those that it considers to be incompatible with human rights.[97]

While the SARC must give independent consideration to the human rights impact of new legislation, the statements of compatibility play an important role in informing its deliberations. The SARC has noted that in approaching its new reporting function in relation to provisions that may test or infringe a Charter right, it 'will consider a statement of compatibility as having the same status as an explanatory memorandum and where the Committee considers a Statement to be inadequate the Committee will draw this to the attention of Members'.[98] The Chair of the SARC, Carlo Carli, has noted that the depth of analysis in the compatibility statement is 'a good guide as to whether the government department or agency has undertaken a proper human rights impact assessment', and has acknowledged that some tensions emerged over this issue in the first few months of the Charter's operation.[99]

The SARC was particularly critical of the perfunctory compatibility statement accompanying the Infertility Treatment Amendment Bill 2007 (Vic), which would authorise therapeutic cloning of embryos for research purposes, stating that:

> where there is a reasonable prospect that a provision in a
> Bill may test or infringe Charter compatibility that issue

should be drawn to the attention of the Parliament and
a reasoned, even if brief, analysis of why the provision
is nevertheless considered compatible with the Charter
should be outlined.[100]

The SARC considered that the Bill might affect enjoyment of
the right to life and more clearly the right of egg donors not
to be subject to medical experimentation without consent. The
SARC held a public hearing and took evidence on the health
risks posed by egg donation, and on issues regarding consent to
donations. The Minister's response to the Committee's report
agreed to raise its concerns regarding consent issues with the
National Health and Medical Research Council, but did not
address the issue of the adequacy of the compatibility statement,
an omission that was not lost on the SARC.[101]

The SARC also queried the approach taken by the government
to the acknowledged discrimination against same sex-couples in
a Bill allowing contribution splitting under the Emergency Services Superannuation Scheme.[102] The splitting provisions applied
only to spouses, and excluded same-sex partners. However, the
compatibility statement found that the breach of the equality
right was justified under s. 7(2) because the government was
constrained by discriminatory Commonwealth superannuation
laws. The SARC rejected this analysis, and questioned whether
in such a case:

> even the strongest and most cogent section 7(2)
> [reasonable limitations] analysis can ever conclude
> that a law which discriminates on the basis of sexual
> orientation without any further qualification can be
> rendered compatible simply because a benefit may be
> obtained by other persons without that attribute.[103]

The SARC considered that the constraints imposed by the
Commonwealth laws might amount to exceptional circum-

stances for the purposes of an override declaration. However, this suggestion was rejected by the Minister, who did not consider it necessary to amend the compatibility statement that had previously been settled by counsel.[104]

The SARC gave detailed consideration to the Graffiti Prevention Bill 2007 (Vic), and noted particular concerns about provisions that criminalise graffiti that would 'offend a reasonable person', even where the owner of the property consents to that graffiti. The SARC reiterated the view of the European Court of Human Rights that freedom of expression 'is applicable not only to information or ideas that are favourably received or regarded as inoffensive or as a matter of indifference, but also to those that offend, shock or disturb the State or any sector of the population'.[105]

The developing dialogue between the SARC and the Executive can also be seen in the exchange of views over the Drugs, Poisons and Controlled Substances Amendment Bill 2008 (Vic). In the context of a proposed broad discretion to grant permits to administer particular categories of scheduled drugs (which included marijuana, heroin and LSD), the SARC suggested that, based on case law on a similar provision of the Canadian Charter of Rights and Freedoms, the 'right to liberty and security' under s. 21 was engaged. The government rejected this view, maintaining that the legislative history of the section showed that it did not extend to guarantees of personal autonomy or access to medical procedures. The Committee responded that, whatever the position under s. 21, regulation of access to certain types of drugs may nonetheless engage the rights to life, freedom from cruel or inhuman or degrading treatment, and the right to privacy.[106]

Other provisions on which the SARC has taken a different view from the government on human rights issues include clauses allowing the publication of photographs of convicted offenders;[107] the removal of self-defence as a lawful excuse in relation to the possession of controlled weapons (in cases where a weapon is picked up in a situation of immediate threat);[108] retrospective alterations to the assessment and compensation for spinal injuries;[109] a provision that would allow the Director of Public Transport to determine that specified classes of overseas students are ineligible for student concessions for public transport and expressly providing that such determination does not constitute race discrimination;[110] provisions regarding the entry into private property and questioning of people over suspected cruelty to animal offences;[111] powers of compulsion in relation to the provision of documents and information 'relevant to the operation of the *Energy Efficiency Target Act 2007* (Vic)';[112] provisions formalising sentencing discounts for pleading guilty;[113] and whether the right to be presumed innocent is relevant only while there are ongoing criminal proceedings, or has a broader application.[114]

In early 2008, serious conflict emerged within the SARC over the scrutiny of the Police Integrity Bill 2008 (Vic), and the alleged failure of the Chair and the Executive Officer to facilitate a public hearing into the Bill as directed by the Committee. The Bill re-established the Office of Police Integrity (OPI) under a stand-alone Act, and strengthened some of the powers of the OPI and its Director. Non-government members of the SARC issued a minority report in which they expressed 'strong disappointment at the attempts to misuse the SARC Committee to shut down effective scrutiny' of the Bill, which they described as 'the first real test of the Labor Government's Human Rights Charter'.[115] The minority report also suggested that the SARC had a mandate to consider policy issues in undertaking Charter scrutiny functions, a suggestion rejected by government members of the Committee.[116] In June 2008 a public hearing on the Police Integrity Bill was eventually held by the SARC after the Bill was referred back to it by the Legislative Council for inquiry, and the Committee's further report on the Bill addresses Charter concerns in more detail than its earlier scrutiny report.[117]

In its review of the compatibility statements and SARC comments on Bills introduced into Parliament during 2007, the VEOHRC noted that there had been a significant number of cases in which the analysis of Bills by the SARC differed from that contained in the government's compatibility statement. While in some cases both analyses reached the same conclusion, in other cases the SARC did not agree with the government's statements on compatibility and sought further clarification from the government. In further cases, the SARC's comments raised human rights issues that had not been identified in the compatibility statements.[118] The VEOHRC concluded that 'SARC's responsibilities under the Charter are generating dialogue between the Executive and legislature'.[119] The Commission's optimistic assessment continued:

> When reflecting on the Charter's overall impact on the legislative process during 2007, the Commission believes it is informative to ask one very simple question: if it was not for the Charter, would the human rights dimensions of these 93 Bills have been identified, analysed and debated? In all but a very few cases, the answer is clearly 'no'. For this reason alone, the initial impact of the Charter is significant: it has already comprehensively expanded the parameters of public policy analysis to include the transparent assessment of new laws against a human rights framework. This is a substantial achievement.[120]

At the same time, the VEOHRC noted that only one Bill had been amended in response to the SARC's comments and expressed its concern that 'SARC's comments do not simply become an end in themselves, but form part of a robust, genuine exchange on human rights'.[121]

The courts and tribunals

Under the staged implementation of the Victorian Charter, provisions in Part 3, including the interpretive obligation, referral of Charter issues to the Supreme Court, declarations of inconsistent interpretation, the duty of public authorities to comply with the Charter and the possibility of bringing legal proceedings based on a breach of Charter rights, did not come into force until 1 January 2008. However, the substantive human rights in Part 2 of the Charter came into effect on 1 January 2007. This staggered introduction of the Charter was further complicated by the transitional provision, s. 49(2), which provides that the Charter 'does not affect any proceedings commenced or concluded before [1 January 2007].' This provision continued to have a stifling effect on many of the Charter arguments raised in 2008, and may exclude the application of Charter rights in ongoing criminal and other proceedings that could conclude years after the Charter's commencement.[122]

The first significant case to consider the Victorian Charter was *R v Williams*,[123] where it was raised by Peter Faris QC, one of the Charter's most vocal critics.[124] Faris sought to rely on the right of an accused person to choose his or her legal representative in s. 25(d) of the Charter to support his client's case for a lengthy adjournment of his trial until his chosen counsel became available. Under the transitional provisions in s. 49(2), the sections of the Charter providing for relief against a violation of a protected right to be sought in ongoing proceedings did not apply to proceedings commenced before 1 January 2007. Faris argued that 'proceedings' referred to the hearing of the trial, which had not yet commenced. However, Justice King held that the 'proceedings' in this case had commenced when Mr Williams was charged in 2004, and that the Charter therefore had no application to the case. Although this was sufficient to dispose of the matter, Justice King went on to consider Canadian authorities, and noted that, even if the Charter had applied in this case, the rights were not absolute and would not require the court to delay proceedings indefinitely to accommodate Mr Williams' choice of counsel.[125]

The Victorian Charter was cited in other matters in 2007, including a bail case in which it was referred to in support of the rejection of an argument that a defendant had acquiesced in the delay of his trial,[126] in criticising the government over the plight of a forensic patient who had to be held in prison because of the lack of beds in a secure psychiatric facility,[127] and in tribunal cases in equal opportunity matters in which exemptions were sought from the operation of anti-discrimination legislation.[128] Justice Bongiorno also considered the Charter in assessing security measures to be put in place in a terrorism trial, concluding that a perspex construction around the dock was unnecessary and would be contrary to the right to a fair trial of the accused.[129]

The commencement of the Part 3 powers of the courts and tribunals under the Charter on 1 January 2008 did not increase litigation discernibly. In the first six months of 2008, the Charter was referred to in 15 reported decisions of Victorian courts and tribunals, but had a decisive impact in only two of those cases.[130] In five of these decisions, the transitional provision was found to exclude any Charter arguments because the proceedings had commenced before 1 January 2007.

The first of the cases in which the Victorian Charter was applied, and in which it had an impact, was the bail application in *Gray v Director of Public Prosecutions (Vic)*.[131] The defendant was charged in late 2007 with aggravated burglary and remanded in custody awaiting trial in Mildura. The prosecution could not provide any evidence as to when the case was likely to be heard, and appeared not to have appreciated the relevance of the Charter in bail proceedings.[132] Justice Bongiorno considered the likelihood that the time spent on remand might exceed any custodial sentence eventually imposed to be a significant factor, in light of the Charter.[133] He noted that the only remedy open in such circumstances, short of a permanent stay, would be to release the accused on bail.[134] Accordingly, the defendant was released on bail, under strict conditions of supervision.

The Charter was also raised in proceedings regarding the suppression in Victoria of the television series *Underbelly*, a fictionalised account of the 'gangland murders' that were the subject of criminal prosecutions. On 16 February 2008, Justice King widened a suppression order to extend to all Victorians, after a publican showed patrons the first episode of the series on cable television.[135] Lawyers for the television station argued that the ban 'struck at the heart' of the right to freedom of expression under the Charter.[136] An appeal against the suppression order included an argument based on this Charter right. Although this ground of appeal was eventually abandoned, the Court of Appeal commented that it considered it 'highly unlikely' that Channel 9 could rely upon the right of free speech in the Charter, and noted that in any case freedom of media expression was always subject to the guarantee of a fair trial.[137] The doubt presumably arose from the appellant's status as a corporation, though the Court did not consider the rights of the potential audience to receive information, which is a fundamental part of the right to freedom of expression.[138]

As in the ACT, the early cases that have been considered by the Victorian courts and tribunals have tended to refer generally to Charter rights, and in some cases to apply them, without clearly identifying the basis on which the right may be relevant. The possible mechanisms for invoking Charter rights are the interpretive obligation, the public authority obligation, the remedy for breach by a public authority, and (perhaps more speculatively) a direct application of a human rights by the court or tribunal pursuant to the application clause in s. 6(2)(b).[139]

The decision of the Victorian Civil and Administrative Tribunal in *Guss v Aldy Corporation Pty Ltd*[140] is a notable exception. In this case, the Tribunal clearly applied the interpretive power to a clause of the *Civil and Administrative Tribunal Act 1998* (Vic), giving effect to the Charter right to a fair trial by allowing for a re-hearing of a matter that had been struck out. This overturned a previous interpretation of the same clause by the Tribunal.

One concern that has emerged about the operation of the Charter is the obligation of the Supreme Court and the County Court to give notice to the Attorney-General when a Charter issue arises in proceedings or has been referred to the Supreme Court. As Justice Bongiorno pointed out in *R v Benbrika*,[141] the need to give notice to various parties under the Charter is unlikely to encourage counsel to invoke Charter arguments, at least where there is a need for an urgent resolution of an issue.[142] He recommended that the Charter be amended to give a judge discretion 'to relieve a party from giving notice where to do so would unduly disrupt or delay a proceeding or for other good reason'.[143]

The enactment of the Victorian Charter was an important milestone in the history of bills of rights in Australia. The early years of its implementation have already had an appreciable impact on the operations of the government and the legislature. The initiatives in training and in the assessment of legislation and policy so far undertaken by most government departments and agencies in Victoria indicate a genuine commitment to the implementation of the Charter. The reasoned assessments of compatibility of all new legislation with the Charter, and the consideration of human rights issues by the SARC, provide a clear picture of the beginnings of a human rights dialogue in Victoria. The quality of this dialogue, and the responsiveness of the government to human rights concerns raised by the legislature, is likely to increase as the courts begin to take a greater role in the review of legislation, and provide an additional level of accountability for the implementation of human rights. So far, use of the Charter in the courts and tribunals has not been extensive, as it has been hampered by a delayed commencement and the effect of transitional provisions. A number of issues remain to be resolved regarding the operation and effect of the Charter provisions. However, the high level of interest in the Charter among the legal profession is likely to ensure that the Victorian jurisprudence will continue to evolve and mature. One ongoing challenge will be to sustain the broad community engagement with human rights, which was tapped so effectively through the Charter consultation process, to involve the wider community in the development of a human rights culture in Victoria.

6

Towards an Australian bill of rights

At the ceremonial sitting to mark the centenary of the Commonwealth Parliament in 2001, Prime Minister John Howard celebrated the enduring success of Australian democracy, which was, he said, built on the idea of the 'fair go'. He argued that the effectiveness of democracy in Australia was built on three great institutions: a robust parliamentary system, an independent judiciary and a strong and sceptical media.[1] On this analysis, a bill of rights was not only unnecessary, but also threatening to Australian democracy.

Since Federation, Australians have been wary of the language of human rights, and Australia is now the only Western democracy without some form of a bill of rights. This fact is not in itself an argument for change, but it illustrates how thoroughly Australians have been persuaded that the discourse of human rights is contrary to traditions of mateship and the fair go, and that human rights are a form of special pleading out of place in an egalitarian society. This dismissiveness glosses over the gaps in Australia's system of governance that allow breaches of human rights to go unremedied.

Despite the limited legal advances in protecting human rights, there is little consciousness of the limitations of the Australian human rights system in the community at large. A survey conducted for Amnesty International in 2006 on Australians' knowledge of human rights protections in the context of anti-terrorism laws discovered that many people overestimate the level of formal rights protection. For example, 61 per cent of the survey group thought that human rights were already protected under the Australian Constitution or by a bill of rights.[2]

The developments in bills of rights described in earlier chapters illustrate how, in the Australian federal system, a single State or Territory can serve as an exemplar to test law reform, which can then influence other States or the Commonwealth.[3] In a similar way, political scientist Katharine Gelber has predicted that '[t]he Australian federal system and its opportunities for diversity and experimentation may provide us with an institutional framework that allows the Australian debate to move forward in a unique way'.[4] The country's first legislative bill of rights, adopted in 2004, broke through the resistance and suspicion surrounding the issue after a string of failures to introduce a bill of rights at the national level. The *Human Rights Act 2004* (ACT) (ACT HRA) paved the way for larger scale consultation in Victoria and the enactment of the *Charter of Human Rights and Responsibilities Act 2006* (Vic) (Victorian Charter). This in turn has contributed to the body of knowledge about how a bill of rights might operate in the broader Australian political landscape.

The impetus generated by the ACT HRA and the Victorian Charter led to public consultations on legislative bills of rights in Tasmania in 2006 and in Western Australia in 2007. We provide an overview of these consultation processes and their outcomes in the first section of this chapter, then focus on the national consultation about the protection of human rights to which the Australian Labor Party (ALP) made a commitment during the 2007 election campaign. We identify the lessons that the developments at State and Territory level offer for this process and offer suggestions for the content of a national bill of rights.

State consultation processes

Tasmania

In February 2006, Tasmanian Attorney-General Judy Jackson asked the Tasmania Law Reform Institute to investigate options for human rights protection in Tasmania and, in particular, to consider whether Tasmania should have a bill or charter of rights.[5] A Human Rights Community Consultation Committee was established to assist the Law Reform Institute.[6] Compared to the processes in the ACT and Victoria, the Tasmanian consultation was run on a very small budget.[7] The work of conducting public consultations, writing an issues paper, and the preparation of the final report, fell largely to the Committee Chair, Terese Henning, an academic at the University of Tasmania Law School, and research officers at the Law Reform Institute.

The Institute issued its report, *A Charter of Rights for Tasmania*, in October 2007. Of the 407 submissions received from individuals and organisations, an overwhelming majority (94 per cent) supported the enactment of a Charter of Human Rights.[8] The report makes a thoughtful contribution to the bill of rights debate, providing a thorough analysis of the nuances of the ACT and Victorian models, and the areas in which both could be improved. The report recommended that a Charter of Human Rights and Responsibilities be enacted in Tasmania. The format favoured by the Institute drew heavily on the ACT HRA and the Victorian Charter, but went further in some areas. In particular, the Institute recommended the inclusion of a range of economic, social and cultural rights in a Tasmanian Charter, stating that the arguments for excluding economic, social and cultural rights were not compelling and '[spoke] of timidity rather than rationality'.[9]

The position of Attorney-General had changed hands by the time the report was delivered. The new Attorney-General, Steve Kons, initially welcomed the report and promised to examine its contents and brief Cabinet,[10] but little further was heard on the matter. The prospects for implementation of the Institute's recommendations were dampened by a Cabinet reshuffle in early 2008, in which David Llewellyn was appointed Attorney-General. Llewellyn was cautious in his first public comments on the report,[11] and his later remarks implied that Tasmania would await the outcome of national consultation.[12]

Western Australia

The Attorney-General of the Western Australian Labor government, Jim McGinty, announced the government's intention to conduct community consultation about a Human Rights Act for Western Australia on 3 May 2007. McGinty followed the lead of the Victorian Government by issuing a prescriptive Statement of Intent for the consultation. However, the Western Australian government took a different approach to the previous consultations by releasing a draft Human Rights Bill to serve as the focus for the consultation, and to indicate the government's preferred model.[13] Although the draft Bill drew heavily on the Victorian Charter and the ACT HRA, it was overall more limited than either of its predecessors.

The Attorney-General appointed a four-person Consultation Committee for a proposed WA Human Rights Act. The Committee was chaired by Fred Chaney, a former Liberal federal parliamentarian who had held a number of ministerial portfolios.[14] The Committee conducted extensive public meetings and consultations, and devolved consultations with disadvantaged groups.

The Committee submitted its report, *A WA Human Rights Act*, in November 2007, which revealed majority support for a Human Rights Act. Of the 377 written submissions received by the Committee, 50 per cent were in favour, 34 per cent were opposed and 16 per cent did not express a clear view.[15] A telephone survey commissioned by the Committee showed stronger support for a Human Rights Act, with 89 per cent of respondents agreeing that Western Australia should have a law to protect individuals' human rights.[16] The devolved consultations also showed high levels of support for a Human Rights Act.[17]

The report recommended a number of changes to the draft Human Rights Bill to reflect concerns raised during the consultation. The most significant amendment was the addition of economic, social and cultural rights, in particular those relating to health, education, housing, cultural life and property.[18] The Committee found the arguments against the inclusion of such rights 'less than compelling, particularly in light of the "dialogue" model of human rights protection adopted in the draft Bill'.[19] It recommended a number of other amendments as well, with the overall effect of bringing the draft Bill generally into line with the Victorian Charter.[20] The Committee went beyond existing models in recommending the establishment of a multi-layered complaint and conciliation system to deal with human rights breaches by government agencies, in addition to court remedies.[21]

The report was launched on 20 December 2007. Attorney-General McGinty welcomed the report but made no commitment to take its recommendations any further. Indeed, he suggested that any Western Australian bill of rights would be put on hold pending developments at Commonwealth level:

> Ideally human rights should be shared by all Australians
> and not be subject to change when you cross State
> borders. Human rights protection is an objective best
> pursued at a national level … We are keen to contribute
> to a national discussion about the possible introduction
> of a Commonwealth human rights charter.[22]

These comments are surprising in light of the strong support initially given by the government to the proposed Human Rights Act, and comments previously made by the Attorney-General about the need for human rights legislation at both levels of government.[23]

It appears that the change of heart was caused by State politics. The Carpenter government had lost its majority in the Legislative Council in November 2007, following the expulsion of MP Shelley Archer from the Labor Party. This controversy left the newly independent Archer holding the balance of power in the Upper House, and unlikely to support McGinty's social reform agenda.[24] Following the election of a Liberal government in Western Australia in September 2008, it is doubtful that the Human Rights Bill will be revived.

Dialogue between the States and Territories

The reports of the ACT, Victorian, Tasmanian and Western Australian consultative committees have generated a conversation between the States and Territories about consultation methodology and the content of bills of rights. The discussion has continued beyond the initial consultations, and is likely to influence the reviews required under the ACT HRA and the Victorian Charter, as well as consultation in relation to a national bill of rights.

The effects of the dialogue are evident in the ratcheting-up of human rights protection in the Victorian Charter and the ACT HRA, as each statute has been shaped or revised in response to the other. The ACT HRA began as a relatively modest legislative bill of rights, with no explicit legal obligations on public authorities to implement those rights. It was feared that the limitations of the ACT HRA could constrain other Australian bills of rights that might be modelled on it.[25] Indeed, this concern was given substance by the Victorian Government's initial Statement of Intent on human rights.[26] However, with the evidence of only modest use being made of the ACT HRA in the courts, the Victorian Government was emboldened to go further with its Charter, incorporating duties on public authorities and a limited remedy provision. The ACT Government in turn amended the HRA in 2008 to incorporate the clearer interpretive provision in the Victorian Charter and a similar duty on public authorities. This raised the bar once more with a more generous and straightforward remedy provision, and a novel 'opt-in' provision for entities to take on human rights obligations as public authorities. The ratcheting-up effect is also evident in the reports of the Tasmanian and Western Australian consultations, which recommended that charters in their States should go further than either the ACT HRA or the Victorian Charter by incorporating economic, social and cultural rights.

Although there are persuasive arguments for a uniform system of human rights protection across the Commonwealth, State and Territory governments, in the short term there are some advantages in the present diversity, with the variations between models allowing useful comparisons to be made about the effectiveness of different provisions. There may also be constitutional reasons for having State bills of rights covering the limited areas of State government that are beyond the reach of Commonwealth laws, although a constitutional bill of rights applicable to both Commonwealth and State governments would avoid this problem.[27] State and Territory bills of rights may well be able to offer a higher level of protection than a national scheme, whether by including a broader range of rights, providing for more generous interpretations of rights, or limiting permissible restrictions.[28] The ability of the States and Territories to improve their bills of rights unilaterally could also serve as a catalyst for the progressive improvement of human rights protection across the board, something that is less likely to occur in a more centralised system. Even if bills of rights are not enacted in all States and Territories, their existence in some jurisdictions has the potential to exert an influence over any uniform legislation developed as part of cooperative schemes at State and Territory level.[29] For example, the bills of rights in the ACT and Victoria should mean that any legislation agreed to as part of a cooperative federal program would have to meet the human rights standards mandated by those statutes.

A national bill of rights

Proposal for a national consultation on human rights

The development of the ACT HRA and the Victorian Charter, and the consultation processes that followed in other States, were in part motivated by the lack of movement at Commonwealth level towards a national bill of rights. Former Prime Minister John Howard, who led the Liberal-National Coalition government for over eleven years from March 1996, was a staunch opponent of bills of rights, maintaining that 'responsive democratic institutions and an active civil society provide more effective protection for the rights of Australian citizens than any charter of rights could hope to achieve'.[30]

The position at the national level changed with the election of a Labor government in November 2007. The ALP has supported a national bill of rights since the 1960s,[31] and each of the previous attempts to establish a national bill of rights was instigated by a Labor government. In the lead-up to the 2007 election, the ALP amended its national platform from an unqualified endorsement of a bill of rights to an undertaking to 'initiate a public inquiry about how best to recognise and protect the human rights and freedoms enjoyed by all Australians'[32] and to 'establish a process of consultation which will ensure that all Australians will be given the chance to have their say on this important question for our democracy'.[33] The platform added:

> Labor will engage with Australians in deciding which democratic, industrial and community rights recognised in international treaties and conventions ratified by Australia should be protected. Any proposal for legislative change in this area must maintain [the] sovereignty of the Parliament and shall not be based on the United States Bill of Rights.[34]

Soon after the election, the new Attorney-General, Robert McClelland, broadcast his aspirations to 'sign a landmark charter enshrining the rights and responsibilities of the nation's legislators' within the first term of the government.[35] This would be preceded by a national public consultation about the rights and responsibilities to be protected by Parliament. McClelland declared that:

> the debate should visit not only a charter of rights but a
> charter of responsibilities, such as aspirations to protect
> the environment and enhance community building ...
> This is not a prescriptive process. The important thing is
> that we are committed to a series of public discussions as
> to whether the public are interested in it and, if they are,
> what its contents would be.[36]

The issue appeared to lose momentum in the national agenda until the Commonwealth Government's 2020 Summit in April 2008. This involved 1000 participants discussing ideas on a range of areas including constitutional reform and governance. While the Summit became a focus for heated media debate about the prospect of a national charter of rights, much of it negative,[37] the Summit stream devoted to governance recommended a national charter of rights as a priority. A bill of rights was also recommended by two other Summit groups, the group focusing on 'strengthening communities and supporting working families' and the group focusing on Indigenous issues.[38] Prime Minister Kevin Rudd later re-affirmed the Labor Party's commitment to a consultation on a legislative charter.[39] However, within the broader ALP community there remains considerable divergence of views on the desirability of a bill of rights.[40]

Lessons from the States and Territories

Unlike the previous campaigns for a national bill of rights, the 21st century movement has the benefit of working examples of legislative bills of rights in the ACT and Victoria, and of completed public consultations in Tasmania and Western Australia. There are also significant comparable models overseas, including those in the United Kingdom and New Zealand. The developments at State and Territory level provide an important body of evidence to inform developments at the Commonwealth level. We outline some lessons from these experiences below.

Political leadership

A bill of rights is dependent upon political will and leadership for its enactment. The commitment of ACT Chief Minister Jon Stanhope and Victorian Attorney-General Rob Hulls, in the face of distinct lack of enthusiasm from their Cabinet colleagues, was decisive in the achievement of the first bills of rights in Australia. The fate of the Tasmanian consultation, which lost its political backing after the resignation of Attorney-General Judy Jackson, suggests that even a high level of community support manifested in a public consultation is unlikely to over-come government apathy or hostility to the issue. Conversely, although a political champion is necessary, it is not sufficient to ensure the adoption of a rights charter, as the efforts of Lionel Murphy and Gareth Evans in the federal sphere attest.[41] Leader-ship must be supported by a well-managed process and strong grassroots support.

The consultation process

The model of an independent public consultation on the issue of a bill of rights, which began with the ACT and has been adopted with modifications in Victoria, Tasmania and Western Australia, has played a role in informing and legitimating the process and final proposals. It has also educated and catalysed new sectors of the community to engage with the debate. Although a legisla-tive bill of rights could be developed and negotiated through the Commonwealth Parliament, as with any other government Bill, the traditional divisiveness of the issue makes public consultation crucial. Australian experience suggests some important elements of a human rights consultation.

First, the appointment of an independent committee to conduct the public consultation has some advantages over a government-run consultation, or referral to an existing law reform body. An independent committee formed around this single issue is likely to generate more interest and momentum and to be more accessible to the community than an existing organisation that faces the constraints of established procedures and public preconceptions about its enquiries, although the very effective consultation run by the Law Reform Institute of Tasmania on a minimal budget is an exception. The existing relationship of a law reform body with government may also affect the prospects of its recommendations being adopted. For example, despite their high quality, a significant proportion of Australian Law Reform Commission reports have not been implemented or only partially implemented,[42] and there is often a long delay in recommendations being taken up.[43]

Second, the composition of a consultative committee is important to the legitimacy of the consultation. A bill of rights is relevant to everyone in Australian society, but this relevance can be obscured if a consultation process appears to be a technical affair dominated by lawyers. Committee members should be open-minded or represent a range of views on the issue so that it remains possible that the committee might not recommend a bill of rights. On the other hand, some members should have expertise in human rights law so that complex legal issues can be dealt with. The various State and Territory committees have included representatives from Indigenous communities, disability advocates, sportspeople, a poet and a religious leader, each of whom contributed significantly to the accessibility of the consultation process. It is also desirable that the committee be bipartisan (or non-partisan), rather than closely associated with the agenda of the political party in power. The appointment of respected former Liberal politicians Haddon Storey and Fred Chaney to the Victorian and Western Australian committees respectively, both commissioned by Labor governments, enhanced the credibility of those consultations.

Terms of reference

The terms of reference of the consultation body are critical to the conduct of the debate and its outcomes. While it is useful for governments to clarify their views – for example, ruling out constitutional amendment if that would not be acceptable – the terms should otherwise be broad. The Western Australian process of producing a draft bill as part of the consultation documents seemed overly prescriptive, and the detail and anomalies of the draft distracted attention from broader issues. Draft legislation may also suggest that the issue has been prejudged, whatever level of community support emerges in the consultation.

Possible terms of reference include requiring the consultation process to receive evidence on whether internationally guaranteed human rights and fundamental freedoms are protected in Australia and enjoyed in practice by all members of the community and others within Australian jurisdiction; the nature and extent of any inadequacies in that protection; whether a bill of rights in some form would contribute to the better protection and enjoyment of those rights and, if so, what model would be appropriate; what rights should be included; and what procedures should be established for ensuring the observance of those rights and remedies for breach of them. The committee should be asked to consider the results of the previous Australian consultations, as well as the experience under the two statutory bills of rights already in operation.

Education

One difficulty faced by a rights-consultation process is the relatively low level of knowledge in the Australian community about the existing legal system and current protections for human rights. A large-scale survey in 1994 revealed that only 18 per cent of Australians had an understanding of the contents of the Constitution, and that a majority reported feeling only a 'little bit' informed, or had only a 'vague idea' about their rights and responsibilities as Australian citizens.[44] As noted above, a 2006 poll found that 61 per cent of respondents mistakenly thought that their rights were protected by an Australian bill of rights.[45] The deliberative poll commissioned by the ACT Bill of Rights Consultative Committee indicated the value of expert debate and peer discussion in helping those who were undecided on the issue to reach an informed view either for or against a bill of rights.[46] The challenge of a consultation process is to make this educational opportunity open to the wider community.

Public seminars and the distribution of community discussion papers and summaries in a range of formats, platforms and languages are important starting points, but may not be sufficient to reach a mass audience. Full-page newspaper advertisements including clear factual information, such as that published as part of the Western Australian consultation, are one method of reaching the wider public.[47] This type of information could also be distributed by electronic media. Another strategy used effectively in the Victorian consultation was to build education into the consultation process with small groups, thus allowing misconceptions to be addressed as part of a two-way dialogue.[48]

Accessibility

A related challenge is to involve the broader community in the consultation, to reach ordinary individuals and groups who would not normally think of taking part in law reform inquiries. Critics have suggested that the consultation process is likely to be dominated by the legal profession and special interest groups to the exclusion of 'regular plumbers, secretaries and teachers'.[49] In fact, in the State and Territory consultations held so far, a majority of submissions have been made by individual citizens, rather than groups. The volume of submissions received, particularly in Victoria, far exceeded that normally generated by law reform inquiries and indicates the enthusiasm and passions the issue of a bill of rights generated. These results also reflect the many face-to-face meetings held by the consultative committees with diverse groups in remote, regional and metropolitan areas. The use of other strategies such as devolved consultations to reach disadvantaged populations,[50] and telephone opinion polling,[51] may also increase the accessibility of the consultation process. Technological developments, such as social networking and video-sharing sites, could further expand the reach of consultation.

Dealing with special interests

The four Australian consultations have underlined the need to work with groups who may have particular anxieties, whether well-based or unfounded, about the effects of a bill of rights. For example, religious groups have voiced consistent concerns about the impact of bills of rights on their beliefs and practices, including whether a right to non-discrimination would affect the selection of staff for denominational or faith-based schools and institutions;[52] and whether the right to life, if defined to commence from the time of birth, would justify liberal abortion laws.[53] The articulation of such concerns typically pits religion against human rights, although more sophisticated understandings of religious traditions seek an accommodation with human rights. Thus, the Compendium of the Social Doctrine of the Church acknowledges that:

> The movement towards the identification and
> proclamation of human rights is one of the most
> significant attempts to respond effectively to the
> inescapable demands of human dignity ... The Church's
> Magisterium has not failed to note the positive value of
> the Universal Declaration of Human Rights, adopted by
> the United Nations on 10 December 1948, which Pope

John Paul II defined as 'a true milestone on the path of humanity's moral progress'.[54]

There is no necessary inconsistency between respect for religious freedom and the protection of human rights, and it is important that the religion/human rights debate take this into account. Although the Australian tendency has been to create particular exemptions from human rights obligations for religious institutions,[55] these have not been adequately justified in human rights terms.

Other groups, such as public servants and law enforcement agencies, may have concerns about how a bill of rights will affect their work, and it is important to engage with them early in the consultation process. The interdepartmental committee established to shadow the Victorian consultation was highly successful in engaging government agencies throughout, and in contributing to practical and workable recommendations.[56] The public support of the Victorian Police Commissioner was particularly significant in avoiding the perception that a bill of rights would give unfair advantages to criminals.[57]

The media

Media commentary about the bill of rights debate can play a positive role in publicising the consultation and informing the community about the issues involved. The media also has the potential to undermine a consultation process if its coverage is unbalanced, or if it promotes misconceptions about bills of rights exploiting the lack of public understanding. This was a particular challenge in the 2007 Western Australian consultation, where the major State newspaper ran a series of negative articles and opinion pieces about the proposed Human Rights Act.[58] It is important to engage with the media at any early stage of the consultation and to educate journalists and commentators about the complex questions involved. Presentation of a spectrum of views on the wisdom of introducing a bill of rights in the media is valuable, but this should be based on an informed understanding of the issues, rather than on prejudices for or against.

The content of a national bill of rights

The bills of rights adopted in the ACT and Victoria, and recommended in Tasmania and Western Australia, have each drawn heavily on the United Kingdom and New Zealand models of rights protection. These aim to encourage governmental accountability for human rights, while stimulating dialogue between the arms of government and the community about their application. This legislative model has its limitations, not least that it can be overridden at any time by a future parliament. On the other hand, while some supporters aspire ultimately to the protection of human rights through a bill of rights entrenched in the Australian Constitution, this approach has failed to gain public support in previous campaigns. Constitutional protection may also be counterproductive for the cause of human rights in the longer term. Conor Gearty argues that according special, entrenched status to a bill of rights risks artificially separating the protection of human rights from politics:

> Large-scale human rights instruments ... particularly those planted on the summit of the law at its highest constitutional peak, may look like tremendous successes from the slopes below, especially from the base camp of politics from which the ascent necessarily commences. But ... it is a dangerous climb, one whose success can do harm to the very fabric of human rights, demoralising many of those left at base and rendering more adventurous climbs impossible in the future.[59]

By contrast, the ACT and Victorian bills of rights, while according a significant role to the courts, preserve the position of the legislature as the final arbiter of the balance between human rights and other community objectives, overcoming many of the criticisms levelled at entrenched bills of rights. In the medium term at least, it seems likely that the legislative dialogue model will be the preferred option in Australia. Within this general category, however, there is considerable variation and a range of choices to be made about the content and mechanisms of human rights protection. There are also constitutional and structural issues particular to a Commonwealth bill of rights that would need to be considered as part of a national consultation.

Jurisdictional scope

An issue of particular relevance to a national consultation is whether a Commonwealth bill of rights should seek to cover the areas of legislative competence historically exercised by the States under the Constitution. This might be achieved using the external affairs power, which allows the Commonwealth Parliament to enact laws implementing the provisions of international treaties to which Australia is a party, as well as drawing on other heads of Commonwealth legislative power.[60] The relevant treaties in the human rights field include the International Covenant on Civil and Political Rights 1966 (ICCPR) and the International Covenant on Economic, Social and Cultural Rights 1966 (ICESCR). A bill of rights of this scope would impose human rights compatibility requirements on State and Territory laws as well as on Commonwealth legislation. Although such a model would have the advantage of providing uniform coverage of human rights, it might well prompt debilitating political opposition.[61] It could also give rise to constitutional problems insofar as it regulated core functions of State government, such as the drafting of legislation by the State Executive, consideration and passage of legislation by State parliaments, and statutory interpretation of State laws by State courts.[62] Another approach would be to seek the cooperation of the States and Territories in enacting human rights legislation that corresponded to a Commonwealth bill of rights.

If a national bill of rights were limited in its application to Commonwealth laws and public authorities, it would nevertheless be possible to achieve wide coverage of protection for human rights. For example, the Commonwealth has taken on a significant role in service delivery in areas where States have primary responsibility, such as education, health and housing, and the relevant Commonwealth laws, and actions by public authorities, would fall within the scope of an Australian bill of rights.

Choice and formulation of rights

The statutory models adopted so far have been cautious about the selection of rights to be given specific protection. The ACT, Tasmanian and Western Australian consultative committees all recommended the inclusion of economic, social and cultural rights, in addition to civil and political rights, in a legislative charter of rights. Although the recommendations were based on significant public support, they have not yet been adopted in any Australian jurisdiction. The failure to include economic, social and cultural rights in the ACT and Victorian bills of rights is based on an inadequate appreciation of their nature. There is now a considerable body of international and comparative jurisprudence that recognises that economic, social and cultural rights can be adjudicated and applied in a similar manner to civil and political rights. For example, in South Africa the courts have developed techniques for the interpretation of economic and social rights that focus on whether measures taken by the government to protect such rights are reasonable. In *South Africa v Grootboom*,[63] the Constitutional Court examined the meaning of the right to housing and children's right to shelter. Justice Yacoob said:

> A court considering reasonableness will not enquire
> whether other or more desirable or favourable measures
> could have been adopted, or whether public money

could have been better spent. It is necessary to recognise that a wide range of possible measures could be adopted by the state to meet its obligations. Many of these would meet the test of reasonableness.[64]

In a later case, the Court held that '[a]ll that is possible, and all that can be expected of the state, is that it act reasonably to provide *access* to the socio-economic rights'.[65] On this analysis, under both constitutional and statutory bills of rights the legislature will have the final say over budgetary allocations that may be relevant to the realisation of these rights. The protection of economic, social and cultural rights will be revisited in 2009 in the five-year review of the ACT HRA and in 2011 in Victoria's review of its Charter.[66]

A significant issue in the protection of human rights is that of permissible limitations. The ACT and Victorian laws include a general limitation provision, which allows rights to be subject to reasonable limits contained in legislation where these are demonstrably justifiable in a free and democratic society.[67] Such a provision may be useful in providing a clear and consistent mechanism for the proportionate balancing of human rights and community objectives. However, it is arguable that a general limitation should replace, rather than add to, the specific limits on individual rights in the international treaties to avoid their being further watered down.[68] Additional restrictions, such as those in the Victorian Charter restricting the right to vote to 'eligible persons',[69] limiting the provision of legal assistance to those 'eligible' under the *Legal Aid Act 1978* (Vic),[70] and allowing courts to be closed to the public where permitted by another law,[71] reduce governmental transparency and accountability for human rights, and may not meet the standards required by the ICCPR.[72]

Mechanisms for human rights protection

Mechanisms for protection of human rights under modern bills of rights include compatibility and scrutiny requirements for new legislation; an obligation on courts and others to interpret legislation consistently with human rights; the ability of courts to make declarations of incompatibility; and the provision of remedies for breach of human rights by public authorities. They may also include education, auditing and complaints handling by an independent human rights commission or an ombudsman.

Statements of compatibility

The ACT HRA and Victorian Charter both require government to assess new bills against human rights standards, and to certify whether they are compatible with human rights,[73] a procedure that has proved effective in improving the quality of legislation and compliance with human rights. Indeed, in the four years of operation of the ACT HRA, the compatibility mechanism has had a more significant impact on the protection of rights than the exercise by the courts of the powers given to them, despite the lack of published reasons for the compatibility assessment in all but two cases.[74] The more rigorous requirement in the Victorian Charter for reasoned statements of compatibility[75] has generated detailed analyses of the human rights effects of each new bill. This has allowed the community to observe the process of human rights reasoning adopted by the government. Both the Tasmanian and Western Australian consultation committees recommended that bills of rights in their States should require the government to give reasons as part of statements of compatibility.[76]

Scrutiny committees

The role of a parliamentary scrutiny committee is important in providing an independent review of the decisions of government on compatibility, and in stimulating a dialogue between the Executive government and the legislature about the justification for incursions on human rights. Access to reasoned compatibility statements, as in Victoria, is of great benefit to a scrutiny committee because it allows analysis of the methodology applied by the government and of possible justifications for limitations on human rights. Ultimately, however, the ability of a scrutiny committee to influence legislative outcomes depends upon the level of dominance of the legislature by the Executive, and the political muscle of the committee.[77]

Interpretive provision

A requirement that courts, tribunals and government decision-makers interpret all legislation consistently with human rights can be a significant step in enhancing the protection of rights. An interpretive provision can shape the exercise of statutory discretions to fully implement human rights principles, and may remedy past interpretations of legislation that have not given adequate consideration to human rights.

An interpretive provision can also, however, be a controversial aspect of the dialogue model of bills of rights, if it allows judges to adopt interpretations of legislation that override the clear intention of the legislature in enacting a particular law. As we discussed in chapter 3, this issue has arisen in the United Kingdom, and indicates the potential of human rights interpretation to affect the balance of power between the legislature and the judiciary.[78] Seeking to avoid this, the Western Australian consultative committee recommended a very narrow interpretive provision, which would bring human rights into play only where a legislative provision was ambiguous, or obscure, or would lead to a result that is manifestly absurd or unreasonable.[79] In our view, this provision is too limited, achieving little more than the common law principle of statutory interpretation, which presumes that the legislature does not intend to override fundamental rights without clear wording.[80] The interpretive provisions contained in the ACT HRA (s. 30) and the Victorian Charter (s. 32), and that proposed by the Tasmanian

Law Reform Institute,[81] strike a better balance between respecting human rights and honouring the intent of the legislature, by providing that legislation must be interpreted in a way that is compatible with human rights so far as it is possible to do so, consistent with the purpose of that legislation.[82]

Declaration of incompatibility

The power given to the courts to declare legislation to be incompatible or inconsistent with human rights is often seen as an integral feature of the dialogue model of bills of rights. While not invalidating legislation, a declaration allows the judiciary to participate in a conversation with the legislature about the application of human rights principles which may lead to more carefully framed laws. The potential for such a review is also likely to ensure that the compatibility statement requirement is taken seriously by government. The power to issue a declaration of incompatibility has been seen as complementary to the interpretive mechanism, providing an avenue of redress (through potential amendment by the legislature) where a law cannot be interpreted to be consistent with human rights. In the United Kingdom, the Parliament has been very responsive to judicial declarations of incompatibility, amending or repealing most incompatible provisions.[83]

However, several commentators have raised concerns that the declaration of incompatibility mechanism, developed in the context of the unitary legal system of the United Kingdom, does not sit easily with the limitations on the functions that courts can perform under the Australian Constitution.[84] A strand of High Court authority has interpreted the Constitution to prohibit the giving of advisory opinions by courts exercising Commonwealth judicial power.[85] The High Court has held that federal jurisdiction is limited to legal 'matters' requiring some 'immediate right, duty or liability to be established by the determination of the Court'.[86] It has been suggested that the declaration of incompatibility may not meet these criteria because it does not have a sufficiently determinative effect.[87] However, others have argued that the declaration provision is likely to meet the constitutional requirements of a legal matter because declarations would be made in the context of a concrete pre-existing dispute, and would have some (albeit limited) legal consequences in requiring the government to table the declaration and a response in the Parliament.[88]

These issues will need to be considered in any consultation relating to a national bill of rights. The uncertainty surrounding the constitutional validity of a declaration of incompatibility mechanism is unlikely to be resolved until such a provision is considered by the High Court. It would be possible to include a declaration provision in a national bill of rights that is severable from the remaining provisions; thus a negative determination by the High Court on this issue would not invalidate the remainder of the bill of rights. It has also been suggested that the declaration provision could simply be omitted altogether.[89] Other options would be to strengthen the determinative effect of a declaration of incompatibility, while maintaining parliamentary sovereignty. The Canadian Charter (s. 33) provides one model that gives greater power to the courts to strike down incompatible laws, but subject to an override power exercisable by the legislature, which can re-enact the law and immunise it from court scrutiny. Another possibility would be to design a declaration of incompatibility that has a delayed effect of invalidating a law or relevant provision if it is not re-affirmed by the Parliament within a specific time-frame, for example six months.

Direct duty upon public authorities

A direct duty on public authorities to comply with human rights is an important mechanism for promoting a culture of human rights within government. Although it had been thought that the obligation to interpret legislation consistently with human rights would encourage ACT public servants to engage with the ACT HRA in their decision-making, cultural changes brought about by the Act have been largely confined to those officers directly involved in the development of legislation and the compatibility process.[90] A direct obligation to comply with human rights in decision making, such as that in the Victorian Charter,[91] and in the amended ACT HRA,[92] is likely to have more immediate relevance to frontline decision-makers. A direct duty will also extend the reach of a bill of rights to the significant sphere of executive action which is not directly regulated by statute.[93]

An open-ended definition of a 'public authority' is critical in the context of the increasing tendency of governments to outsource their traditional functions to private entities. This ensures that a government agency cannot 'contract out' of its human rights obligations. The approach of the Victorian Charter and the ACT HRA is to spell out functional criteria to identify a public authority. This seeks to avoid the overly restrictive approach that has been taken by the courts in the United Kingdom, but the delineation of the 'functions of government' may still require determination by the courts.[94] The amendments to the ACT HRA introduced in 2008 include a provision to allow entities to 'opt in' to assume the obligations of public authorities.[95] While this provision would allow commercial entities to assume human rights duties voluntarily, it could also allow government agencies to request contractors to opt in as public authorities, thus avoiding uncertainties about the latter's human rights obligations.

There are some aspects of the ACT and Victorian bills of rights that could be improved in a national instrument. The exclusion of the courts as public authorities, except in their administrative capacities,[96] undermines the utility of a range of human rights, such as the right to a fair trial and rights in criminal proceedings, which should be respected by the courts in the application and development of the common law. This omission reflected constitutional concerns over the ability of the States and Territories to disturb the development of the 'unified' common law of Australia,[97] but this issue does not appear to arise in the same way in relation to a national bill of rights.[98] The ability of the Victorian Government to modify the definition of public authority to exclude certain entities by regulation, without transparent justification, is also problematic.[99] The government has already relieved adult and youth parole boards from obligations under the Charter (at least temporarily),[100] undermining the expectation that these authorities should comply with human rights such as the right to a fair hearing, as well as equality, humane treatment, privacy and freedom of expression.

Remedy provision

A direct duty upon public authorities should be coupled with an effective remedy mechanism. The Human Rights Act 1998 (UK) (UK HRA) provides a useful model. It allows the courts to grant any relief or remedy or make any order they consider just and appropriate, but limits the award of damages to cases where such an award is clearly necessary.[101] Legislative bills of rights in Australia have so far taken a more cautious approach, excluding damages altogether, apparently to avoid increased litigation and potential financial liability. However, experience in the United Kingdom suggests that such caution may be unwarranted. A review of the UK HRA in 2006 noted that the courts had awarded damages in only three reported cases.[102] In the great majority of cases, relief such as a declaration, the substitution of a new decision by the court or an order for a public authority to take a particular action will be sufficient to uphold human rights requirements. However, in the rare cases where no other remedy is adequate to compensate for a serious breach of human rights, it would be preferable to allow an award of damages to ensure that these rights are respected. Apart from its omission of damages, the straightforward remedy provision adopted by the ACT Government in its 2008 amending legislation is a significant improvement on the overly complex and opaque provision in the Victorian Charter.[103]

Human Rights Commission

The role of an independent human rights commission is central in developing a culture of human rights around a statutory charter of rights. The UK HRA did not initially provide for such a commission, but it became apparent that a body independent from government was needed to provide public education about the importance of human rights. The Parliament's Joint Committee on Human Rights argued in 2003 that a human rights commission could also act as a 'critical friend' to government:

> The enthusiasm to make the [UK HRA] come alive as a measure which places positive duties on public authorities, and which should promote a culture of respect for human rights in every aspect of public life, needs to be rekindled. A human rights commission probing, questioning and encouraging public bodies could have a real impact in driving forward the development of that culture by guiding, advising and assisting those involved in the work of public authorities.[104]

The Equality and Human Rights Commission commenced on 1 October 2007, replacing previous discrimination commissions with a single body with broad educational and inquiry powers under the UK HRA and the existing anti-discrimination legislation.

The ACT HRA and the Victorian Charter have each expanded the jurisdiction of existing discrimination bodies to incorporate functions under those bills of rights, although the ACT Human Rights Commission has a more extensive role than its Victorian counterpart. In the ACT, the power of the Human Rights Commissioner to initiate audits of human rights compliance has been particularly effective in achieving improvements in the areas of corrections and youth detention.[105] Neither commission has a human rights complaint-handling function.

At the national level, the Human Rights and Equal Opportunity Commission is well placed to assume the role of a 'critical friend' to the Australian government. It already has responsibilities for human rights education and inquiries, and deals with individual complaints alleging violations of federal anti-discrimination law and the ICCPR.

The Commonwealth Ombudsman also has a mandate that includes some human rights issues, where maladministration involves the violation of a human right. The Ombudsman provides an important oversight mechanism to monitor and improve the quality of administrative decision making by government agencies, and to ensure that laws and policies are properly implemented in individual cases.[106] While the Ombudsman contributes to the protection of human rights in a practical way, this role is not a substitute for a bill of rights.[107] The Ombudsman does not use an explicit human rights framework for his or her investigative and reporting powers, and works to improve administration within the constraints of existing laws, rather than critically assessing those laws against human rights standards.

What difference would a national bill of rights make?

The effect of a bill of rights translating international human rights standards to the Australian context would depend on its structure. If it followed the models of the ACT and Victorian bills of rights, an Australian bill of rights would draw attention to human rights protection at all levels of government. The early evidence from the ACT and Victoria is that a bill of rights primarily affects the development of government policy, the drafting and adoption of legislation, and the delivery of services to the community. The courts play a vital but not dominant role in interpreting legislation to be consistent with human rights and alerting the government and the community to breaches of human rights.

Bills of rights have been particularly useful in challenging the rigid application of policies in ways that ignore the realities of human lives. A 2006 study of the effect of the UK HRA outside the courts illustrates the value of recourse to human rights guarantees to improve the quality of basic services. For example, a woman with a disability required a special bed so that her carers, employed by a local authority, could lift her for baths; she requested a double bed so her husband could share it, but this was denied, although she had offered to pay the extra costs. Eventually the woman invoked her right to privacy and family life under the UK HRA, which led immediately to a change in policy.[108] Other examples in this study show how human rights concepts, such as human dignity, can transform long-entrenched practices.

The development and passage of the 2005 Commonwealth terrorism legislation indicates how easily human rights concerns can be sidelined in national politics.[109] That law introduced a series of mechanisms, such as 'control orders' and 'preventative detention', which were inconsistent with human rights standards. Given the Coalition government's Senate majority, and Opposition support for the legislation, little attention was paid to breaches of human rights in parliamentary debates. The Australian media generally also offered uncritical support for the laws. It would, of course, remain possible under a dialogue style of bill of rights for a legislature to enact any laws it pleases, subject to the Constitution, but issues of human rights would assume more prominence at all levels of governmental and public scrutiny. The government would be required to address and justify potential human rights breaches specifically, instead of invoking the obfuscating mantle of national security to avoid criticism.

The Australian judicial system is unable to address human rights breaches in Commonwealth laws if legislation comes within a constitutional head of power.[110] One striking example is the High Court's decision in *Al-Kateb v Godwin*.[111] Ahmed Ali al-Kateb, born in Kuwait in 1976 to Palestinian parents, arrived by boat in Australia in December 2000 claiming refugee status, and was placed in detention. There was no dispute that he was a stateless person because Kuwait did not consider him a citizen and Palestine did not have the capacity to grant citizenship. Mr Al-Kateb applied for, but was refused, a protection visa to stay in Australia. After failed legal challenges to this decision, he wrote to the Minister for Immigration in 2002 asking to be sent back either to Kuwait or Gaza. However, no country would accept him. The *Migration Act 1958* (Cwlth), as amended by the *Migration Reform Act 1992* (Cwlth), states that a non-citizen unlawfully in Australia who asks to be removed from Australia must be removed 'as soon as reasonably practicable'.[112] It also requires the continued detention of such a person 'until' they are removed.[113]

The High Court had to determine whether or not under the *Migration Act* the Minister for Immigration could detain an individual in Mr Al-Kateb's situation until another country was prepared to accept him. Members of the High Court conceded that the likelihood of Mr Al-Kateb's acceptance by another country was remote in current circumstances and that his detention in Australia would be indefinite, but a majority of the Court held that the *Migration Act* validly allowed his detention. Justice McHugh acknowledged that the outcome for Mr Al-Kateb was 'tragic', but there was no reason why Parliament could not legislate for indefinite detention. Justice McHugh argued that the lack of an Australian bill of rights justified his narrow reading of the *Migration Act*.[114] He implied that an Australian bill of rights would provide authority for the judiciary to look beyond Australia's borders and to take human rights principles into account in interpreting domestic law.[115] Mr Al-Kateb was released from detention soon after the High Court's decision, perhaps because of the publicity his case had attracted. The legal principle that indefinite detention is possible under Australian law remains, however.

A legislative bill of rights would provide a structure that would allow the human rights issues in *Al-Kateb* to be articulated and considered. It is possible that the plight of stateless persons seeking removal from Australia after unsuccessful applications for refugee status may have emerged in the process of developing human rights-compatible amendments to the *Migration Act*. The preparation of a statement of human rights compatibility at the time of the legislation's introduction into Parliament would also have allowed the issue to be identified. If the human rights of stateless persons only emerged at a later stage, then judicial power to interpret the legislation consistently with human rights could have resolved the issue.[116] Alternatively, a judicial declaration of incompatibility in relation to the relevant provisions of the *Migration Act* could exert political pressure for change.

Depending on its scope, an Australian bill of rights could allow Australia to implement fully the obligations it has accepted under international human rights treaties. The preservation of parliamentary supremacy in similar human rights legislation has led, however, to criticism that the mechanism of human rights interpretation is inadequate to protect human rights. For example, the UN Human Rights Committee has questioned the efficacy of the New Zealand and United Kingdom human rights laws, recommending that both countries revise them to allow courts to strike down legislation inconsistent with the rights set out in the ICCPR.[117] The Human Rights Committee's approach may be based, however, on a failure to appreciate the more subtle and pervasive operation of a dialogue form of bill of rights.

The ACT and Victorian statutory bills of rights, which were adopted with significant community support, suggest that the general suspicion of human rights in Australia is waning. Their enactment has nevertheless generated predictions of dire consequences for Australian democracy. Much of this opposition depends on incorrect, outdated or misleading arguments and data. The 'democracy objection' to an Australian bill of rights understands democracy as essentially majority rule,[118] but this approach does not respond to cases where majoritarian democracy delivers injustice, or when the interests of minorities are not taken into account. Moreover, the notion of democracy has a much broader context and potential and has a symbiotic, rather than antagonistic, relationship with human rights. On this analysis, it is possible to argue that '[d]emocracy depends on the protection of human rights. At the same time, the protection of human rights depends on democracy'.[119] In Australia's political system, a statutory bill of rights would be likely to improve the quality of democracy by requiring human rights standards to be taken into account in governmental actions and policy; it would not be a panacea for all rights violations, but would be likely to make the violations more obvious and subject to scrutiny.

A bill of rights would also serve as a significant symbolic statement of Australian values. It would set out the rights that were considered the basis of dignified and valued lives in Australia. Apart from any direct legal or political effect of a bill of rights, it has, as the poet Seamus Heaney has observed of the Universal Declaration of Human Rights, the capacity to offer redress in a more diffuse sense.[120] Heaney borrowed the idea of redress from Simone Weil, who argued that 'if we know in what direction the scales of society are tilted, we must do what we can to add weight to the lighter side of the scale'.[121] A bill of rights then, like the Universal Declaration, 'adds this kind of weight and contributes thereby to the maintenance of an equilibrium – never entirely achieved – between individual rights and majoritarian politics'.[122]

Notes

Foreword

1   Philip Alston (ed.), *Towards an Australian Bill of Rights* (1994).
2   Philip Alston 'An Australian bill of rights: by design or default?' ibid 1, 1.
3   Stuart Scheingold, *The Politics of Rights: Lawyers, public policy, and political change* (2nd edn, 2004), xxxii.
4   Consultation Committee for a Proposed WA Human Rights Act, *A WA Human Rights Act: Report of the Consultation Committee for a proposed WA Human Rights Act* (2007) ch. 4.
5   Jack Straw, 'Towards a Bill of Rights and Responsibility' (Speech delivered 21 January 2008), available at <http://www.justice.gov.uk/>.
6   See Malcolm Langford (ed.), *Social Rights Jurisprudence: Emerging trends in comparative and international law* (2008); and Varun Gauri & Daniel Brinks (eds), *Courting Social Justice* (2008).
7   Jack Straw, 'Modernising the Magna Carta' (Speech delivered at George Washington University, Washington, DC, 13 February 2008), available at <http://www.justice gov.uk/>.

Chapter 1: What are human rights?

1   See Sophocles, *Antigone*, lines 450–70; Tony Burns, 'Sophocles' *Antigone* and the history of the concept of natural law' (2002) 50 *Political Studies* 545.
2   Amartya Sen, 'Human rights and Asian values' (Speech delivered at the 16th Annual Morgenthau Memorial Lecture on Ethics and Foreign Policy, New York, 25 May 1997) 18–23, available at <http://www.cceia. org>.
3   Ibid. 17–18; Joseph Chan, 'A Confucian perspective on human rights for contemporary China' in Joanne R Bauer & Daniel A Bell (eds), *The East Asian Challenge for Human Rights* (1999) 212.
4   A C Grayling, *Towards the Light: The story of the struggles for liberty and rights that made the modern west* (2007) 34–5.
5   Ibid. 59–69.
6   Andrew Clapham, *Human Rights: A very short introduction* (2007) 6.
7   John Locke, 'The second treatise of government: An essay concerning the true origin, extent, and end of civil government' in Peter Laslett

(ed.), *John Locke – Two Treatises of Government* (1988) 265.

8   Ibid.

9   Translation by the Avalon Project, available at <http://www.yale.edu/>.

10   The Declaration is reproduced in Micheline Ishay (ed.), *Human Rights Reader: Major political essays, speeches and documents from the Bible to the present* (1997) 140.

11   See Allen Douglas, 'Gouges, Olympe de, 1748–1793' in Fedwa Malti-Douglas (ed.), *Encyclopedia of Sex and Gender* (2007) vol 2, 657, 657–8; Lynn Hunt, *Inventing Human Rights: A history* (2007) 171.

12   See Micheline Ishay, *The History of Human Rights: From ancient times to the globalization era* (2004) 107–16.

13   See, e.g. Karl Marx, 'On the Jewish question' in Micheline Ishay (ed.), *Human Rights Reader* (1997) 189, 196.

14   Ishay, *History of Human Rights*, above n. 12, 155.

15   Ibid. 138–41.

16   Ibid. 125.

17   Ibid. 123.

18   See Jenny S Martinez, 'Slave trade on trial: lessons of a great human-rights law success' (2008) 117 *Yale Law Journal* 550.

19   Ishay, *History of Human Rights*, above n. 12, 157.

20   See Pamela Bromley, 'Human rights and the League of Nations: How ideas about human rights came to be included in the charter and work of the League of Nations' (Paper presented at the Annual Meeting of the Western Political Science Association, San Diego, 20 March 2008) available at <http://www.allacademic.com>.

21   See the discussion in Jerome J Shestack, 'The philosophic foundations of human rights' (1998) 20 *Human Rights Quarterly* 201; James W Nickel, *Making Sense of Human Rights* (2nd edn, 2007) 70–91; Michael Freeman, 'The philosophical foundations of human rights' (1994) 16 *Human Rights Quarterly* 491; Anthony J Langlois, 'Human rights and modern liberalism: A critique' (2003) 51 *Political Studies* 509.

22   See, e.g. Alan Dershowitz, *Rights from Wrongs: A secular theory of the origins of rights* (2004) 9, cited in Nickel, above n. 21, 71–2; Jack Donnelly, *Universal Human Rights in Theory and Practice* (2nd edn, 2002), cited in Nickel, above n. 21, 73.

23   For example, Henry Shue describes a rights demand as 'a rationally justified demand for social guarantees against standard threats': Shue, *Basic Rights: Subsistence, affluence, and US foreign policy* (2nd edn, 1996) 17.

24   See Grayling, above n. 4, 260–1; Martha Nussbaum, *Women and Human Development: The capabilities approach* (2000).

25   'Act only according to that maxim whereby you can at the same time will that it should become a universal law': Immanuel Kant, *Grounding for the Metaphysics of Morals* (James W Ellington trans, 1993 edn) 30 [trans of: *Grundlegung zur Metaphysik der Sitten* (1785)].

26   Christian Tomuschat, *Human Rights: Between idealism and realism* (2003) 3.

27   See, e.g. Jack Donnelly, 'The social construction of international

human rights' in Tim Dunne & Nicholas J Wheeler (eds), *Human Rights in Global Politics* (1999) 71, 81–2. But see Marie-Bénédicte Dembour, *Who Believes in Human Rights? Reflections on the European Convention* (2006) 246–7 (pointing to the tension between these dual justifications).

28　See, e.g. Anthony J Langlois, *The Politics of Justice and Human Rights: Southeast Asia and universalist theory* (2001), especially chs 4, 5; Abdullahi Ahmed An-Na'im & Francis Mading Deng (eds), *Human Rights in Africa: Cross-cultural Perspectives* (1999).

29　Jeremy Bentham, *Anarchical Fallacies; Being an examination of the declarations of rights issued during the French Revolution* (1843).

30　Edmund Burke, *Reflections on the Revolution in France and on the Proceedings in Certain Societies in London Relative to that Event* (2nd edn, 1790) 46.

31　Alasdair MacIntyre, *After Virtue: A study in moral theory* (2nd edn, 1984) 69.

32　David Kennedy, 'The international human rights movement: Part of the problem?' (2002) 15 *Harvard Human Rights Journal* 101.

33　See, e.g. Prime Minister Mahathir Mohamad of Malaysia, quoted in Don Greenlees, 'Great divide on human rights', *The Australian* (Sydney), 20 August 1997, 1. For more extensive examinations of the issue, see Upendra Baxi, *The Future of Human Rights* (2nd edn, 2006); Balakrishnan Rajagopal, *International Law from Below: Development, social movements and third world resistance* (2005) 171–232.

34　See the account of the involvement of Charles Malik (Lebanon) & Chang Peng-chun (China) in Mary Ann Glendon, *A World Made New: Eleanor Roosevelt and the Universal Declaration of Human Rights* (2001); Johannes Morsink, *The Universal Declaration of Human Rights* (1999) 28–31.

35　Yash Ghai, 'Human rights and governance: The Asian debate' (1994) 10 *Australian Yearbook of International Law* 1.

36　See, e.g. Catharine A MacKinnon, *Are Women Human?* (2006); Elizabeth Kingdom, *What's Wrong with Rights? Problems for feminist politics of law* (1991); Hilary Charlesworth, Christine Chinkin & Shelley Wright, 'Feminist approaches to international law' (1991) 85 *American Journal of International Law* 613; Andrew Byrnes, 'Women, feminism and international human rights law – methodological myopia, fundamental flaws or meaningful marginalisation?' (1992) 12 *Australian Yearbook of International Law* 205.

37　See S James Anaya, *Indigenous Peoples in International Law* (2nd edn, 2004).

38　*Economic and Social Rights and the Right to Health* (1995) 13.

39　Dembour, above n. 27, 3.

40　Langlois, *Politics of Justice*, above n. 28, using the concept developed by Cass Sunstein (see, e.g. Cass R Sunstein, 'Incompletely theorized agreements in constitutional law' (2007) 74 *Social Research* 1).

41　Langlois, *Politics of Justice*, above n. 28, 112–13.

42　*Instructions for the Government of Armies of the United States in the*

Field, General Order No 100, 24 April 1863.

43 Convention for the Amelioration of the Condition of the Wounded in Armies in the Field 1864.

44 Geneva Convention for the Amelioration of the Condition of the Wounded and Sick in the Armed Forces in the Field 1949 (First Geneva Convention); Geneva Convention for the Amelioration of the Condition of Wounded, Sick and Shipwrecked Members of Armed Forces at Sea 1949 (Second Geneva Convention); Geneva Convention relative to the Treatment of Prisoners of War 1949 (Third Geneva Convention); Geneva Convention relative to the Protection of Civilian Persons in Time of War 1949 (Fourth Geneva Convention).

45 These included Poland, Czechoslovakia, Yugoslavia, Romania, Greece, Hungary, Austria, Bulgaria, and Turkey. Albania, Lithuania, Estonia, Latvia and Iraq accepted obligations with respect to national minorities as part of the conditions on which they were admitted to the League of Nations.

46 Treaty of Peace between the Allied and Associated Powers and Germany, and Protocol 1919 ('Treaty of Versailles').

47 ILO Constitution 1919, Preamble.

48 Louis Henkin, 'Introduction' in Louis Henkin (ed.), *The International Bill of Rights* (1981) 1, 8–10.

49 The General Assembly also adopted the First Optional Protocol to the ICCPR in 1966 and a Second Optional Protocol to the ICCPR, aiming at the abolition of the death penalty, in 1989.

50 A wide range of international human rights instruments have also been adopted within the framework of regional systems for the protection of human rights, in particular within the framework of the Council of Europe, the Organisation of American States and the African Union (formerly the Organisation of African Unity).

51 Supplemented by an Optional Protocol 1999.

52 Supplemented by an Optional Protocol 2002.

53 Supplemented by an Optional Protocol on the Involvement of Children in Armed Conflicts 2000 and an Optional Protocol on the Sale of Children, Child Prostitution and Child Pornography 2000.

54 Supplemented by an Optional Protocol 2006.

55 Annemarie Devereux, *Australia and the Birth of the International Bill of Human Rights 1946–1966* (2005) 1.

56 The Australian delegation to the Human Rights Commission working group on implementation submitted that: 'States therefore must take action to ensure that their national laws cover the contents of the Bill, so that no executive or legislative organs or government can override them, and that the judicial organs alone shall be the means whereby the rights of citizens set out in the Bill are protected.' UN Doc E/CN.4/AC.4/SR.2, 1–2 (1947).

57 Australia has also accepted procedures that allow other states to complain about human rights violations under the ICCPR (art. 41) and CAT (art. 21). CERD (art. 11) also allows a similar procedure.

58 Cynthia Banham, 'Australia to sign torture treaty at last', *Sydney*

Morning Herald (Sydney), 1 March 2008, 1; Robert McClelland, 'Australia and international human rights: Coming in from the cold' (Speech given at Australia's International Human Rights Engagement: Coming in From the Cold? Human Rights Law Seminar, Sydney, 8 May 2008) available at <http://www.hreoc.gov.au>.

59   McClelland, above n. 58, [27].
60   See generally, Hilary Charlesworth et al, *No Country is an Island: Australia and international law* (2006) 64–105.
61   Daryl Williams (Attorney-General), 'CERD Report Unbalanced' (Press Release, 26 March 2000).
62   Alexander Downer (Minister for Foreign Affairs), Daryl Williams (Attorney-General) & Philip Ruddock (Minister for Immigration and Multicultural Affairs), 'Improving the Effectiveness of United Nations Committees' (Press Release, 29 August 2000).
63   See, e.g. Sarah Smiles, 'UN Bid to Mend Fences with Canberra', *The Age* (Melbourne), 17 March 2008, 8.

Chapter 2: A short history of Australian bills of rights

1   Claims for the recognition and granting of political rights in the Australian colonies (in particular in the colony of New South Wales), including demands for expanded male suffrage and responsible government, date from at least the 1840s and in many respects follow developments in Britain. See generally Peter Cochrane, *Colonial Ambition: Foundations of Australian democracy* (2006).
2   The draft is reproduced as an appendix to John Reynolds, 'A I Clark's American sympathies and his influence on Australian Federation' (1958) 32 *Australian Law Journal* 62.
3   Andrew Inglis Clark, *Studies in Australian Constitutional Law* (1901) 386–7.
4   See, e.g. *Schenck v US*, 249 US 47 (1919); *Abrams v US*, 250 US 616 (1919).
5   Proposed by Clark in an amendment to the draft Constitution in 1897.
6   See George Williams, *Human Rights under the Australian Constitution* (1999) 37–42.
7   *Official Record of the Debates of the Australasian Federal Convention*, Melbourne, 8 February 1898, 688.
8   Ibid.
9   Ibid. 683.
10   See, e.g. James Bryce, *Studies in History and Jurisprudence* (1901) 447–8.
11   Robert Moffatt, 'Philosophical foundations of the Australian constitutional tradition' (1965) 5 *Sydney Law Review* 59, 85–6.
12   Brian Galligan, 'Australia's rejection of a bill of rights' (1990) 28 *Journal of Commonwealth and Comparative Politics* 344, 350.
13   Ibid. 351.
14   Ibid. 350–2.
15   Ibid. 354.
16   Ibid. 355.

17 Commonwealth, *Parliamentary Debates*, Senate, 21 November 1973, 1972.
18 Commonwealth, *Parliamentary Debates*, House of Representatives, 21 March 1979, 944–5.
19 Commonwealth, *Parliamentary Debates*, Senate, 25 September 1979, 918.
20 A Human Rights Commission Bill was introduced into Parliament in 1977 and a revised Bill in 1979.
21 See, e.g. Commonwealth, *Parliamentary Debates*, Senate, 8 November 1979, 2093; 13 November 1979, 2213.
22 *The Age* (Melbourne), 26 October 1983, 1.
23 Jon Faine & Michael Pearce, 'An interview with Gareth Evans: Blueprints for reform' (1983) 8 *Legal Service Bulletin* 117, 118.
24 *The Australian* (Sydney), 24 October 1984.
25 Senate Standing Committee on Constitutional and Legal Affairs, Commonwealth Parliament, *A Bill of Rights for Australia? An exposure report for the consideration of senators* (1985).
26 Australian Human Rights Bill 1985.
27 Brian Galligan, Rainer Knopff & John Uhr, 'Australian federalism and the debate over a bill of rights' (1990) 20(4) *Publius* 53, 60.
28 George Williams, *A Charter of Rights for Australia* (2007) 60.
29 See Enid Campbell, 'Fashioning and refashioning the Constitution' (2001) 24 *University of New South Wales Law Journal* 620, 627.
30 The other proposals related to the length of parliamentary terms and simultaneous elections for the Senate and House of Representatives (*Constitutional Alteration (Parliamentary Terms) 1988*), ensuring fair and democratic Commonwealth, State and Territory elections (*Constitutional Alteration (Fair Elections) 1988*), and the constitutional recognition of local government (*Constitutional Alteration (Local Government) 1988*).
31 Commonwealth, *Parliamentary Debates*, Senate, 27 September 2001, 28110–11.
32 Another draft bill of rights, the Australian Bill of Rights Bill 2001, was introduced into the House of Representatives by Dr Andrew Theophanous, a former Labor member, but in 2001 an independent Member of Parliament. It was not passed.
33 See <http://www.newmatilda.com>.
34 See the campaign website at <http://www.humanrightsact.com.au>.
35 Richard McGregor, 'Howard firm on state rights', *The Australian* (Sydney), 26 February 2000, 5.
36 *Official Records of the Debates of the Australasian Federal Convention*, Melbourne, 8 February 1898, 689.
37 Robert Menzies, *Central Power in the Australian Commonwealth* (1967) 54.
38 For a comprehensive guide to Australian human rights laws, see Nick O'Neill, Simon Rice & Roger Douglas, *Retreat from Injustice: Human rights law in Australia* (2nd edn, 2004). See also Australia's reports to the United Nations, in particular its core document setting out the

various laws and institutions at federal and state levels: *Core Document Forming Part of the Reports of States Parties: Australia*, UN Doc HRI/CORE/AUS/2007 (2007), 11–17.

39   Article 8.

40   Article 22.

41   See chapter 1 at 20–21.

42   For details of pending and recent cases and government responses, see Attorney-General's Department, *Human Rights Communications*, available at <http://www.ag.gov.au>.

43   Treaty violations were found in one of nine cases brought under the CAT (one case was inadmissible); one of six cases under CERD (two cases were inadmissible) and 17 of 54 cases under the ICCPR (31 cases were inadmissible). See *The United Nations Human Rights Treaties Jurisprudence: Australia*, available at <http://www.bayefsky.com>.

44   *Toonen v Australia*, Communication No 488/1992: Australia. 04/04/94, UN Doc CCPR/C/50/D/488/1992 (1994).

45   See NSW Council for Civil Liberties, *Does Australia Violate Human Rights?*, available at <http://www.nswccl.org.au> (list of cases in which UN Human Rights Committee has found Australia in violation of the ICCPR and the Australian government's response). See also Hilary Charlesworth, *Human Rights: Australia versus the UN* (2006) Democratic Audit of Australia, available at <http://democratic.audit.anu.edu.au>.

46   There are many statutes that provide legislative protection of aspects of human rights or legislative framework for the enjoyment of rights, without explicit reference to the rights or being 'human rights legislation': see generally the overview provided in *Core Document*, above n. 38.

47   See Chris Ronalds, *Discrimination Law and Practice* (3rd edn, 2008); Neil Rees, Katherine Lindsay & Simon Rice, *Australian Anti-Discrimination Law: Text, cases and materials* (2008).

48   On privacy law, see, e.g. Australian Law Reform Commission, *Review of Australian Privacy Law*, Discussion Paper 72 (2007); on freedom of information, see, e.g. Commonwealth Ombudsman, *Scrutinising Government: Administration of the* Freedom of Information Act 1982 *in Australian government agencies* (2006).

49   *HREOC Act 1986* (Cwlth) s. 11(e). HREOC also has a responsibility under the *Native Title Act 1993* (Cwlth) to report on the enjoyment of the human rights of Indigenous people with regard to native title (a function carried out by the Aboriginal and Torres Strait Islander Social Justice Commissioner), and certain functions under the *Workplace Relations Act 1996* (Cwlth) in relation to federal awards and equal pay (a function carried out by the Sex Discrimination Commissioner).

50   See, e.g. *HREOC Act 1986* (Cwlth) s. 11(g), (h), (j), (n).

51   The appended treaties are the ICCPR, the CRC and the Convention Concerning Discrimination in Respect of Employment and Occupation 1958. Non-treaty instruments are the Declaration on the Rights of the Child, GA Res 1386 (1959), the Declaration on the Rights of Disabled

Persons, GA Res 2856 (1971) and the Declaration on the Rights of
Mentally Retarded Persons, GA Res 3447 (1975).

52 However, under s. 46 of the *HREOC Act 1986* (Cwlth), the Aboriginal
and Torres Strait Islander Commissioner is required to have regard to
the Universal Declaration of Human Rights, ICESCR, CERD and other
instruments the Commissioner considers relevant in carrying out his or
her functions in relation to Aboriginal and Torres Strait Islanders.

53 Except in relation to Div. 4 of the Act, which extends the Convention
Concerning Discrimination in Respect of Employment and Occupation
1958 to the States and Territories.

54 See Christine Fougere, 'The intervention and *amicus curiae* functions
of the Human Rights and Equal Opportunity Commission and its
commissioners' (Paper presented at the National Conference of
Community Legal Centres, Fremantle, WA, 2–5 September 2001),
available at <http://www.hreoc.gov.au>.

55 *HREOC Act 1986* (Cwlth) s. 11(1), (o).

56 *HREOC Act 1986* (Cwlth) s. 31(j).

57 *Racial Discrimination Act 1975* (Cwlth) s. 20(1)(e); *Sex Discrimination
Act 1984* (Cwlth) s. 48(1)(gb); *Disability Discrimination Act 1992*
(Cwlth) s. 67(1)(l); *Age Discrimination Act 2004* (Cwlth) s. 53(1)(g).

58 As of June 2008, HREOC had intervened in 54 cases. See also Julie
O'Brien, 'Human rights: Intervention powers of the Human Rights
Commission' (2006) 44 *Law Society Journal* 39.

59 See HREOC, *Guidelines on Applications for Interventions in Court
Proceedings* (2003), available at <http://www.hreoc.gov.au>.

60 Human Rights Legislation Amendment Bill (No 2) 1998 (Cwlth).

61 Australian Human Rights Commission Legislation Bill 2003 (Cwlth).

62 The Human Rights Commissioner, the Race Discrimination
Commissioner, the Sex Discrimination Commissioner, the Disability
Discrimination Commissioner and the Aboriginal and Torres Strait
Islander Social Justice Commissioner.

63 *HREOC Act 1986* (Cwlth) s. 49P. See HREOC, *Commission Guidelines
for the Exercise of the* Amicus Curiae *Function under the Human Rights
and Equal Opportunity Commission Act* (2007), available at <http://
www.hreoc.gov.au>. For details of cases in which the commissioners
have sought to appear as amici, see HREOC, *Submission to Court as
Intervener and* Amicus Curiae, available at <http://www.hreoc.gov.au>.

64 HREOC, *Bringing Them Home: Report of the national inquiry into
the separation of Aboriginal and Torres Strait Islander children from
their families* (1997). See Antonio Buti, *Sir Ronald Wilson: A matter of
conscience* (2007) 330–47.

65 See Ronalds, above n. 47; Rees, Lindsay & Rice, above n. 47.

66 See Australian Institute of Family Studies: National Child Protection
Clearinghouse, *Children's Commissioners: A national snapshot*,
available at <http://www.aifs.gov.au>.

67 The Constitution (Declaration of Rights) Bill 1959 (Qld) was introduced
by the Country-National Party Premier Frank Nicklin into the
Queensland Parliament in December 1959. The Bill sought to entrench

democratic rights, the independence of the judiciary and rights on arrest or detention, but was abandoned due to fierce opposition.

68   See chapter 5.

69   See chapter 4.

70   Constitutional Development Committee, Parliament of Northern Territory, *A Northern Territory Bill of Rights?*, Discussion Paper No 8 (1995). For the final report, see Sessional Committee on Constitutional Development, Parliament of Northern Territory, *Foundations for a Common Future* (1996) vol 1, [5–12] – [5–13]. The issue re-emerged in 2007: see Statehood Steering Committee, Parliament of Northern Territory, *Constitutional Paths to Statehood*, Community Discussion Paper (2007) 60–3.

71   Legal, Constitutional and Administrative Review Committee, Parliament of Queensland, *The Preservation and Enhancement of Individuals' Rights and Freedoms in Queensland: Should Queensland adopt a bill of rights?* (1998).

72   Standing Committee on Law and Justice, Parliament of New South Wales, *A NSW Bill of Rights* (2001).

73   Galligan, above n. 12, 345.

74   Ibid. 352–3.

75   See above n. 67.

76   See ABC-Radio National, 'A bill of rights for an age of terror', *The National Interest*, 13 November 2005, available at <http://www.abc.net.au>.

77   See, e.g. Bob Carr, 'Only people – not bills – protect rights', *The Australian* (Sydney), 9 January 2001, 17; John Hatzistergos, 'Busting myths about the need for our own charter of rights', *The Australian* (Sydney), 7 March 2008, 30.

78   Australian Labor Party, *National Platform and Constitution* (2007) 206–7 [4], available at <www.alp.org.au>.

79   Ibid. 207[9].

Chapter 3: Bills of rights: models and controversies

1   Philip Alston, 'Bills of rights: An analytical framework' in Philip Alston (ed.), *Promoting Human Rights through Bills of Rights: Comparative perspectives* (1999) 1, 7 (citation omitted).

2   The procedure, under art. V of the United States Constitution, involves the proposal of an amendment approved by two-thirds of both Houses of Congress or by a constitutional convention called on the application of two-thirds of the State legislatures, and requires the ratification of the proposed amendment by three-quarters of the State legislatures or State constitutional conventions.

3   See, e.g. Mark Tushnet, *Taking the Constitution Away from the Courts* (2000); Frank Brennan, *Legislating Liberty: A bill of rights for Australia* (1998).

4   Proposed amendments must be approved by the House of Commons, the Senate, and a two-thirds majority of the provincial legislatures representing at least 50 per cent of the national population: ss. 38–49.

5   Parliamentary Information and Research Service (Canada), *The Notwithstanding Clause of the Charter*, Background Paper PRB 194E (2005) 10–13.

6   The Constitution can only be amended by legislation passed by a supermajority in the National Assembly or, in certain circumstances, a supermajority of the ten-member National Council of Provinces (s. 74).

7   See Johannes Chan & Yash Ghai (eds), *The Hong Kong Bill of Rights: A comparative approach* (1993); Andrew Byrnes, 'And some have bills of rights thrust upon them: The experience of Hong Kong's Bill of Rights' in Alston above n. 1, 318.

8   *A Bill of Rights for New Zealand: A White Paper* (1985).

9   For signs of the judicial development of such a procedure, see *R v Poumako* [2000] NZCA 69.

10 Pursuant to s. 92J(I) of the Human Rights Act (inserted by s. 6 of the Human Rights Amendment Act 2001 with commencement on 1 January 2002). In *Howard v. Attorney-General (No 3)* [2008] NZHRRT 10 the Tribunal granted a declaration that statutory provisions, the effect of which was to provide lesser vocational rehabilitation support after personal injury for those who are near 65 and older than for younger people, was inconsistent with s. 19 of the Bill of Rights Act. See also *Child Poverty Action Group v Attorney-General* [2005] NZHRRT 28; *Attorney-General v Human Rights Tribunal and Child Poverty Action Group* (2006) 16 PRNZ 295, [2007] NZAR 67.

11 Peter Hogg & Allison Bushell, 'The *Charter* dialogue between courts and legislatures (or perhaps the *Charter of Rights* isn't such a bad thing after all)' (1997) 35 *Osgoode Hall Law Journal* 75.

12 Peter Hogg, Allison Thornton & Wade Wright, '*Charter* dialogue revisited – or "much ado about metaphors"' (2007) 45 *Osgoode Hall Law Journal* 1, 7; Julie Debeljak, 'Parliamentary sovereignty and dialogue under the *Victorian Charter of Human Rights and Responsibilities*: Drawing the line between judicial interpretation and judicial law-making' (2007) 33 *Monash University Law Review* 9, 22–35; Leighton McDonald, 'New directions in the Australian bill of rights debate' (2004) 12 *Public Law* 22.

13 For an overview, see the articles in (2007) 45 *Osgoode Hall Law Journal* 1–202 (special issue on '*Charter* Dialogue Ten Years Later').

14 Hogg, Thornton & Wright, '*Charter* dialogue revisited', above n. 12, 4.

15 Peter Hogg, Allison Thornton & Wade Wright, 'A reply on "*Charter* dialogue revisited"' (2007) 45 *Osgoode Hall Law Journal* 193, 194.

16 Hogg, Thornton & Wright, '*Charter* dialogue revisited', above n. 11, 4.

17 Christopher Manfredi & James Kelly, 'Six degrees of dialogue: A response to Hogg and Bushell' (1999) 37 *Osgoode Hall Law Journal* 513, 520–1.

18 Debeljak, above n. 12, 25–39.

19 Peter Hogg & Allison Thornton, 'Reply to "Six degrees of dialogue"' (1999) 37 *Osgoode Hall Law Journal* 529, 536.

20 Debeljak, above n. 12, 68–70; Priyanga Hettiarachi, 'Some things borrowed, some things new: An overview of judicial review of

legislation under the *Charter of Human Rights and Responsibilities'*
(2007) 7 *Oxford University Commonwealth Law Journal* 61, 89–90.
21 Debeljak, above n. 12, 25–39.
22 Ibid. 35–9.
23 See generally George Williams, *A Charter of Rights for Australia* (2007)
    18–50.
24 ABC Television, 'UN's Committee Process "out of whack": Howard',
    The 7.30 Report, 30 August 2000, available at <http://www.abc.net.au>.
25 Daryl Williams (Attorney-General), 'CERD report unbalanced' (Press
    Release, 26 March 2000).
26 Victorian Human Rights Consultation Committee (Victorian
    Committee), *Rights, Responsibilities and Respect: The Report of
    the Human Rights Consultation Committee* (2005) 14; Tasmanian
    Law Reform Institute, *A Charter of Rights for Tasmania, Report No
    10* (2007) 27; Consultation Committee for a Proposed WA Human
    Rights Act (WA Committee), *A WA Human Rights Act: Report of the
    Consultation Committee for a Proposed WA Human Rights Act* (2007)
    40–4.
27 WA Committee, above n. 26, 44.
28 See, e.g. John Hatzistergos, 'A charter of rights or a charter of wrongs?'
    (Speech delivered at the Sydney Institute, Sydney, 10 April 2008);
    George Pell, 'Four fictions: An argument against a charter of rights'
    (2008) 52(8) *Quadrant* 24, 24.
29 See, e.g. Justice Michael McHugh, 'Does Australia need a bill of rights?'
    (Paper presented to NSW Bar Association Forum, Sydney, 7 August
    2007) 36–7, available at <http://www.nswbar.asn.au>.
30 Victorian Committee, above n. 26, 6; Tasmanian Law Reform Institute,
    above n. 25, 28–39; WA Committee, above n. 26, 27–9.
31 Victorian Committee, above n. 26, 14; Tasmanian Law Reform Institute,
    above n. 26, 49; WA Committee, above n. 26, 23, 40–2.
32 Tasmanian Law Reform Institute, above n. 26, 32–3; WA Committee,
    above n. 26, 30–2, 40–2.
33 The NSW Parliamentary Inquiry, while accepting the limited nature
    of coverage and consequent problems, was not persuaded that a bill
    of rights was the answer, seeing a more vigilant role for parliament as
    the appropriate response: Standing Committee on Law and Justice,
    Parliament of New South Wales, *A NSW Bill of Rights* (2001) chs. 7, 8.
34 See, e.g. Williams, above n. 23; McHugh, above n. 29, 14–37.
35 Victorian Committee, above n. 26, 12; WA Committee, above n. 26,
    39; *Report of the Human Rights Committee*, GAOR, 55th sess., Supp
    No 40, [514]–[515], UN Doc A/55/40 (2000); Committee on Economic,
    Social and Cultural Rights, *Report on the Twenty-Second, Twenty-Third
    and Twenty-Fourth Sessions*, UN ESCOR, 22nd, 23rd and 24th sess.,
    Supp No 2, [378]–[379], [389], UN Doc E/2001/22 (2001).
36 See, e.g. Bob Carr, 'The rights trap: How a bill of rights could
    undermine freedom' (2001) 17(2) *Policy* 19.
37 See, e.g. Tom Campbell, 'Does anyone win under a bill of rights? A
    response to Hilary Charlesworth's "Who wins under a bill of rights?"'

(2006) 25 *University of Queensland Law Journal* 55, 60.

38   Mac Darrow & Philip Alston, 'Bills of rights in comparative perspective' in Alston above n. 1, 465, 498 (quoting R Dworkin). See also Hilary Charlesworth, 'Who wins under a bill of rights?' (2006) *University of Queensland Law Journal* 39, 52–3.

39   Darrow & Alston, above n. 38, 500.

40   Carr, above n. 36, 19–20; Campbell, above n. 37; James Allan, 'A defence of the status quo' in Tom Campbell, Jeffrey Goldsworthy & Adrienne Stone (eds), *Protecting Human Rights: Instruments and institutions* (2003) 175.

41   Darrow & Alston, above n. 38, 514–17.

42   Charlesworth, above n. 38, 46. See also Adrienne Stone, 'Judicial review without rights: Some problems for the democratic legitimacy of structural judicial review' (2008) 28 *Oxford Journal of Legal Studies* 1.

43   Australasian Institute of Judicial Administration, *Judges and Magistrates (% of Women)* (2008) available at <http://www.aija.org.au>. See also Attorney General's Department, *Judicial Appointments: Procedure and criteria* (1993).

44   Darrow & Alston, above n. 38, 501 (citing the work of Michael Zander).

45   Former High Court Chief Justice Sir Harry Gibbs, an opponent of a constitutional bill of rights, conceded that the arguments against an entrenched bill of rights 'do not apply with the same force' to a statutory charter, though he noted that legislators might feel reluctant to repeal such a statute despite its status as ordinary legislation: 'Does Australia need a bill of rights?' in *Upholding the Australian Constitution: Proceedings of the Sixth Conference of the Samuel Griffith Society* (1996) 74, 78.

46   Ibid.

47   Conor Gearty, *Can Human Rights Survive?* (2006) 96.

48   James Allan, 'The Victorian *Charter of Human Rights and Responsibilities*: Exegesis and criticism' (2006) 30 *Melbourne University Law Review* 906, 909.

49   Ibid.

50   [2004] UKHL 30 ('*Ghaidan*').

51   Ibid [30] (Lord Nicholls).

52   [2001] UKHL 25.

53   See, e.g. the comments of Lord Steyn in *Ghaidan* [2004] UKHL 30, [42]–[46].

54   See Chief Justice J J Spigelman, 'Legitimate and spurious interpretation' (Third lecture in the 2008 McPherson Lectures: Statutory Interpretation and Human Rights, Brisbane, 12 March 2008) 16, available at <http://www.lawlink.nsw.gov.au>; Hettiarachi, above n. 20, 82–6. See also *Raytheon Australia Pty Ltd and ACT Human Rights Commission* [2008] ACTAAT 19 (*Raytheon*), [69]–[81].

55   Allan, 'Exegesis and criticism', above n. 48, 912–14. See also Manfredi & Kelly, above n. 17.

56   Allan, 'Exegesis and criticism', above n. 48, 914.

57 *R (on the application of H) v Mental Health Review Tribunal for the North and East London Region* [2001] EWCA Civ 415.

58 *Re an Application for Judicial Review by McR* [2002] NIQB 58.

59 *Blood and Tarbuck v Secretary of State for Health* (Unreported, Sullivan J, 28 February 2003).

60 *Bellinger v Bellinger* [2003] UKHL 21.

61 *R (on the application of Hooper) v Secretary of State for Work and Pensions* [2003] EWCA Civ 875.

62 *A v Secretary of State for the Home Department* [2004] UKHL 56.

63 Laurence Tribe, Jeremy Waldron & Mark Tushnet, 'On judicial review' (2005) 52(3) *Dissent* 81. See also Jeremy Waldron, 'The core of the case against judicial review' (2006) 115 *Yale Law Journal* 1346, 1370.

64 Tribe, 'On judicial review', above n. 63, 83.

65 Jeremy Webber, 'A modest (but robust) defence of statutory bills of rights' in Tom Campbell, Jeffrey Goldsworthy & Adrienne Stone (eds), *Protecting Rights Without a Bill of Rights: Institutional performance and reform in Australia* (2006) 263, 276.

66 Ibid. 284.

67 WA Committee, above n. 26, 36–9.

68 Ibid. 34–5, 37–8 (citing UK experience); Victorian Committee, above n. 26, 10–12 (citing UK and ACT experiences).

69 Tasmanian Law Reform Institute, above n. 26, 72–3; WA Committee, above n. 26, 37–8. See also The Audit Commission, *Human Rights: Improving public service delivery* (2003); Ministry of Justice (UK), *Human Rights Insight Project*, Ministry of Justice Research Series 1/08 (2008). The 2001 NSW Parliamentary Committee concluded that many of the concerns supporting the case for such a bill of rights could be addressed by the adoption of an explicit parliamentary scrutiny function to be conferred on a specialist committee: Standing Committee on Law and Justice, above n. 33, ch. 8.

70 Department for Constitutional Affairs (UK) (DCA), Review of the Implementation of the Human Rights Act (2006) 4.

71 Andrew Butler & Petra Butler, *The New Zealand Bill of Rights Act: A commentary* (2005) 197–208 (Attorney-General's duty to report to Parliament); 1103–6 (impact on the law-making process more generally).

72 Department of Justice and Community Safety (ACT) (JACS), *Human Rights Act 2004: Twelve-month review – report* (2006) 15; Gabrielle McKinnon, 'The ACT Human Rights Act – The second year' (Paper presented at the Australian Bills of Rights Conference, Canberra, 21 June 2006).

73 See Victorian Equal Opportunity and Human Rights Commission, *Compatibility Statements for 2007 under the Charter of Human Rights and Responsibilities* (2008), available at <http://www.humanrightscommission.vic.gov.au>.

74 DCA, above n. 70, 4.

75 British Institute of Human Rights, *The Human Rights Act – Changing lives* (2006) 5.

76   Audit Commission, above n. 69; Ministry of Justice, above n. 69.
77   Tasmanian Law Reform Institute, above n. 26, 76-7; WA Committee, above n. 26, 47–50.
78   See, e.g. Carr, above n. 36, 20.
79   DCA, above n. 70, 10.
80   Tom Mullen et al, 'Human Rights in the Scottish Courts' (2005) 32 *Journal of Law and Society* 148, 152.
81   Ibid. 160.
82   Ibid. 168.
83   See JACS, above n. 72, 11–13.
84   DCA, above n. 70, 30–4.
85   Ibid. 13; *Brown v Stott* [2000] UKPC D3.
86   For example, the UK courts have held that the role of the Home Secretary in determining the minimum period that a person serving a life sentence must serve before that person becomes eligible for parole was incompatible with human rights (*R (Anderson) v Secretary of State for the Home Department* [2002] UKHL 46), as was a policy allowing prison staff to search a prisoner's legally privileged correspondence in his absence (*R (Daly) v Secretary of State for the Home Department* [2001] UKHL 26).
87   For example, the decision in *R v Askov* [1990] SCC 45 staying actions under the Canadian Charter for delay in criminal proceedings, and the prospect of similar stays under the Hong Kong Bill of Rights, led the governments concerned to allocate additional resources to reduce delays in the criminal justice system: Byrnes, above n. 7, 377.
88   With respect to the ACT and Victoria, see chs. 4 and 5. The advent of the BORO in Hong Kong led to review of the primary and secondary legislation in relation to prison administration, evidentiary presumptions in criminal statutes, and laws relating to freedom of expression, with mixed results: Byrnes, above n. 7, 345–6.
89   See Richard Refshauge, 'Impact on criminal law and procedure' (Paper presented at the Protecting Human Rights Conference, University of Melbourne, 25 September 2007); Justice Terry Connolly, 'Practicing criminal law under the Human Rights Act: No rogue's charter' (Paper presented at the Conference of Australian Prosecutors, Canberra, 14 July 2005). See also DCA, above n. 70, 1; WA Committee, above n. 26, 57.
90   DCA, above n. 70, 30.
91   See Carr, above n. 36, 20.
92   See, e.g. Gibbs, above n. 45.
93   ACT HRA ss. 43, 44; Victorian Charter ss. 44, 45.
94   See, e.g. ACT HRA s. 7; Victorian Charter s. 5.
95   Darrow & Alston, above n. 38, 502–9.
96   See, e.g. Bill Stefaniak, 'The need to balance a bill of rights' (2005) 86 *The Parliamentarian* 251.
97   Darrow & Alston, above n. 38, 494.
98   Gearty, above n. 47, 60–98 (although Gearty sees a bill of rights such as the UK HRA as preserving important dimensions of the politics of human rights: ibid. 93–8).

Chapter 4: The ACT *Human Rights Act 2004*

1   See Jack Waterford, 'How a model ACT Self-Government Act might look' in Philip Grundy et al, *Reluctant Democrats: The transition to self-government in the Australian Capital Territory* (1996) appendix 9.

2   Section 23 of the Act limits the power of the ACT legislature to make laws in relation to censorship or the acquisition of property other than on just terms.

3   Attorney-General's Department (ACT), *A Bill of Rights for the ACT?: Issues Paper* (1993).

4   See Attorney-General's Department (ACT), *A Bill of Rights for the ACT: Proceedings of a Seminar 7 May 1994* (1994).

5   See ACT, *Parliamentary Debates,* 3 May 1995, 108 (Terry Connolly) (speech on moving the Bill of Rights Bill 1995).

6   Standing Committee on Legal and Constitutional Affairs, Commonwealth Parliament, *Half Way to Equal: Report of the Inquiry into Equal Opportunity and Equal Status for Women in Australia* (1992).

7   Monika Boogs, 'ACT needs a bill of rights – Stanhope', *The Canberra Times* (Canberra), 18 August 2001, 5; Crispin Hull, 'Charting a course for rights', *The Canberra Times* (Canberra), 25 August 2001, 3.

8   Daniel Landon, 'Stefaniak against bill of rights', *The Canberra Times* (Canberra), 24 August 2001, 6.

9   David McLennan, 'Stanhope begins building bill of rights committee', *The Canberra Times* (Canberra), 11 December 2001, 2.

10 ACT Bill of Rights Consultative Committee (ACT Committee), *Towards an ACT Human Rights Act: Report of the ACT Bill of Rights Consultative Committee* (2003) [1.3].

11 These are described at ibid. [1.6]–[1.18].

12 Ibid., appendix 3. For a discussion of the poll, see Rachael Eggins et al, 'Citizen participation in a deliberative poll: Factors predicting attitude change and political engagement' (2002) 59 *Australian Journal of Psychology* 94.

13 See the Preamble to the Human Rights Bill 2003 in ACT Committee, above n. 10, appendix 4, 3.

14 Articles 6(1) of the ICCPR and 11(1), (2) of the ICESCR respectively. See ACT Committee, above n. 10, appendix 4, 15.

15 ACT, *Parliamentary Debates*, 9 April 2002, 832–5 (Bill Stefaniak).

16 See ACT Parliamentary Counsel's Office, *What We Do*, available at <http://www.pco.act.gov.au>.

17 ACT, *Parliamentary Debates*, 25 November 2003, 4577.

18 Roderick Campbell, 'Libs seek change to bill of rights', *The Canberra Times* (Canberra), 1 March 2004, 2.

19 ACT, *Parliamentary Debates*, 2 March 2004, 511 (Jacqui Burke).

20 ACT, *Parliamentary Debates*, 2 March 2004, 456 (Steve Pratt).

21 See, e.g. ACT, *Parliamentary Debates*, 25 November 2003, 4581–3 (Kerrie Tucker).

22 Ibid.

23 ACT HRA s. 43.

24 ACT, *Parliamentary Debates*, 18 August 2004, 3883 (Bill Stefaniak). For the history and an analysis of this Bill, see Lara Kostakidis-Lianos & George Williams, 'Bills of responsibility: Is one needed to counter the excesses of the ACT *Human Rights Act 2004*?' (2005) 30 *Alternative Law Journal* 58.

25 This would have been possible through Commonwealth legislation under the Territories power set out in s. 122 of the *Australian Constitution*.

26 Sophie Morris, 'Howard axe hangs over ACT's landmark Bill of Rights', *The Australian* (Sydney), 3 March 2004, 3.

27 John Laws, Interview with John Howard, Prime Minister of Australia (Sydney, 8 March 2004).

28 The concept of inter-institutional 'dialogue' under a bill of rights is discussed in chapter 3.

29 Explanatory Statement, Human Rights Act Bill 2003 (ACT) 3.

30 ICCPR art. 20. There is separate protection against vilification on the grounds of race and religion under the *Discrimination Act 1991* (ACT).

31 ICCPR art. 22.

32 Department of Justice and Community Safety (ACT) (JACS), *Human Rights Act 2004: Twelve-Month Review – Report* (2006) recommendation 10.

33 The *Canberra Times* argued that the ACT HRA affected the interpretation of the *Discrimination Act 1991* (ACT) in *Emlyn-Jones v Federal Capital Press* (ACT Discrimination Tribunal, heard 11 July 2006, decision reserved). Cf *Vosame Pty Ltd and ACT Planning & Land Authority* [2006] ACTAAT 12.

34 This has the unfortunate effect that the ACT HRA provides that some rights which are not subject to any limitation or derogation under the ICCPR (such as the right not to be subjected to torture or cruel, inhuman or degrading treatment) are in theory subject to limitation under the ACT HRA.

35 *Human Rights Amendment Act 2008* (ACT) s. 4.

36 *Legislation Act 2001* (ACT) s. 13.

37 See Jeremy Gans' discussion of the same issue in relation to the Victorian Charter: Jeremy Gans, *Can Public Authorities Limit Rights?* (2008), available at <http://charterblog.wordpress.com>.

38 JACS, above n. 32, 3.

39 The history, content and impact of the Victorian Charter are discussed in chapter 5.

40 Explanatory Statement, Human Rights Amendment Bill 2007 (ACT) 3.

41 [1999] NZCA 329 ('*Moonen*').

42 [2007] NZSC 7 ('*Hansen*').

43 See the discussion by Carolyn Evans & Simon Evans, *Australian Bills of Rights: The law of the* Victorian Charter *and ACT* Human Rights Act (2008) 99–102 (preferring the approach based on *Hansen*). Cf Andrew Butler & Petra Butler, *The New Zealand Bill of Rights Act: A commentary* (2005) 119–22 (arguing for an approach based on *Moonen*).

44 See, e.g. *Evans v New South Wales* [2008] FCAFC 130, [68]–[78].

45 See generally Nihal Jayawickrama, *The Judicial Application of Human Rights Law* (2002) 159–73.

46 *Human Rights Amendment Act 2008* (ACT) s. 2, and s. 7 (inserting a new Part 5A into the ACT HRA). The new right to commence proceedings is in addition to any existing right of action, but the nature of the ACT HRA-based action (judicial review, tort action, or both) and its relationship to existing actions and procedures (such as judicial review – the ACT HRA allows a longer period to lodge a challenge, but it is not clear whether the procedures in the *Administrative Decisions (Judicial Review) Act 1989* (ACT) would be available) is unclear.

47 *Human Rights Amendment Act 2008* (ACT) s 7 (inserting a new s. 40D in the ACT HRA).

48 Explanatory Statement, Human Rights Amendment Bill 2007 (ACT) 7–8.

49 See, e.g. Robin Creyke, 'The performance of administrative law in protecting rights' in Tom Campbell, Jeffrey Goldsworthy & Adrienne Stone (eds), *Protecting Rights Without a Bill of Rights: Institutional performance and reform in Australia* (2006) 101, and Max Spry, 'ACT's human rights bill cannot achieve its purpose', *The Canberra Times* (Canberra), 3 February 2004, 11.

50 See the list of publications on the JACS Human Rights Act website, available at <http://www.jcs.act.gov.au>

51 See, e.g. ACT, *Parliamentary Debates*, 30 August 2007, 2538 (Deb Foskey).

52 Kate Eastman, *Terrorism (Extraordinary Temporary Powers) Bill 2006 (ACT): Memorandum of advice* (2006), available at <http://acthra.anu. edu.au>, tabled by Simon Corbell, ACT, *Parliamentary Debates*, 3 May 2006, 1126.

53 The Standing Committee on Legal Affairs (performing the duties of a Scrutiny of Bills and Subordinate Legislation Committee) (Scrutiny Committee).

54 Scrutiny Committee, Parliament of ACT, *Scrutiny Report No 54* (2008) 24.

55 JACS, above n. 32, recommendation 3.

56 ACT, *Parliamentary Debates*, 6 December 2007, 4156 (Simon Corbell).

57 Explanatory Statement, Children and Young People Bill 2008 (ACT) 2.

58 See Scrutiny Committee, Parliament of ACT, *Scrutiny Report No 53* (2008) 1. The Committee went on to note further human rights issues, such as strict liability offences and provisions relating to Indigenous children: ibid. 11, 13–21.

59 Elizabeth Kelly, 'Government in the ACT: A human rights dialogue' (Paper presented at the Conference Assessing the First Year of the ACT *Human Rights Act*, ANU, 29 June 2005); Jon Stanhope (Speech delivered at the ACT Human Rights Community Forum, Canberra, 1 May 2006); both available at <http://acthra.anu.edu.au>.

60 See, e.g. ACT, *Parliamentary Debates*, 14 November 2006, 3417 (Deb Foskey).

61   See John Paget (Director, ACT Prisons Project), 'Human rights, prisons
      and women prisoners' (Paper delivered at the Fifth National CSAC
      Female Offenders Conference, Sydney, 20 April 2005), available at
      <http://www.cs.act.gov.au>.
62   ACT Committee, above n. 10, 41.
63   ACT Human Rights Act Research Project, interviews with ACT
      government officers (Canberra, 2006–2008).
64   See *Annual Reports (Government Agencies) Act 2004* (ACT) s. 5(2)(a).
65   Chief Minister's Department (ACT), *Chief Minister's 2007–2010 Annual
      Report Directions* (2007) 33.
66   *Human Rights Commission Act 2005* (ACT) s. 27(2).
67   See, e.g. Helen Watchirs, *Request for Advice on Discrimination and
      Human Rights Implications of Commonwealth Emergency Measures
      in NT Indigenous Communities Announced on 21 June 2007* (2007),
      Human Rights Commission, available at <http://www.hrc.act.gov.au>.
68   See the list of submissions at *Human Rights and Discrimination
      Commissioner/Submissions*, available at <http://www.hrc.act.gov.au>.
69   [2005] ACTSC 125 ('*SI v KS*').
70   *Emlyn-Jones v Federal Capital Press* (ACT Discrimination Tribunal,
      heard 11 July 2006, decision reserved).
71   ACT Human Rights Office, *Human Rights Audit of Quamby Youth
      Detention Centre* (2005), available at <http://www.hrc.act.gov.au>.
72   ACT Human Rights Commission, *Human Rights Audit on the
      Operation of ACT Correctional Facilities under Corrections Legislation*
      (2007), available at <http://www.hrc.act.gov.au>.
73   See ACT, *Parliamentary Debates*, 18 August 2007, 2909–11 (Katy
      Gallagher).
74   ACT, *Parliamentary Debates*, 12 February 2008, 73 (Simon Corbell)
75   The Victorian Charter confers on the Ombudsman the power to 'enquire
      into or investigate whether any administrative action is incompatible
      with a human right set out in the Charter': *Ombudsman Act 1973* (Vic)
      s. 13(1A), inserted by cl. 2 of the schedule to the Charter.
76   Interview with Professor John McMillan, Commonwealth and ACT
      Ombudsman (Canberra, 24 July 2007).
77   See, e.g. ACT, *Parliamentary Debates*, 5 April 2005, 1364 (Richard
      Mulcahy), and ACT, *Parliamentary Debates*, 15 March 2007, 656
      (Bill Stefaniak). Under the leadership of Zed Seselja, however, the
      Opposition's policy of repeal may be reconsidered: see, e.g. ACT,
      Parliamentary Debates, 4 March 2008, 383 (Zed Seselja) (commenting
      that the Liberal Party will take an 'open mind' to the five-year review of
      the ACT HRA).
78   See, e.g. ACT, *Parliamentary Debates*, 29 June 2005, 2479–80 (Jacqui
      Burke, Richard Mulcahy, Zed Seselja).
79   ACT, *Parliamentary Debates,* 1 December 2004, 188 (Jacqui Burke).
80   ACT, *Parliamentary Debates,* 6 April 2005, 1412–16 (Vicki Dunne,
      Richard Mulcahy).
81   ACT, *Parliamentary Debates,* 5 April 2005, 1352–3 (Jacqui Burke).
82   ACT, *Parliamentary Debates*, 18 August 2005, 2867–8 (Vicki Dunne).

83   ACT, *Parliamentary Debates*, 20 September 2005, 3350–1 (Jacqui Burke).
84   ACT, *Parliamentary Debates*, 4 May 2005, 1754 (Brendan Smyth).
85   ACT, *Parliamentary Debates*, 10 March 2005, 887 (Brendan Smyth).
86   ACT, *Parliamentary Debates*, 14 November 2006, 3417–19 (Deb Foskey).
87   ACT, *Parliamentary Debates*, 16 February 2006, 264ff (debate on the Crimes (Offences against Pregnant Women) Amendment Bill 2005 (ACT)).
88   See, e.g. ACT, *Parliamentary Debates*, 16 February 2006, 248ff (debate on the use of the *Land (Planning and Environment) Act 1991* (ACT) in relation to the Alexander Maconochie Centre).
89   See, e.g. ACT, *Parliamentary Debates*, 20 October 2005, 3928ff (debate on the Criminal Code Harmonisation Bill 2005 (ACT)); ACT, *Parliamentary Debates*, 31 May 2007, 1335ff (Zed Seselja) (debate on the Corrections Management Bill 2006 (ACT)).
90   ACT, *Parliamentary Debates*, 29 March 2006, 798–805.
91   ACT, *Parliamentary Debates*, 28 February 2007, 109 (Zed Seselja).
92   ACT, *Parliamentary Debates*, 8 March 2007, 346 (Bill Stefaniak). See also the comments of Vicki Dunne on open and accountable government: ACT, *Parliamentary Debates*, 8 March 2007, 1752.
93   ACT, *Parliamentary Debates*, 31 May 2007, 1333ff.
94   ACT, *Parliamentary Debates*, 14 November 2006, 3413ff (debate on the Health Legislation Amendment Bill 2006 (No 2)).
95   Council of Australian Governments, *Council of Australian Governments Communiqué: Special meeting on counter-terrorism* (2005), available at <http://www.coag.gov.au>.
96   ACT, *Parliamentary Debates*, 9 May 2006, 1335 (Bill Stefaniak).
97   ACT, *Parliamentary Debates*, 9 May 2006, 1348–50.
98   Andrew Byrnes & Gabrielle McKinnon, 'The ACT *Human Rights Act 2004* and the Commonwealth *Anti-Terrorism Act (No 2) 2005*: A triumph for federalism or a federal triumph?' in Penelope Mathew & Miriam Gani (eds), *Fresh Perspectives on the 'War on Terror'* (2008) 361.
99   Three reports in the Fifth Assembly, and 56 in the Sixth Assembly (to 30 June 2008). For an overview of the issues raised by the Scrutiny Committee in its reports from the beginning of 2007 and government responses to these comments, see the table of Scrutiny Reports available at <http://acthra.anu.edu.au>.
100 The ACT HRA does not expressly require the Committee to consider the consistency of delegated legislation with the Act.
101 Scrutiny Committee, Parliament of ACT, *Scrutiny Report No 34* (2006). The proposed new s. 59A was removed pursuant to an amendment proposed by the Minister for Health: ACT, *Parliamentary Debates*, 14 November 2006, 3424, 3426–7 (Katy Gallagher).
102 Scrutiny Committee, Parliament of ACT, *Scrutiny Report No 46* (2007) appendix (response by Minister John Hargreaves to comments by the Committee in *Scrutiny Report 43*).

103 See, e.g. Scrutiny Committee, Parliament of ACT, *Scrutiny Report No 15* (2005).

104 ACT, *Parliamentary Debates*, 20 October 2005, 3933–4 (Jon Stanhope, Chief Minister).

105 Standing Committee on Legal Affairs, Parliament of ACT, *Strict and Absolute Liability Offences* (2008).

106 'Role of the Committee' as set out in the preface to each Scrutiny Report. See, e.g. Scrutiny Committee, Parliament of ACT, *Scrutiny Report No 56* (2008).

107 See Peter Bayne (legal adviser to the Scrutiny Committee), 'The *Human Rights Act 2004* (ACT): Developments in 2004' (2005) 8 *Canberra Law Review* 137, 149.

108 See, e.g. Scrutiny Committee, Parliament of ACT, *Scrutiny Report No 16* (2005) 4 (discussing the Court Procedures (Protection of Public Participation) Amendment Bill 2005 (ACT)).

109 Standing Committee on Planning and Environment, Parliament of ACT, *Draft Variation to the Territory Plan No 256 Kingston Group Centre Part Section 22* (2006).

110 *Emlyn-Jones v Federal Capital Press* (ACT Discrimination Tribunal, heard 11 July 2006, decision reserved).

111 *Griffin v The Queen* [2008] HCA Trans 72.

112 See *Merritt and Commissioner for Housing* [2004] ACTAAT 37; *Z and Commissioner for Housing* [2007] ACTAAT 12, [65]. See also *Dunne/Barden and ACT Department of Education and Training* [2007] ACTAAT 26.

113 See, e.g. *IF v Commissioner for Housing* [2005] ACTSC 80, [59]. See also *R v PJ* [2006] ACTSC 37, [11]-[12] (relevance of ACT HRA to provisions of the *Crimes Act 1900* (ACT) authorising the issue of search warrants); *Re an Application for the Adoption of TL* [2005] ACTSC 49 ('*TL*'), [11] (relevance of ACT HRA to interpretation of *Adoption Act 1993* (ACT)); *R v Rao* [2006] SCC No 164 (unreported, Gray J, 11 August 2006) (relevance of s. 18 of the ACT HRA to s. 9C of the *Bail Act 1992* (ACT)).

114 [2007] ACTSC 84.

115 *Z and Commissioner for Housing* [2007] ACTAAT 12.

116 *Kingsley's Chicken Pty Ltd v Queensland Investment Corporation* [2006] ACTCA 9, [49]–[52]. See also *Capital Property Projects (ACT) Pty Ltd v ACT Planning & Land Authority* [2006] ACTSC 122, [20]–[22]. But see Chief Justice J J Spigelman 'The application of quasi-constitutional laws' (Second lecture in the 2008 McPherson Lectures: Statutory Interpretation and Human Rights, Brisbane, 11 March 2008) 14–15, available at <http://www.lawlink.nsw.gov.au>; *Raytheon* [2008] ACTAAT 19.

117 [2004] UKHL 30.

118 Ibid. [30].

119 See Spigelman, above n. 116, 14–15. Cf Explanatory Statement, Human Rights Amendment Bill 2007 (ACT) 3.

120 [2005] ACTSC 125. See Gabrielle McKinnon, 'An opportunity missed?

Comment on *SI bhnf CC v KS bhnf IS* [2005] ACTSC 125' (2006) 9 *Canberra Law Review* 21.

121 See also *Pappas v Noble* [2006] ACTSC 39.

122 The UK HRA s. 3 provides, 'So far as it is possible to do so, primary legislation and subordinate legislation must be read and given effect in a way which is compatible with the Convention rights.'

123 *Capital Property Projects (ACT) Pty Ltd v ACT Planning & Land Authority* [2008] ACTCA 9 ('*Capital Property Projects*'), [39]. See also *Raytheon* [2008] ACTAAT 19, [69]–[81].

124 *R v YL* [2004] ACTSC 115, [31].

125 See *R v Rao* [2006] SCC No 164 (Unreported, Gray J, 11 August 2006).

126 *TL* [2005] ACTSC 49; *Re Adoption of D* [2008] ACTSC 44.

127 *West v New South Wales* [2007] ACTSC 43, [19]–[22].

128 *Al-Rawahi v Niazi* [2006] ACTSC 84, [39] (referring to s. 21 of the ACT HRA).

129 *R v YL* [2004] ACTSC 115.

130 *Hausmann v Shute* [2007] ACTCA 5, [37].

131 Ibid. [39].

132 *S v DPP (ACT)* [2007] ACTSC 100, [7].

133 *King v Fricker* [2007] ACTSC 101, [28]–[30].

134 *R v PJ* [2006] ACTSC 37, [11]. See also *R v Caruso* [2006] ACTSC 45, [30].

135 See, e.g. *Stevens v McCallum* [2006] ACTCA 13, [138].

136 *R v Upton*, [2005] ACTSC 52, [23]. See also *R v Martiniello* [2005] ACTSC 9.

137 *Perovic v CW*, No CH 05/1046 (Unreported, Magistrate Somes, 1 June 2006).

138 Andrew Byrnes, 'And some have bills of rights thrust upon them: The experience of Hong Kong's Bill of Rights' in Philip Alston (ed.), *Promoting Human Rights Through Bills of Rights: Comparative perspectives* (1999) 318.

139 [2007] ACTCA 6.

140 Ibid. [4]. See also *R v Upton* [2005] ACTSC 52, [18] ('the right to trial without undue delay [in ACT HRA s. 22(2)(c)] may confer a great power on this Court than the common law position'); *R v DA* [2008] ACTSC 26, [7]; *Capital Property Projects* [2008] ACTCA 9, [40].

141 [2005] ACTSC 52.

142 See also *Perovic v CW*, No CH 05/1046 (Unreported, Magistrate Somes, 1 June 2006), where Magistrate Somes relied on jurisprudence from the European Court of Human Rights.

143 See, e.g. *Stevens v McCallum* [2006] ACTCA 13, [139].

144 Gerard McCoy, 'Sibylline observations: The *Human Rights Act 2004* (ACT)' (Paper presented at the Conference Assessing the First Year of the ACT Human Rights Act, ANU, 29 June 2005) available at <http://acthra.anu.edu.au>.

145 European Court of Human Rights, *Key Case-law Issues: Exhaustion of domestic remedies* (2006), available at <http://www.echr.coe.int>.

146 ACT, *Parliamentary Debates*, 6 December 2007, 4031 (Simon Corbell,

Attorney-General) (presentation speech for Human Rights Amendment Bill 2007).

Chapter 5: The Victorian *Charter of Human Rights and Responsibilities 2006*

1   For detailed analysis of the legislation, see Alistair Pound & Kylie Evans, *An Annotated Guide to the Victorian* Charter of Human Rights and Responsibilities (2008); Carolyn Evans & Simon Evans, *Australian Bills of Rights: The law of the Victorian* Charter *and ACT* Human Rights Act (2008).
2   See, e.g. Greg Taylor, *The Constitution of Victoria* (2006) 51–2.
3   Statute Law Revision Committee, Parliament of Victoria, *Progress Report on the Constitution Act 1975: A Bill of Rights*, Parl Paper D-No 9 (1979) 1.
4   Ibid. 11.
5   Senate Standing Committee on Constitutional and Legal Affairs, Commonwealth Parliament, *A Bill of Rights for Australia? An exposure report for the consideration of Senators* (1985). See further, chapter 2.
6   Legal and Constitutional Committee, Parliament of Victoria, *Report on the Desirability or Otherwise of Legislation Defining and Protecting Human Rights* (1987) 1.
7   Ibid. 3–4.
8   Ibid. 53–61.
9   Alison Moran, 'The Constitution (Declaration of Rights and Freedoms) Bill 1988 (Vic): A doomed legislative proposal' (1990) 17 *Melbourne University Law Review* 418, 429.
10   Victorian Legal and Constitutional Committee, above n. 6, 1.
11   As noted by Moran, above n. 9, 434.
12   For a useful discussion of this Bill and the political context, see ibid.
13   Rick Wallace, 'Hulls breaking the curse', *The Australian* (Sydney), 5 January 2008, 16.
14   Attorney-General (Victoria), *Attorney-General's Justice Statement: New directions for the Victorian justice system 2004–2014* (2004) 52.
15   Ibid. 53–6.
16   Attorney-General's Department (Victoria), 'Hulls appoints panel to lead discussion on human rights' (Press release, 17 April 2005).
17   Department of Justice (Victoria), *Human Rights in Victoria: Statement of intent* (2005), reproduced in Victorian Human Rights Consultation Committee (Victorian Committee), *Rights, Responsibilities and Respect: The Report of the Victorian Human Rights Consultation Committee* (2005) 61–4.
18   Ibid. 62.
19   Ibid.
20   George Williams, 'The Victorian *Charter of Human Rights and Responsibilities*: Origins and scope' (2006) 26 *Melbourne University Law Review* 880, 887.
21   Victorian Committee, above n. 17, 141.
22   Williams, above n. 20, 889.

23   Victorian Committee, above n. 17, 165–7.
24   Williams, above n. 20, 890.
25   Victorian Committee, above n. 17, v.
26   Ibid. 146. If petitions and form letters are included in the total, the level of support increases to 94 per cent.
27   Ibid. 27.
28   Ibid.
29   Ibid. vi (recommendation 2).
30   Ibid. vi (recommendations 5, 6).
31   Ibid. vi–viii (recommendation 7).
32   Ibid. 29.
33   Draft Charter of Human Rights and Responsibilities Act 2006, preamble (annexed to Victorian Committee, above n. 17).
34   Attorney-General's Department (Victoria), 'Victoria leads the way on human rights' (Press release, 20 December 2005).
35   Draft Charter of Human Rights and Responsibilities Act 2006, above n. 33, cl. 35.
36   Spencer Zifcak, *Not Bad but Not Yet Good: Victoria's new Charter of Rights and Responsibilities* (2006) Centre for Policy Development, available at <http://www.cpd.org.au>.
37   Charter of Human Rights and Responsibilities Bill 2006 (Vic) cl. 37.
38   Draft Charter of Human Rights and Responsibilities Act 2006, above n. 33, cl. 35.
39   Charter of Human Rights and Responsibilities Bill 2006 (Vic) cl. 31.
40   Victoria, *Parliamentary Debates*, Legislative Assembly, 15 June 2006, 2211.
41   However, there is no explicit right to compensation for unlawful arrest or detention or for wrongful conviction, as provided for by ACT HRA ss. 18(7), 23.
42   Victorian Charter s. 48.
43   See, e.g. Shadow Attorney-General Robert Clark's comments in Victoria, *Parliamentary Debates*, Legislative Assembly, 17 April 2007, 924 (debate on the Infertility Treatment Amendment Bill 2007 (Vic)).
44   See discussion in chapter 4, 82–3.
45   The limitations permitted by the existing laws referred to in s. 24 of the Victorian Charter seem on their face to be largely in compliance with the relevant ICCPR obligations. ACT HRA s. 21 sets out specific criteria for limitation of this right, which are taken from art. 14 of the ICCPR.
46   See the criticism by Jeremy Gans, *Evidence Law Under Victoria's Charter*, University of Melbourne Legal Studies Research Paper No 260 (2007) 15–16, available at <http://ssrn.com>.
47   Victorian Charter s. 3(1) defines 'discrimination' in relation to a person as meaning 'discrimination (within the meaning of the *Equal Opportunity Act 1995*) on the basis of an attribute set out in s. 6 of that Act'. These include age, impairment, political belief or activity, race, religious belief or activity, sex and sexual orientation.
48   If an issue of interpretation arises in any lower court or tribunal, it may be referred to the Supreme Court of Victoria for determination (s. 33).

49　Cf ACT HRA ss. 40B(1), (2).

50　For a critical analysis of the development and content of this provision, see Jeremy Gans, 'The Messy Origins of Charter s. 39(1)' (2008) Charterblog, available at <http://charterblog.wordpress.com>.

51　Previously the Equal Opportunity Commission.

52　*Ombudsman Act 1973* (Vic) s. 13(1A) (inserted by Victorian Charter sch. Cl. 2).

53　See, e.g. Evans & Evans, *Australian Bills of Rights*, above n. 1, 13–14.

54　See, e.g. Priyanga Hettiarachi, 'Simple and Complex: Interactions between the common law, private sphere and human rights legislation in Australia' (2008) 10–13, available at <http://www.hrlrc.org.au>

55　Victorian Solicitor-General Pamela Tate SC, legal counsel to the Committee, has noted that, due to constitutional considerations, the Charter 'could not and does not' impose direct duties on Victorian courts to develop the common law consistently with human rights: 'Protecting human rights in a federation' (2008) 33 *Monash University Law Review* 217, 241.

56　See e.g. *Kortel v Mirik* [2008] VSC 103 ('*Kortel*').

57　See chapter 4, 85–6.

58　The Victorian Charter also amended the *Public Administration Act 2004* (Vic) to add human rights as a new public sector value and employment principle. The amendment came into force on 1 January 2007.

59　Victorian Charter s. 38(2).

60　Victorian Charter s. 38(3).

61　Victorian Charter s. 38(4). Cf the view of the UK Joint Committee on Human Rights, that the right of a religious organisation to manifest a religious belief – in contrast with the freedom of conscience to hold a religious belief – is not absolute, and must be weighed against the individual rights of service users: Joint Committee on Human Rights, Parliament of United Kingdom, *The Meaning of Public Authority under the Human Rights Act* (2007) [101].

62　See, e.g. the approach of the Victorian Civil and Administrative Tribunal in *MH6 v Mental Health Review Board (General)* [2008] VCAT 846 ('*MH6*'); Evans & Evans, *Australian Bills of Rights*, above n. 1, ch. 5; Jeremy Gans, 'Can Public Authorities Limit Rights?' (2008) Charterblog, available at <http://charterblog.wordpress.com>.

63　Parole boards have been temporarily excluded from the obligations of public authorities under this definition: *Charter of Human Rights and Responsibilities (Public Authorities) (Interim) Regulations 2007* (Vic).

64　See Tate, above n. 55.

65　Gans, *Evidence Law*, above n. 46, 34.

66　See, e.g. UK Joint Committee on Human Rights, above n. 61. The Chair of the Joint Committee, Andrew Dinsmore, has introduced a Private Member's Bill, the Human Rights Act (Meaning of Public Function) Bill 2007, to clarify the meaning of 'public function'. The Bill is yet to be debated.

67　Simon Evans & Carolyn Evans, 'Legal Redress under the Victorian *Charter of Human Rights and Responsibilities*' (2006) 17 *Public Law*

Review 264, 274.

68   The Ombudsman also has jurisdiction in relation to complaints that public authorities have failed to comply with the Charter.

69   Department of Justice (Victoria), *Statement of Intent*, above n. 17, 163.

70   Ron Merkel, *Memorandum of Advice on the Interpretation and Application of s. 39 of the Charter of Human Rights and Responsibilities Act 2006 (Vic)* (2007), available at <http://www.hrlrc. org.au>.

71   It appears that judicial review would in any case be available where a public authority has failed to interpret legislation in accordance with the Charter under s. 32, but this would not necessarily provide a remedy for a breach of the more extensive obligations of public authorities in s. 38.

72   See, e.g. Larissa Dubecki, 'Victoria to be first state to adopt a human rights charter', *The Age* (Melbourne), 8 December 2007, 11; Nick Higginbottom, 'Charter protects rights: Victoria leads way', *Herald Sun* (Melbourne), 29 December 2007, 10.

73   These Private Member's Bills related to body piercing, decriminalisation of abortion and consent to fluoridisation of water. The Register includes summaries of reasons for compatibility, the comments of the SARC, and any Ministerial correspondence, and is a useful record of the early human rights dialogue between the executive and the Parliament. It is available on the VEOHRC website at <http://www. humanrightscommission.vic.gov.au>.

74   See Victorian Government Solicitor's Office, *Charter of Human Rights Newsletter* (Issue 3, March 2007) 3.

75   Legal advice on the consistency of bills with the Bill of Rights Act 1990 (NZ) is published at <http://www.justice.govt.nz>.

76   See VEOHRC, *First Steps Forward: The 2007 report on the operation of the Charter of Human Rights and Responsibilities* (2008) appendix 2.

77   See, e.g. Rick Wallace, 'Lawyers eye off Charter breaches', *The Australian* (Sydney), 9 January 2008, 2.

78   Liquor Control Reform Amendment Bill 2007 (Vic).

79   Graffiti Prevention Bill 2007 (Vic).

80   Victoria, *Parliamentary Debates*, Legislative Assembly, 10 October 2007, 3435–6 (Louise Asher). See also Suzy Freeman-Greene, 'Urban scrawl: Shades of grey', *The Age* (Melbourne), 12 January 2008, 5.

81   Victorian Charter sch. cl. 7.

82   See VEOHRC, *First Steps Forward*, above n. 76, chs 3–6.

83   Attorney-General's Department (Victoria), *2006/2007 Budget Statement: Victoria leads the way on human rights* (2006), available at <http:// acthra.anu.edu.au>.

84   Department of Justice (Victoria), *Annual Report 2006–07* (2007) 41.

85   Victoria Police, *Annual Report 2006–07* (2007) 44–5.

86   VEOHRC, *First Steps Forward*, above n. 76, 27.

87   Ibid.

88   E.g. noting that the Department of Treasury and Finance had not demonstrated anything beyond preliminary engagement with the Charter: ibid. 19.

89 Ibid. appendix 3.

90 [2008] VSC 103.

91 Ombudsman Victoria, *Annual Report 2007* (2008) 10–11, 46.

92 Victoria, *Parliamentary Debates*, Legislative Council, 22 May 2007, 1292 (Edward O'Donoghue).

93 Victoria, *Parliamentary Debates*, Legislative Assembly, 8 August 2007, 2587 (in relation to the Summary Offences (Upskirting) Bill 2007 (Vic)).

94 Victoria, *Parliamentary Debates*, Legislative Assembly, 21 June 2007, 2150.

95 Statement of Compatibility, Magistrates' Court and Coroners Court Acts Amendment Bill 2007 (Vic).

96 Victoria, *Parliamentary Debates*, Legislative Assembly, 21 June 2007, 2150.

97 *Subordinate Legislation Act 1994* (Vic) s 21.

98 SARC, Parliament of Victoria, *Alert Digest No 4 of 2007* (2007) 10, now codified in SARC, *Practice Note No 2* (2007), available at <http://www.parliament.vic.gov.au>.

99 Carlo Carli, 'The Victorian *Charter of Rights and Responsibilities* and Scrutiny in Victoria' (Speech delivered at Australasian Scrutiny of Legislation Conference, Wellington, 1 August 2007).

100 SARC, Parliament of Victoria, *Alert Digest No 9 of 2007*, 10.

101 Response of Bronwyn Pike in SARC, Parliament of Victoria, *Alert Digest No 9 of 2007* (2007) 10.

102 Superannuation Legislation Amendment (Contribution Splitting and Other Matters) Bill 2007 (Vic).

103 SARC, Parliament of Victoria, *Alert Digest No 7 of 2007* (2007) 14.

104 Response of Tim Holding in SARC, Parliament of Victoria, *Alert Digest No 9 of 2007* (2007) 12–13.

105 SARC, Parliament of Victoria, *Alert Digest No 13 of 2007* (2007) 17, citing *Handyside v United Kingdom* (1976) 1 EHRR 737.

106 SARC, Parliament of Victoria, *Alert Digest No 4 of 2008* (2008) 37–40.

107 SARC, Parliament of Victoria, *Alert Digest No 10 of 2007* (2007) 8, 9 (in relation to the Justice and Road Legislation Amendment (Law Enforcement) Bill 2007 (Vic)).

108 SARC, Parliament of Victoria, *Alert Digest No 12 of 2007* (2007) 15–16 (in relation to the Justice Legislation Amendment Bill 2007 (Vic)).

109 SARC, Parliament of Victoria, *Alert Digest No 13 of 2007* (2007) 22–3 (in relation to the Transport Accident and Accident Compensation Acts Amendment Bill 2007 (Vic)).

110 Ibid. 29–30 (in relation to the Transport Legislation Amendment Bill 2007 (Vic)).

111 SARC, Parliament of Victoria, *Alert Digest No 14 of 2007* (2007) 6–7 (in relation to the Animals Legislation Amendment (Animal Care) Bill 2007 (Vic)).

112 SARC, Parliament of Victoria, *Alert Digest No 15 of 2007* (2007) 39–40 (in relation to the Victorian Energy Efficiency Target Bill 2007 (Vic)).

113 SARC, Parliament of Victoria, *Alert Digest No 16 of 2007* (2007) 7–10 (in relation to the Criminal Procedure Legislation Amendment Bill 2007

(Vic)).

114 SARC, Parliament of Victoria, *Alert Digest No 4 of 2008* (2008) 41–4 (in relation to the Working with Children Amendment Bill 2007 (Vic)).

115 *Minority Report: Scrutiny of Acts and Regulations Committee on Police Integrity Bill 2008*, appended to SARC, *Report on the Police Integrity Bill 2008* (2008) 19ff.

116 See, e.g. Victoria, *Parliamentary Debates*, Legislative Assembly, 11 June 2008, 2218 (Colin Brooks).

117 SARC, *Report on the Police Integrity Bill 2008* (2008). Cf SARC, Parliament of Victoria, *Alert Digest No 4 of 2008* (2008) 25–30.

118 VEOHRC, *First Steps Forward*, above n. 76, 42. For tables categorising the various Bills, see ibid. 43–50.

119 Ibid. 42.

120 Ibid.

121 Ibid. 51.

122 One example is *R v Benbrika (Ruling No 20)* [2008] VSC 80 (*'Benbrika'*), the trial of a number of persons accused of terrorism offences where the accused had all been arrested by March 2006. In February 2008, the accused sought a stay of proceedings on the basis of the conditions in which they were being held and transported to court, relying on common law principles and also referring to s. 25 of the Charter. Justice Bongiorno doubted that, in view of s. 49(2), the Charter would have any application and reliance on it would require notice to be given to various parties (at [16]–[19]), though he did not explicitly address the alternate argument that s. 22 of the Charter applied to Corrections Victoria and its treatment of the accused (at [20]), and decided the case without reliance on the Charter.

123 [2007] VSC 2.

124 See, e.g. Peter Faris, 'Lawyers' picnic for your rights', *Herald Sun* (Melbourne), 1 January 2008, 16.

125 See also *Tomasevic v Travaglini* [2007] VSC 337; *Ragg v Magistrates' Court of Victoria* [2008] VSC 1.

126 *Re Unumadu* [2007] VSC 258.

127 *R v White* [2007] VSC 142.

128 *Towie v Victoria* [2007] VCAT 1489, [33]; *Boeing Australia Holdings Pty Ltd (Anti Discrimination Exemption)* [2007] VCAT 532.

129 *R v Benbrika (Ruling No 12)* [2007] VSC 524R, [29].

130 The Charter was mentioned in *DPP(Vic) v Zierk* [2008] VSC 184; DPP(Vic) v Ali [2008] VSC 167; *Swain v Department of Infrastructure (General)* [2008] VCAT 848; *MH6* [2008] VCAT 846; *R v Rich* [2008] VSC 141; *Guss v Aldy Corporation Pty Ltd* [2008] VCAT 912 (*'Guss v Aldy'*); *Kortel* [2008] VSC 103; *General Television Corporation Pty Ltd v DPP(Vic)* [2008] VSCA 49 (*'General Television'*); *Benbrika* [2008] VSC 80; *Guneser v Magistrates' Court of Victoria* [2008] VSC 57; *C v Chief Commissioner of Police* [2008] VSC 51; *Halwood Corporation (in liq) v Roads Corporation* [2008] VSC 28; *R v A* [2008] VSC 73; *Ferguson v Walkley* [2008] VSC 7; *Gray v DPP(Vic)* [2008] VSC 4 (*'Gray'*). It was decisive only in *Gray* and *Guss v Aldy*. See also the

decision of the Victorian Mental Health Review Board: *P 09-003* [2008] VMHRB 1 which discusses a number of Charter issues in some detail.

131 [2008] VSC 4.

132 Ibid. [10].

133 Ibid. [12].

134 Ibid.

135 *R v A* [2008] VSC 73.

136 See, e.g. Milanda Rout, 'Nine wins right to speed up appeal on Underbelly,' *The Australian* (Sydney), 16 February 2008, 11.

137 *General Television* [2008] VSCA 49, [38] (Warren CJ, Vincent and Kellam JJA).

138 See Gans, *Evidence Law*, above n. 46, 38–9.

139 See, e.g. *MH6* [2008] VCAT 846, where the Tribunal member applied a proportionality analysis to an assessment of the detention of a patient in a mental health facility, without clarifying the basis for this exercise.

140 [2008] VCAT 912.

141 *Benbrika* [2008] VSC 80.

142 See also *Kortel* [2008] VSC 103.

143 [2008] VSC 80, [17]–[18].

Chapter 6: Towards an Australian bill of rights

1 John Howard, 'Democracy built on a fair-go ethic', *The Australian* (Sydney), 10 May 2001, 11.

2 Roy Morgan Research, *Anti-Terrorism Legislation Community Survey* (2006), available at <http://acthra.anu.edu.au>.

3 See *New State Ice Co v Liebmann*, 285 US 262, 311 (1932) (Brandeis J).

4 Katharine Gelber, 'Beyond Australia's first bill of rights' (Paper presented at the Conference Assessing the First Year of the ACT Human Rights Act, ANU, 29 June 2005) 6.

5 Tasmanian Law Reform Institute, *A Charter of Rights for Tasmania?*, Issues Paper No 11 (2006) 1.

6 Apart from the Chair, members of the Consultation Committee were Mat Rowell, Tasmanian Council of Social Services; Lisa Hutton, Department of Justice; Julian Eades, Advocacy Tasmania; Jamie Cox, former captain of the Tasmanian Tigers, the State's cricket team; and Alan Stevenson, disability advisor to the Committee.

7 The Tasmanian government contributed a total of $50 000 to this project: Tasmanian Law Reform Institute, *Annual Progress and Financial Report 2006* (2007) 3. See also Tasmania Law Reform Institute, *A Charter of Rights for Tasmania, Report No 10* (2007) 153.

8 Tasmanian Law Reform Institute, *A Charter of Rights Report*, above n. 7, 15.

9 Ibid. 122.

10 David Killick, 'Law reformers want human rights charter', *The Mercury* (Hobart), 13 October 2007, 7.

11 Maria Rae, 'Law boss Llewellyn coy on rights charter', *The Mercury* (Hobart), 23 February 2008, 12.

12 Maria Rae, 'Rights charter stranded', *The Mercury* (Hobart), 12 March

2008, 12.

13 Consultation Committee for a Proposed WA Human Rights Act (WA Committee), *A WA Human Rights Act: Report of the Consultation Committee for a proposed WA Human Rights Act* (2007) appendix B.

14 The other members were Dr Peter Carnley, former Anglican Archbishop of Perth; Lisa Baker, Chief Executive of the Western Australian Council of Social Service; and Associate Professor Colleen Hayward, Manager of the Kulunga Research Network.

15 WA Committee, above n. 13, 19.

16 Ibid. appendix E.

17 Ibid. appendix F.

18 Ibid. recommendation 7.

19 Ibid. 76.

20 One area of difference was in relation to the human rights interpretive principle, discussed below at 159–60.

21 WA Committee, above n. 13, recommendation 61. The Committee recommended that complaints first be dealt with internally, and then referred to the Equal Opportunity Commission for conciliation if unresolved.

22 Attorney-General's Department (WA), 'Human Rights Report completed' (Press release, 20 December 2007).

23 See, e.g. Western Australia Council of Social Services, *Event Report: Community perspectives: A WA Human Rights Act* (2007) 3, available at <http://wacoss.org.au>.

24 See, e.g. Paige Taylor, 'MP rebel threatens McGinty reforms', *The Australian* (Sydney), 20 November 2007, 9.

25 Hilary Charlesworth & Gabrielle McKinnon, 'Australia's first bill of rights: The Australian Capital Territory's *Human Rights Act*' (*Law and Policy Paper No 28*, Centre for International and Public Law, ANU, 2006) 25.

26 See chapter 4, 111–12.

27 See *Austin v Commonwealth* (2003) 215 CLR 185; [2003] HCA 3.

28 The two-tiered constitutional protection of rights is seen in the United States, where individual State constitutions contain guarantees of rights (in particular economic and social rights) in addition to those contained in the federal Constitution: see Peter J Galie, 'State courts and economic rights' (1988) 496 *Annals of the American Academy of Political and Social Science* 76.

29 See, e.g. Andrew Byrnes & Gabrielle McKinnon, 'The ACT *Human Rights Act 2004* and the Commonwealth *Anti-Terrorism Act (No 2) 2005*: A triumph for federalism or a federal triumph?' in Miriam Gani & Penelope Mathew (eds), *Fresh Perspectives on the 'War on Terror'* (2008) 361.

30 John Howard, 'A sense of balance: The Australian achievement in 2006' (Speech delivered at the Australia Day Address to the National Press Club, Canberra, 25 January 2006).

31 See chapter 2, 27ff.

32 Australian Labor Party, *National Platform and Constitution* (2007) 207

[7], available at <http://www.alp.org.au>.

33 Ibid. [9].

34 Ibid.

35 Jonathan Pearlman, 'Do-it-yourself charter to right future wrongs', *The Sydney Morning Herald* (Sydney), 1 December 2007, 26.

36 Ibid. See also Michael Pelly, 'Labor to push on with new charter', *The Australian* (Sydney), 7 December 2007, 29.

37 See, e.g. Paul Maley, 'Christian lobby fears bill of rights', *The Australian* (Sydney), 16 April 2008, 7; Paul Maley, 'Alarmist tactics spark rift in ALP over rights bill', The Australian (Sydney), 14 April 2008, 4; Alex Boxsell, 'A-G rejects dangerous rights charter', *Australian Financial Review* (Sydney), 11 April 2008, 52; James Allan, 'Mad game to tinker with our great system', *The Australian* (Sydney), 11 April 2008, 12.

38 Australia 2020, *Australia 2020 Summit: Final Report* (2008) 173, 308, available at <http://www.australia2020.gov.au>.

39 Karen Middleton, Interview with Kevin Rudd (Canberra, 20 April 2008), available at <http://www.pm.gov.au>. The May 2008 Budget made an allocation for a consultation on the issue: see Attorney-General's Department (Commonwealth), *Portfolio Budget Statements 2008–09: Attorney-General's Portfolio* (2008) 28.

40 See, e.g. Ashleigh Wilson, 'Young Labor votes to reject charter of rights', *The Australian* (Sydney), 7 June 2008, 10; Janet Albrechtsen, 'Even young progressives don't want to give unelected judges more power', *The Australian* (Sydney), 7 June 2008, 22.

41 See chapter 2, 28–32.

42 Australian Law Reform Commission, *Annual Report 2006–07*, Report No 106 (2007) appendix F indicates that of 73 final reports, 27 have not been implemented or only partially (as opposed to substantially) implemented.

43 Former Australian Law Reform Commission President Alan Rose noted that five-to-ten-year timeframes are the norm for commissions to have their recommendations adopted: quoted in Victorian Law Reform Commission, 'VLRC: VLRC turns five' (2006) 80(5) *Law Institute Journal* 73.

44 Civics Expert Group, *Whereas the People: Civics and citizenship education* (1994) 133, 155.

45 Roy Morgan Research, above n. 2, 4.

46 Issues Deliberation Australia, *The ACT Deliberates: An ACT bill of rights?* (2002).

47 See WA Committee, above n. 13, 8. The advertisement was published in *The West Australian* on 24 July 2007.

48 George Williams, 'The Victorian *Charter of Human Rights and Responsibilities*: Origins and scope' (2006) 30 *Melbourne University Law Review* 880, 889.

49 James Allan, quoted in Nicola Berkovic, 'Make bill of rights debate open to all', *The Australian* (Sydney), 25 April 2008, 31.

50 Human Rights Consultation Committee (Victorian Committee), *Rights, Responsibilities and Respect* (2005) appendix C; WA Committee, above

n. 13, appendix F.

51　WA Committee, above n. 13, appendix E.

52　See, e.g. Cardinal George Pell, 'Four fictions: An argument against a charter of rights' (2008) 52(8) *Quadrant* 24.

53　See chapter 5, 114.

54　Pontifical Council for Justice and Peace, *Compendium of the Social Doctrine of the Church* (2005) [302]–[304], available at <http://www.vatican.va>. See also Pope Benedict XVI, 'Untitled' (Speech delivered to the United Nations General Assembly, 18 April 2008). It should be noted, however, that the Vatican has always been ambivalent about the rights of women: see Hilary Charlesworth, 'The challenges of human rights law for religious traditions' in Mark W Janis & Carolyn Evans (eds), *Religion and International Law* (1999) 401.

55　See chapter 5, 114. See also the religious exemptions to the *Sex Discrimination Act 1984* (Cwlth) (ss. 37, 38).

56　Williams, above n. 48, 890.

57　Cf the WA Police opposition to a charter: see, e.g. Amanda Banks, 'Police attack human rights plan', *The West Australian* (Perth), 3.

58　See, e.g. ibid. The ACT newspaper, *The Canberra Times*, also took a strong negative line against proposals for the ACT HRA.

59　Conor Gearty, *Can Human Rights Survive?* (2006) 69.

60　*Australian Constitution*, s. 51(xxix); *Commonwealth v Tasmania* (1983) 158 CLR 1; [1983] HCA 21. Other heads of power, such as the power to make laws in relation to corporations, may also be relevant.

61　See chapter 2.

62　*Melbourne Corporation v Commonwealth* (1947) 74 CLR 31; [1947] HCA 26.

63　[2001] 1 SA 46.

64　Ibid. [41].

65　*Minister of Health v Treatment Action Campaign* [2002] 5 SA 271, [35].

66　ACT HRA s. 44; Victorian Charter s. 44.

67　ACT HRA s. 28; Victorian Charter s. 7.

68　See generally Jeremy Gans, *Submission on the Proposed WA Human Rights Act* (2007), discussed in WA Committee, above n. 13, 109–10.

69　Victorian Charter s. 18.

70　Victorian Charter s. 25.

71　Victorian Charter s. 24.

72　ICCPR arts. 14(1), (3)(c), 25.

73　ACT HRA s. 37; Victorian Charter s. 28.

74　Reasons for compatibility statements were given in relation to the Mental Health (Treatment and Care) Amendment Bill 2005 (ACT) (dealing with the use of electro-convulsive therapy) and the Terrorism (Extraordinary Temporary Powers) Bill 2006 (ACT).

75　Victorian Charter s. 28.

76　Tasmanian Law Reform Institute, *A Charter of Rights Report*, above n. 7, 84; WA Committee, above n. 13, 140–3.

77　See Victorian Equal Opportunity and Human Rights Commission, *First*

Steps Forward: The 2007 Report on the operation of the Charter of Human Rights and Responsibilities (2008) 42, noting that only one Bill was amended in response to concerns raised by the Scrutiny of Acts and Regulations Committee during 2007.

78 See, e.g. Priyanga Hettiarachi, 'Some things borrowed, some things new: An overview of judicial review of legislation under the *Charter of Human Rights and Responsibilities*' (2007) 7 *Oxford University Commonwealth Law Journal* 61, 64, 89–90.

79 WA Committee, above n. 13, 160.

80 See, e.g. *Coco v The Queen* (1994) 179 CLR 427, 437; [1994] HCA 15, [9]-[11].

81 Tasmanian Law Reform Institute, *A Charter of Rights Report*, above n. 7, 93–5.

82 Another option is a repeal provision for prior inconsistent legislation and an interpretive provision for subsequent legislation, as was contained in the original Hong Kong Bill of Rights Ordinance 1991 s. 3, though this was supplemented by constitutional level protection for subsequent legislation.

83 As at 30 June 2008, 15 declarations of incompatibility had become final and not subject to further appeal. Eight had been remedied by later primary legislation; one was remedied by a remedial order under s. 10 of the UK HRA; three related to provisions that had already been remedied by primary legislation at the time of the declaration; one was the subject of public consultation (in conjunction with the implementation of a judgment of the European Court of Human Rights); two relating to the same subject were the subject of remedial measures before Parliament: *Communication from Human Rights Division of the UK Ministry of Justice*, 14 July 2008. See chapter 3, 61–2 for a discussion of these cases.

84 See, e.g. James Stellios, 'State/Territory human rights legislation in a federal judicial system' (2008) 19 *Public Law Review* 52; Sir Gerard Brennan, 'The Constitution, good government and human rights' (Paper delivered at Human Rights Law Resource Centre Seminar, Melbourne, 12 March 2008) 24.

85 For a more detailed discussion of the issues raised by advisory opinions, see Helen Irving, 'Advisory opinions, the rule of law and the separation of powers' (2004) 4 *Macquarie Law Journal* 105.

86 In *Re Judiciary and Navigation Acts* (1921) 29 CLR 257, 265; [1921] HCA 20; aff'd in a number of decisions, including *Re McBain* (2002) 209 CLR 372; [2002] HCA 16, *Agtrack (NT) Pty Ltd v Hatfield* (2005) 223 CLR 251, 262; [2005] HCA 38, [29].

87 Stellios, above n. 84, 63–4. See also Wendy Lacey & David Wright, 'Highlighting inconsistency: The declaration as a remedy in administrative law and human rights standards' in Chris Finn (ed.), *Shaping Administrative Law for the Next Generation: Fresh perspectives* (2005) 32, 55.

88 Dominique Dalla-Pozza & George Williams, 'The constitutional validity of declarations of incompatibility in Australian charters of rights' (2007) 12 *Deakin Law Review* 1, 25. See also Pamela Tate, 'Protecting human

rights in a federation' (2008) 33 *Monash University Law Review* 217, 233–8. The decision of the High Court in *A-G (Cwlth) v Alinta Ltd* [2008] HCA 2 appears to provide some judicial support for this view: see [33] (Kirby J).

89 George Williams, quoted in Michael Pelly, 'Brennan foresees constitutional glitch with rights charter', *The Australian* (Sydney), 14 March 2008, 33.

90 Gabrielle McKinnon, 'Giving meaning to a "culture of human rights"' (Working Paper No 3, ACT Human Rights Act Research Project, ANU, 2006), available at <http://acthra.anu.edu.au>.

91 Victorian Charter s. 38.

92 ACT HRA s. 40B.

93 Carolyn Evans, 'The *Human Rights Act* and administrative law' (Paper presented to the Conference Assessing the First Year of the *Human Rights Act*, ANU, 29 June 2005) 7–9.

94 See chapter 5, 120–21.

95 ACT HRA s. 40D.

96 Victorian Charter s. 4(1)(j); ACT HRA s. 40(2)(b) (to take effect from 1 January 2009).

97 See *Lipohar v The Queen* (1999) 200 CLR 485, 505-10; [1999] HCA 65, [43]–[59] (Gaudron, Gummow & Hayne JJ).

98 See Tate, above n. 88, 240–2.

99 Victorian Charter s. 4(1)(k).

100 See *Charter of Human Rights and Responsibilities (Public Authorities) (Interim) Regulations 2007* (Vic).

101 UK HRA s. 8. This provision uses the terminology of 'just satisfaction' to incorporate the requirements for an award of damages applied by the European Court of Human Rights.

102 Department of Constitutional Affairs, *Review of the Implementation of the Human Rights Act* (2006) 18.

103 See chapter 5, 122.

104 Joint Committee on Human Rights, Parliament of United Kingdom, *The Case for a Human Rights Commission* (2003) Summary.

105 See chapter 4, 92–3.

106 See John McMillan, 'The role of the Ombudsman in protecting human rights' (Speech delivered at the Legislatures and the Protection of Human Rights Conference, University of Melbourne, 21 July 2006), available at <http://cccs.law.unimelb.edu.au>.

107 But see Robin Creyke, 'The performance of administrative law in protecting human rights' in Tom Campbell, Jeffrey Goldsworthy & Adrienne Stone (eds), *Protecting Rights without a Bill of Rights: Institutional performance and reform in Australia* (2006) 101.

108 British Institute of Human Rights, *The Human Rights Act – Changing Lives* (2006).

109 *Anti-Terrorism Act (No 2) 2005* (Cwlth).

110 See Justice Michael McHugh, 'Does Australia need a bill of rights?' (Paper presented to NSW Bar Association Forum, Sydney, 7 August 2007) 44, available at <http://www.nswbar.asn.au>.

111 (2004) 219 CLR 562; [2004] HCA 37 ('*Al-Kateb*'). See generally Alice Rolls, 'Avoiding tragedy: Would the decision of the High Court in *Al-Kateb* have been any different if Australia had a bill of rights like Victoria?' (2007) 18 *Public Law Review* 119.

112 Section 198.

113 Section 196(1).

114 (2004) 219 CLR 562, 594–5; [2004] HCA 37, [73].

115 Ibid. See also McHugh, above n. 110.

116 The decision of the House of Lords in *A v Secretary of State for the Home Department* [2004] UKHL 56 illustrates the way in which interpretation informed by human rights can deal with legislation allowing indefinite Executive detention. Cf Frank Brennan, 'Getting the Balance Right after the 2020 Summit' (2008) *Eureka Street*, available at <http://www.eurekastreet.com.au>.

117 *Report of the Human Rights Committee*, GAOR, 50th sess, Supp No 40, [176] (New Zealand), [408]–[435] (United Kingdom), UN Doc A/50/40 (1996). For further discussion, see Geoffrey W G Leane, 'Enacting bills of rights: Canada and the curious case of New Zealand's "thin" democracy' (2004) 26 *Human Rights Quarterly* 152.

118 See, e.g. James Allan, 'A defence of the status quo' in Tom Campbell, Jeffrey Goldsworthy & Adrienne Stone (eds), *Protecting Human Rights: Instruments and institutions* (2003) 175, 175–8.

119 Susan Marks & Andrew Clapham, *International Human Rights Lexicon* (2005) 66.

120 Seamus Heaney, 'Human rights, poetic redress', *Irish Times* (Dublin), 15 March 2008, 1.

121 Simone Weil, *Gravity and Grace* (Arthur Wills trans, 1997 edn) 224 [trans of: *La Pesanteur et la Grâce*].

122 Heaney, above n. 120.

Select Bibliography

1. Books

Alston, Philip (ed.), *Promoting Human Rights Through Bills of Rights: Comparative perspectives* (1999), Oxford University Press, Oxford

An-Na'im, Abdullahi Ahmed & Francis Mading Deng (eds), *Human Rights in Africa: Cross-cultural perspectives* (1999), Brookings Institution Press, Washington, DC

Anaya, S James, *Indigenous Peoples in International Law* (2nd edn, 2004), Oxford University Press, Oxford

Baxi, Upendra, *The Future of Human Rights* (2nd edn, 2006), Oxford University Press, Oxford

Brennan, Frank, *Legislating Liberty: A bill of rights for Australia* (1998), University of Queensland Press, Brisbane

Butler, Andrew & Petra Butler, *The New Zealand Bill of Rights Act: A commentary* (2005), Lexis Nexis, Wellington, NZ

Buti, Antonio, *Sir Ronald Wilson: A matter of conscience* (2007), University of Western Australia Press, Perth

Campbell, Tom, Jeffrey Goldsworthy & Adrienne Stone (eds), *Protecting Rights Without a Bill of Rights: Institutional performance and reform in Australia* (2006), Ashgate Publishing, Aldershot, UK

Charlesworth, Hilary, *Writing in Rights: Australia and the protection of human rights* (2002), UNSW Press, Sydney

Charlesworth, Hilary, Madelaine Chiam, Devika Hovell & George Williams, *No Country is an Island: Australia and international law* (2006), UNSW Press, Sydney

Charlesworth, Hilary & Gabrielle McKinnon, 'Australia's first bill of rights: The Australian Capital Territory's Human Rights Act' (Law and Policy Paper No 28, Centre for International and Public Law, ANU, Canberra, 2006)

Clapham, Andrew, *Human Rights: A very short introduction* (2007), Oxford University Press, Oxford

Cochrane, Peter, *Colonial Ambition: Foundations of Australian democracy* (2006), Melbourne University Press, Melbourne

Dembour, Marie-Bénédicte, *Who Believes in Human Rights? Reflections on the European Convention* (2006), CUP, Cambridge

Dershowitz, Alan, *Rights from Wrongs: A secular theory of the origins of rights* (2004), Basic Books, New York

Devereux, Annemarie, *Australia and the Birth of the International Bill of Human Rights 1946–1966* (2005), The Federation Press, Sydney

Donnelly, Jack, *Universal Human Rights in Theory and Practice* (2nd edn, 2002), Cornell University Press, Ithaca, NY

Evans, Carolyn & Simon Evans, *Australian Bills of Rights: The law of the Victorian Charter and ACT Human Rights Act* (2008), Lexis Nexis, Wellington, NZ

Gearty, Conor, *Can Human Rights Survive?* (2006), Cambridge University Press, Cambridge

Glendon, Mary Ann, *A World Made New: Eleanor Roosevelt and the Universal Declaration of Human Rights* (2001), Random House, New York

Grayling, AC, *Towards the Light: The story of the struggles for liberty and rights that made the modern west* (2007), Bloomsbury, London

Harvard Law School, *Economic and Social Rights and the Right to Health* (1995), Harvard University Press, Cambridge, MA

Hunt, Lynn, *Inventing Human Rights: A history* (2007), W W Norton & Co, New York

Ishay, Micheline (ed.), *Human Rights Reader: Major political essays, speeches and documents from the Bible to the present* (1997), Routledge, New York

—— *The History of Human Rights: From ancient times to the globalization era* (2004), University of California Press, Berkeley

Kingdom, Elizabeth, *What's Wrong with Rights? Problems for Feminist Politics of Law* (1991), Edinburgh University Press, Edinburgh

Langlois, Anthony J, *The Politics of Justice and Human Rights: Southeast Asia and universalist theory* (2001), CUP, Cambridge

MacIntyre, Alasdair, *After Virtue: A study in moral theory* (2nd edn, 1984), University of Notre Dame Press, Notre Dame, IN

MacKinnon, Catharine A, *Are Women Human?* (2006), Harvard University Press, Cambridge, MA

Marks, Susan & Andrew Clapham, *International Human Rights Lexicon* (2005), Oxford University Press, Oxford

Menzies, Robert, *Central Power in the Australian Commonwealth* (1967), Cassell, London

Morsink, Johannes, *The Universal Declaration of Human Rights: Origins, drafting and intent* (1999), University of Pennsylvania Press, Philadelphia

Nickel, James W, *Making Sense of Human Rights* (2nd edn, 2007), University of California Press, Berkeley

Nussbaum, Martha, *Women and Human Development: The capabilities approach* (2000), Cambridge University Press, New York

O'Neill, Nick, Simon Rice & Roger Douglas, *Retreat from Injustice: Human rights law in Australia* (2nd edn, 2004), The Federation Press, Sydney

Pound, Alistair & Kylie Evans, *An Annotated Guide to the Victorian* Charter of Human Rights and Responsibilities (2008), Law Book Company, Sydney

Rajagopal, Balakrishnan, *International Law from Below: Development, social movements and third world resistance* (2005), Cambridge University Press, Cambridge

Rees, Neil, Katherine Lindsay & Simon Rice, *Australian Anti-Discrimination Law: Text, cases and materials* (2008), The Federation Press, Sydney

Ronalds, Chris, *Discrimination Law and Practice* (3rd edn, 2008), The Federation Press, Sydney

Shue, Henry, *Basic Rights: Subsistence, Affluence, and US Foreign Policy* (2nd edn, 1996), Princeton University Press, Princeton, NJ

Tomuschat, Christian, *Human Rights: Between idealism and realism* (2003), Oxford University Press, Oxford

Wilcox, Murray, *An Australian Charter of Rights?* (1993), Law Book Company, Sydney

Williams, George, *Human Rights under the Australian Constitution* (1999), Oxford University Press, Melbourne

——, *A Charter of Rights for Australia* (2007), UNSW Press, Sydney

2. Book Chapters

Allan, James, 'A defence of the status quo' in Tom Campbell, Jeffrey Goldsworthy & Adrienne Stone (eds), *Protecting Human Rights: Instruments and institutions* (2003), Ashgate Publishing, Aldershot, UK, 175

Alston, Philip, 'Bills of rights: An analytical framework' in Philip Alston (ed.), *Promoting Human Rights through Bills of Rights: Comparative perspectives* (1999), Oxford University Press, Oxford, 1

Byrnes, Andrew, 'And some have bills of rights thrust upon them: The experience of Hong Kong's Bill of Rights' in Philip Alston (ed.), *Promoting Human Rights Through Bills of Rights: Comparative perspectives* (1999), Oxford University Press, Oxford, 318

Byrnes, Andrew & Gabrielle McKinnon, 'The ACT *Human Rights Act 2004* and the Commonwealth *Anti-Terrorism Act (No 2) 2005*: A triumph for federalism or a federal triumph?' in Pene Mathew & Miriam Gani (eds), *Fresh Perspectives on the 'War on Terror'* (2008), ANU E-Press, Canberra, 361

Chan, Joseph, 'A Confucian perspective on human rights for contemporary China' in Joanne R Bauer & Daniel A Bell (eds), *The East Asian Challenge for Human Rights* (1999), Cambridge University Press, UK, 212

Charlesworth, Hilary, 'The challenges of human rights law for religious traditions' in Mark W Janis & Carolyn Evans (eds), *Religion and International Law* (1999), Martinus Nijhoff Publishers, The Hague, 401

Creyke, Robin, 'The performance of administrative law in protecting
    rights' in Tom Campbell, Jeffrey Goldsworthy & Adrienne Stone
    (eds), *Protecting Rights Without a Bill of Rights: Institutional
    performance and reform in Australia* (2006), Ashgate Publishing,
    Aldershot, UK, 101
Darrow, Mac & Philip Alston, 'Bills of rights in comparative perspective'
    in Philip Alston (ed.), *Promoting Human Rights Through Bills of
    Rights: Comparative perspectives* (1999), Oxford University Press,
    Oxford, 465
Donnelly, Jack, 'The social construction of international human rights' in
    Tim Dunne & Nicholas J Wheeler (eds), *Human Rights in Global
    Politics* (1999), Cambridge University Press, UK, 71
Gibbs, Harry, 'Does Australia need a bill of rights?' in *Upholding the
    Australian Constitution: Proceedings of the Sixth Conference of the
    Samuel Griffith Society* (1996), Samuel Griffith Society, Melbourne,
    74
Henkin, Louis, 'Introduction' in Louis Henkin (ed.), *The International Bill of
    Rights: The covenant on civil and political rights* (1981), Columbia
    University Press, New York, 1
Lacey, Wendy & David Wright, 'Highlighting inconsistency: The declaration
    as a remedy in administrative law and human rights standards'
    in Chris Finn (ed.), *Shaping Administrative Law for the Next
    Generation: Fresh perspectives* (2005), Proceedings of the 2004
    National Administrative Law Forum, Australian Institute of
    Administrative Law, Canberra, 32
Webber, Jeremy, 'A modest (but robust) defence of statutory bills of
    rights' in Tom Campbell, Jeffrey Goldsworthy & Adrienne Stone
    (eds), *Protecting Rights Without a Bill of Rights: Institutional
    performance and reform in Australia* (2006), Ashgate Publishing,
    Aldershot, UK, 263

3. Journal Articles

Allan, James, 'The *Victorian Charter of Human Rights and Responsibilities*:
    Exegesis and criticism' (2006) 30 *Melbourne University Law Review*
    906
Bayne, Peter, 'The *Human Rights Act 2004 (ACT)*: Developments in 2004'
    (2005) 8 *Canberra Law Review* 137
Byrnes, Andrew, 'Women, feminism and international human rights law
    – methodological myopia, fundamental flaws or meaningful
    marginalisation?' (1992) 12 *Australian Yearbook of International
    Law* 205
Campbell, Tom, 'Does anyone win under a bill of rights? A response to
    Hilary Charlesworth's "Who wins under a bill of rights?"' (2006)
    25 *University of Queensland Law Journal* 55
Charlesworth, Hilary, 'The Australian reluctance about rights' (1993) 31
    Osgoode Hall Law Journal 195

—— 'Who wins under a bill of rights?' (2006) *University of Queensland Law Journal* 39

Charlesworth, Hilary, Christine Chinkin & Shelley Wright, 'Feminist approaches to international law' (1991) 85 *American Journal of International Law* 613

Dalla-Pozza, Dominique & George Williams, 'The constitutional validity of declarations of incompatibility in Australian charters of rights' (2007) 12 *Deakin Law Review* 1

Debeljak, Julie, 'Parliamentary sovereignty and dialogue under the *Victorian Charter of Human Rights and Responsibilities*: Drawing the line between judicial interpretation and judicial law-making' (2007) 33 *Monash University Law Review* 9

Evans, Simon & Carolyn Evans, 'Legal redress under the *Victorian Charter of Human Rights and Responsibilities*' (2006) 17 *Public Law Review* 264

Freeman, Michael, 'The philosophical foundations of human rights' (1994) 16 *Human Rights Quarterly* 491

Galie, Peter J, 'State courts and economic rights' (1988) 496 *Annals of the American Academy of Political and Social Science* 76

Galligan, Brian, 'Australia's rejection of a bill of rights' (1990) 28 *Journal of Commonwealth and Comparative Politics* 344

Ghai, Yash, 'Human rights and governance: The Asian debate' (1994) 10 *Australian Yearbook of International Law* 1

Hettiarachi, Priyanga, 'Some things borrowed, some things new: An overview of judicial review of legislation under the *Charter of Human Rights and Responsibilities*' (2007) 7 *Oxford University Commonwealth Law Journal* 61

Hogg, Peter & Allison Bushell, 'The *Charter* dialogue between courts and legislatures (or perhaps the *Charter of Rights* isn't such a bad thing after all)' (1997) 35 *Osgoode Hall Law Journal* 75

Hogg, Peter & Allison Thornton, 'Reply to "Six degrees of dialogue"' (1999) 37 *Osgoode Hall Law Journal* 529

Hogg, Peter, Allison Thornton & Wade Wright, '*Charter* dialogue revisited – or "much ado about metaphors"' (2007) 45 *Osgoode Hall Law Journal* 1

——, 'A reply on "*Charter* dialogue revisited"' (2007) 45 *Osgoode Hall Law Journal* 193

Irving, Helen, 'Advisory opinions, the rule of law and the separation of powers' (2004) 4 *Macquarie Law Journal* 105

Kennedy, David, 'The international human rights movement: Part of the problem?' (2002) 15 *Harvard Human Rights Journal* 101

Kostakidis-Lianos, Lara & George Williams, 'Bills of responsibility: Is one needed to counter the excesses of the ACT *Human Rights Act 2004*?' (2005) 30 *Alternative Law Journal* 58

Langlois, Anthony J, 'Human rights and modern liberalism: A critique' (2003) 51 *Political Studies* 509

Leane, Geoffrey, 'Enacting bills of rights: Canada and the curious case of New Zealand's "thin" democracy' (2004) 26 *Human Rights*

Quarterly 152

McDonald, Leighton, 'New Directions in the Australian Bill of Rights Debate' (2004) 12 *Public Law* 22

McKinnon, Gabrielle, 'An opportunity missed? Comment on *SI bhnf CC v KS bhnf IS* [2005] ACTSC 125' (2006) 9 *Canberra Law Review* 21

—— 'Giving meaning to a "culture of human rights"' (Working Paper No 3, ACT Human Rights Act Research Project, ANU, 2006) <http://acthra.anu.edu.au/publications/index.html>

Manfredi, Christopher & James Kelly, 'Six degrees of dialogue: A response to Hogg and Bushell' (1999) 37 *Osgoode Hall Law Journal* 513

Martinez, Jenny S, 'Slave trade on trial: Lessons of a great human-rights law success' (2008) 117 *Yale Law Journal* 550

Moffatt, Robert, 'Philosophical foundations of the Australian constitutional tradition' (1965) 5 *Sydney Law Review* 59

Moran, Alison, 'The Constitution (Declaration of Rights and Freedoms) Bill 1988 (Vic): A doomed legislative proposal' (1990) 17 *Melbourne University Law Review* 418

Mullen, Tom et al, 'Human rights in the Scottish courts' (2005) 32 *Journal of Law and Society* 148

O'Brien, Julie, 'Human rights: Intervention powers of the Human Rights Commission' (2006) 44 *Law Society Journal* 39

Pell, George, 'Four fictions: An argument against a charter of rights' (2008) 52(8) *Quadrant* 24

Reynolds, John, 'A I Clark's American sympathies and his influence on Australian Federation' (1958) 32 *Australian Law Journal* 62

Rolls, Alice, 'Avoiding tragedy: Would the decision of the High Court in *Al-Kateb* have been any different if Australia had a bill of rights like Victoria?' (2007) 18 *Public Law Review* 119

Shestack, Jerome J, 'The philosophic foundations of human rights' (1998) 20 *Human Rights Quarterly* 201

Stefaniak, Bill, 'The need to balance a bill of rights' (2005) 86 *The Parliamentarian* 251

Stone, Adrienne 'Judicial Review without rights: Some problems for the democratic legitimacy of structural judicial review' 28 *Oxford Journal of Legal Studies* (2008) 1

Stellios, James, 'State/Territory human rights legislation in a federal judicial system' (2008) 19 *Public Law Review* 52

Tate, Pamela, 'Protecting human rights in a federation' (2008) 33 *Monash University Law Review* 217

Tribe, Laurence, Jeremy Waldron & Mark Tushnet, 'On judicial review' (2005) 52(3) *Dissent* 81

Waldron, Jeremy, 'The core of the case against judicial review' (2006) 115 *Yale Law Journal* 1346, 1370

Williams, George, 'The *Victorian Charter of Human Rights and Responsibilities*: Origins and scope' (2006) 26 *Melbourne University Law Review* 880 .

4. Official Documents (Government Papers)

ACT Attorney-General's Department, *A Bill of Rights for the ACT?: Issues Paper* (1993)

ACT Bill of Rights Consultative Committee, *Towards an ACT Human Rights Act: Report of the ACT Bill of Rights Consultative Committee* (2003)

ACT Human Rights Commission, *Human Rights Audit on the Operation of ACT Correctional Facilities under Corrections Legislation* (2007)

ACT Human Rights Office, *Human Rights Audit of Quamby Youth Detention Centre* (2005)

Audit Commission (UK), *Human Rights: Improving Public Service Delivery* (2003)

Consultation Committee for a Proposed WA Human Rights Act, *A WA Human Rights Act: Report of the Consultation Committee for a Proposed WA Human Rights Act* (2007)

Department for Constitutional Affairs (UK), *Review of the Implementation of the Human Rights Act* (2006)

Department of Justice (NZ), *A Bill of Rights for New Zealand: A White Paper* (1985)

Department of Justice and Community Safety (ACT), *Human Rights Act 2004: Twelve-Month Review – Report* (2006)

Human Rights and Equal Opportunity Commission, *Bringing Them Home: Report of the National Inquiry into the Separation of Aboriginal and Torres Strait Islander Children from Their Families* (1997)

Joint Committee on Human Rights, Parliament of United Kingdom, *The Case for a Human Rights Commission* (2003)

—— *The Meaning of Public Authority under the Human Rights Act* (2007)

Legal and Constitutional Committee, Parliament of Victoria, *Report on the Desirability or Otherwise of Legislation Defining and Protecting Human Rights* (1987)

Legal, Constitutional and Administrative Review Committee, Parliament of Queensland, *The Preservation and Enhancement of Individuals' Rights and Freedoms in Queensland: Should Queensland Adopt a Bill of Rights?* (1998)

Ministry of Justice (UK), *Human Rights Insight Project*, Ministry of Justice Research Series 1/08 (2008)

Standing Committee on Law and Justice, Parliament of New South Wales, *A NSW Bill of Rights* (2001)

Tasmanian Law Reform Institute, *A Charter of Rights for Tasmania?*, Issues Paper No 11 (2006)

Tasmanian Law Reform Institute, *A Charter of Rights for Tasmania*, Report No 10 (2007)

Victorian Equal Opportunity and Human Rights Commission, *First Steps Forward: The 2007 Report on the Operation of the* Charter of Human Rights and Responsibilities (2008)

Victorian Human Rights Consultation Committee, *Rights, Responsibilities and Respect: The Report of the Human Rights Consultation Committee* (2005)

5. Other

British Institute of Human Rights, *The Human Rights Act – Changing Lives* (2006)

TABLE OF CASES

AUSTRALIA

ACT

Al-Rawahi v Niazi [2006] ACTSC 84	190
Capital Property Projects (ACT) Pty Ltd v ACT Planning & *Land Authority* [2006] ACTSC 122	189
Capital Property Projects (ACT) Pty Ltd v ACT Planning & *Land Authority* [2008] ACTCA 9	190
Commissioner for Housing in the ACT v Y [2007] ACTSC 84	100
Dunne/Barden and ACT Department of Education and *Training* [2007] ACTAAT 26	189
Emlyn-Jones v Federal Capital Press (ACT Discrimination Tribunal, heard 11 July 2006, decision reserved)	185, 187, 189
Griffin v The Queen [2008] HCA Trans 72	99, 189
Hausmann v Shute [2007] ACTCA 5	190
IF v Commissioner for Housing [2005] ACTSC 80	189
King v Fricker [2007] ACTSC 101	190
Kingsley's Chicken Pty Ltd v Queensland Investment *Corporation* [2006] ACTCA 9	189
Merritt and Commissioner for Housing [2004] ACTAAT 37	189
Pappas v Noble [2006] ACTSC 39	190
Perovic v CW, No CH 05/1046 (Unreported, Magistrate Somes, 1 June 2006)	190
R v Caruso [2006] ACTSC 45	190
R v DA [2008] ACTSC 26	190
R v Griffin [2007] ACTCA 6	104, 190
R v Martiniello [2005] ACTSC 9	190
R v PJ [2006] ACTSC 37	189, 190
R v Rao [2006] SCC No 164 (unreported, Gray J, 11 August 2006)	189, 190
R v Upton [2005] ACTSC 52	190
R v YL [2004] ACTSC 115	190
Raytheon Australia Pty Ltd and ACT Human Rights *Commission* [2008] ACTAAT 19	181–82, 189–90
Re Adoption of D [2008] ACTSC 44	190
Re an Application for the Adoption of TL [2005] ACTSC 49	189, 190
S v DPP (ACT) [2007] ACTSC 100	190
SI bhnf CC v KS bhnf IS [2005] ACTSC 125	92, 100–101, 187

Stevens v McCallum [2006] ACTCA 13	190, 191
Vosame Pty Ltd and ACT Planning & Land Authority [2006] ACTAAT 12	185
West v New South Wales [2007] ACTSC 43	190
Z and Commissioner for Housing [2007] ACTAAT 12	189

Commonwealth

A-G (Cwlth) v Alinta Ltd [2008] HCA 2	202
Agtrack (NT) Pty Ltd v Hatfield (2005) 223 CLR 251; [2005] HCA 38	202
Al-Kateb v Godwin (2004) 219 CLR 562; [2004] HCA 37	166–67, 203
Austin v Commonwealth (2003) 215 CLR 185; [2003] HCA 3	198
Coco v The Queen (1994) 179 CLR 427; [1994] HCA 15	201
Commonwealth v Tasmania (1983) 158 CLR 1; [1983] HCA 21	200
Evans v New South Wales [2008] FCAFC 130	186
In Re Judiciary and Navigation Acts (1921) 29 CLR 257; [1921] HCA 20	201–202
Lipohar v The Queen (1999) 200 CLR 485; [1999] HCA 65	202
Melbourne Corporation v Commonwealth (1947) 74 CLR 31; [1947] HCA 26	200
Re McBain (2002) 209 CLR 372; [2002] HCA 16	202

Victoria

Boeing Australia Holdings Pty Ltd (Anti Discrimination Exemption) [2007] VCAT 532	196
C v Chief Commissioner of Police [2008] VSC 51	197
DPP(Vic) v Ali [2008] VSC 167	196
DPP(Vic) v Zierk [2008] VSC 184	196
Ferguson v Walkley [2008] VSC 7	197
General Television Corporation Pty Ltd v DPP(Vic) [2008] VSCA 49	197
Gray v DPP (Vic) [2008] VSC 4	135–36, 197
Guneser v Magistrates' Court of Victoria [2008] VSC 5	197
Guss v Aldy Corporation Pty Ltd [2008] VCAT 912	136–37, 197
Halwood Corporation (in liq) v Roads Corporation [2008] VSC 28	197
Kortel v Mirik [2008] VSC 103	127, 193, 195, 197

MH6 v Mental Health Review Board (General) [2008] VCAT 846	193, 196, 197
R v A [2008] VSC 73	197
R v Benbrika (Ruling No 12) [2007] VSC 524R	196
R v Benbrika (Ruling No 20) [2008] VSC 80	137, 196, 197
R v Rich [2008] VSC 141	196–97
R v Williams [2007] VSC 2	134–35, 196
R v White [2007] VSC 142	196
Ragg v Magistrates' Court of Victoria [2008] VSC 1	196
Re Unumadu [2007] VSC 258	196
Swain v Department of Infrastructure (General) [2008] VCAT 848	196
Tomasevic v Travaglini [2007] VSC 337	196
Towie v Victoria [2007] VCAT 1489	196
Victorian Mental Health Review Board: P 09-003 [2008] VMHRB 1	197

UNITED KINGDOM

A v Secretary of State for the Home Department [2004] UKHL 56	182, 203
Bellinger v Bellinger [2003] UKHL 21	182
Blood and Tarbuck v Secretary of State for Health (Unreported, Sullivan J, 28 February 2003)	182
Brown v Stott [2000] UKPC D3	183
Ghaidan v Godin Mendoza [2004] UKHL 30	60, 100, 181, 190
R v A (No 2) [2001] UKHL 25	60, 181
R (Anderson) v Secretary of State for the Home Department [2002] UKHL 46	183
R (Daly) v Secretary of State for the Home Department [2001] UKHL 26	183
R (on the application of H) v Mental Health Review Tribunal for the North and East London Region [2001] EWCA Civ 415	182
R (on the application of Hooper) v Secretary of State for Work and Pensions [2003] EWCA Civ 875	182
Re an Application for Judicial Review by McR [2002] NIQB 58	182

NEW ZEALAND

A-G v Human Rights Tribunal (2006) 16 PRNZ 295, [2007] NZAR 67	179
Child Poverty Action Group v A-G [2005] NZHRRT 28	179
Hansen v The Queen [2007] NZSC 7	84–85, 185, 186
Howard v A-G (No 3) [2008] NZHRRT 10	179
Moonen v Film and Literature Board of Review	84–85, 185, 186
R v Poumako [2000] NZCA 69	179

SOUTH AFRICA

Minister of Health v Treatment Action Campaign [2002] 5 SA 271	200
South Africa v Grootboom [2001] 1 SA 46	156–57, 200

UNITED STATES of AMERICA

Abrams v US, 250 US 616 (1919)	174
Schenck v US, 249 US 47 (1919)	174
New State Ice Co v Liebmann, 285 US 262 (1932)	197

CANADA

R v Askov [1990] SCC 45	183

OTHER

Handyside v United Kingdom (1976) 1 EHRR 737	195
Toonen v Australia, Communication No 488/1992: Australia. 04/04/94, UN Doc CCPR/C/50/D/488/1992 (1994)	37–38, 176

TABLE OF STATUTES AND BILLS

AUSTRALIA

ACT

Administrative Decisions (Judicial Review) Act 1989 (ACT)	186
Adoption Act 1993 (ACT)	102, 189
Annual Reports (Government Agencies) Act 2004 (ACT)	187
Bail Act 1992 (ACT)	102, 189
Charter of Responsibilities Bill 2004 (ACT)	78–79
Children and Young People Act 2008 (ACT)	89–90
Children and Young People Bill 2008 (ACT)	88
Corrections Management Bill 2006 (ACT)	88, 188
Court Procedures Rules 2006 (ACT)	102
Court Procedures (Protection of Public Participation) Amendment Bill 2005 (ACT)	189
Crimes Act 1900 (ACT)	189
Crimes (Offences against Pregnant Women) Amendment Bill 2005 (ACT)	188
Criminal Code Harmonisation Bill 2005 (ACT)	188
Director of Public Prosecutions Act 1990 (ACT)	102
Discrimination Act 1991 (ACT)	185
Domestic Animals Amendment Bill 2007 (ACT)	97
Domestic Violence and Protection Orders Act 2001 (ACT)	101
Freedom of Information Act 1989 (ACT)	95
Health Legislation Amendment Bill (No 2) 2006 (ACT)	97
Human Rights Act 2004 (ACT)	41, 53, 63, 73–107, 108, 111, 112, 115, 116, 117, 118, 119, 120, 123, 140, 141, 142, 144–45, 146, 157, 158, 159, 161–62, 163, 164, 185, 186, 187, 188, 189, 190, 192, 193, 200, 201, 202

Human Rights Amendment Act 2008 (ACT)	85, 185, 186
Human Rights Commission Act 2005 (ACT)	187
Land (Planning and Environment) Act 1991 (ACT)	188
Legislation Act 2001 (ACT)	77, 83, 100, 185
Magistrates Court Act 1930 (ACT)	103
Mental Health (Treatment and Care) Amendment Bill 2005 (ACT)	87, 201
Ombudsman Act 1989 (ACT)	93
Supreme Court Act 1933 (ACT)	102, 104
Terrorism (Extraordinary Temporary Powers) Bill 2006 (ACT)	87, 95, 201
Water Resources Bill 2007 (ACT)	97

Commonwealth

Age Discrimination Act 2004 (Cwlth)	40, 177
Anti-Terrorism Act (No 2) 2005 (Cwlth)	95, 203
Australian Bill of Rights Bill 1985 (Cwlth)	31–32, 33
Australian Bill of Rights Bill 2001 (Cwlth)	175
Australian Capital Territory (Self Government) Act 1988 (Cwlth)	74, 184
Australian Human Rights Bill 1985 (Cwlth)	175
Australian Human Rights Commission Legislation Bill 2003 (Cwlth)	177
Constitution of the Commonwealth of Australia	24–27, 28–29, 30, 31, 32–33, 36, 38, 151, 154, 155, 160–61, 185, 200
Constitutional Alteration (Fair Elections) 1988 (Cwlth)	175
Constitutional Alteration (Local Government) 1988 (Cwlth)	175
Constitutional Alteration (Parliamentary Terms) 1988 (Cwlth)	175
Constitutional Alteration (Post-War Reconstruction and Democratic Rights) 1944 (Cwlth)	27
Constitutional Alteration (Rights and Freedoms) 1988 (Cwlth)	33
Constitutional Alteration (War Aims and Reconstruction) Bill 1942 (Cwlth)	26
Disability Discrimination Act 1992 (Cwlth)	177
Human Rights Bill 1973 (Cwlth)	27–29
Human Rights and Equal Opportunity Commission Act 1986 (Cwlth)	32, 38–39, 176, 177

Human Rights Commission Act 1981 (Cwlth)	29–30, 32
Human Rights Legislation Amendment Bill (No 2) 1998 (Cwlth)	177
Human Rights (Sexual Conduct) Act 1994 (Cwlth)	37
Migration Act 1958 (Cwlth)	167–68
Migration Reform Act 1992 (Cwlth)	167
Native Title Act 1993 (Cwlth)	176
Parliamentary Charter of Rights and Freedoms Bill 2001 (Cwlth)	33
Racial Discrimination Act 1975 (Cwlth)	38, 40, 177
Sex Discrimination Act 1984 (Cwlth)	38, 40, 177, 200
Workplace Relations Act 1996 (Cwlth)	176

Victoria

Animals Legislation Amendment (Animal Care) Bill 2007 (Vic)	196
Charter of Human Rights and Responsibilities 2006 (Vic)	41, 53, 60–61, 63, 84, 86, 93, 105, 108–38, 140, 141, 142, 143, 144–45, 146, 151, 152, 153, 157, 158, 159, 162–63, 164, 187, 192, 193, 194, 195, 196, 200, 201, 202
Charter of Human Rights and Responsibilities Bill 2006 (Vic)	113–14
Charter of Human Rights and Responsibilities (Public Authorities) (Interim) Regulations 2007 (Vic)	193, 202
Civil and Administrative Tribunal Act 1998 (Vic)	136
Confiscation Amendment Bill 2007 (Vic)	125
Constitution Act 1975 (Vic)	109, 110
Constitution (Declaration of Rights and Freedoms) Bill 1988 (Vic)	110
Coroners Act 1985 (Vic)	128
Crimes (Decriminalisation of Abortion) Bill 2007 (Vic)	124

Criminal Procedure Legislation Amendment Bill 2007 (Vic)	196
Drugs, Poisons and Controlled Substances Amendment Bill 2008 (Vic)	131
Energy Efficiency Target Act 2007 (Vic)	132
Equal Opportunity Act 1995 (Vic)	117, 193
Graffiti Prevention Bill 2007 (Vic)	125, 131, 194
Infertility Treatment Amendment Bill 2007 (Vic)	124, 128, 129–30, 192
Justice and Road Legislation Amendment (Law Enforcement) Bill 2007 (Vic)	195
Justice Legislation Amendment Bill 2007 (Vic)	195
Legal Aid Act 1978 (Vic)	157
Liquor Control Reform Amendment Bill 2007 (Vic)	194
Ombudsman Act 1973 (Vic)	187, 193
Police Integrity Bill 2008 (Vic)	132
Public Administration Act 2004 (Vic)	193
Road Legislation Further Amendment Bill 2007 (Vic)	125
Summary Offences (Upskirting) Bill 2007 (Vic)	195
Subordinate Legislation Act 1994 (Vic)	195
Superannuation Legislation Amendment (Contribution Splitting and Other Matters) Bill 2007 (Vic)	195
Transport Accident and Accident Compensation Acts Amendment Bill 2007 (Vic)	195
Transport Legislation Amendment Bill 2007 (Vic)	195–96
Victorian Constitution	109, 110
Victorian Energy Efficiency Target Bill 2007 (Vic)	196
Working with Children Amendment Bill 2007 (Vic)	196

Queensland

Constitution (Declaration of Rights) Bill 1959 (Qld)	177–78
Legislative Standards Act 1992 (Qld)	51

Tasmania

Criminal Code Act 1924 (Tas)	37

CANADA

Charter of Rights and Freedoms 1982	46–47, 50–53, 82, 118, 131, 161, 178–79, 183

HONG KONG

Basic Law of the Hong Kong Special Administrative Region of the People's Republic of China	48
Hong Kong Bill of Rights Ordinance 1991 (HK)	48–49, 183, 201

NEW ZEALAND

Bill of Rights Act 1990 (NZ)	49, 52, 53, 104, 105
Human Rights Act 1993 (NZ)	179
Human Rights Amendment Act 2001 (NZ)	179

SOUTH AFRICA

Bill of Rights	47
Constitution of the Republic of South Africa 1996	47, 179

UNITED KINGDOM

Bill of Rights 1689 (UK)	3
Factory Act 1833 (UK)	7–8
Human Rights Act 1998 (UK)	49–51, 52, 53, 60–68, 84, 100, 101, 105, 121, 122, 159, 160, 162, 163, 164, 166, 201, 202
Human Rights Act (Meaning of Public Function) Bill 2007 (UK)	194
Slavery Abolition Act 1833 (UK)	8

UNITED STATES of AMERICA

US Bill of Rights	4, 45–46, 68, 146
US Constitution	4, 8, 24, 26, 45–46, 69, 178, 198

TABLE OF INTERNATIONAL INSTRUMENTS

TREATIES

Convention against Torture and Other Cruel, Inhuman or Degrading Treatment or Punishment 1984 (CAT)	18, 20, 37, 174, 176
Convention Concerning Discrimination in Respect of Employment and Occupation 1958	176–77
Convention for the Amelioration of the Condition of the Wounded in Armies in the Field 1864 (Geneva Convention 1864)	14, 173
Convention on the Elimination of All Forms of Discrimination against Women 1979 (CEDAW)	18, 20
Convention on the Rights of the Child 1989 (CRC)	18, 39, 90, 176
Convention on the Rights of Persons with Disabilities 2006	19, 21
Covenant of the League of Nations 1919	8
European Convention on Human Rights 1950	50, 67, 105
Geneva Convention for the Amelioration of the Condition of the Wounded and Sick in the Armed Forces in the Field 1949 (First Geneva Convention)	14, 173
Geneva Convention for the Amelioration of the Condition of Wounded, Sick and Shipwrecked Members of Armed Forces at Sea 1949 (Second Geneva Convention)	14, 173
Geneva Convention relative to the Treatment of Prisoners of War 1949 (Third Geneva Convention)	14, 173
Geneva Convention relative to the Protection of Civilian Persons in Time of War 1949 (Fourth Geneva Convention)	14, 173
International Convention for the Protection of All Persons from Enforced Disappearance 2006	19, 20
International Convention on the Elimination of All Forms of Racial Discrimination 1965 (CERD)	18, 20, 37, 174, 176, 177
International Convention on the Protection of the Rights of All Migrant Workers and Members of Their Families 1989	18–19, 20

International Covenant on Civil and Political Rights 1966 (ICCPR)	18, 20, 28, 29, 30, 31, 32, 33, 34, 36, 37, 39, 48–49, 50, 70, 76, 81, 82, 95, 113, 117, 155, 157, 165, 168, 173, 176, 184, 185, 192, 201
International Covenant on Economic, Social and Cultural Rights 1966 (ICESCR)	18, 28, 29, 34, 36, 39, 48–49, 76, 81, 155, 177, 184
International Labour Organisation Constitution 1919	173
Treaty of Peace between the Allied and Associated Powers and Germany, and Protocol 1919 (Treaty of Versailles)	14, 173
United Nations Charter 1945	17

OTHER

Declaration on the Rights of Disabled Persons, GA Res 1856 (1971)	177
Declaration on the Rights of Mentally Retarded Persons, GA Res 3447 (1975)	177
Declaration on the Rights of the Child, GA Res 1386 (1959)	177
Declaration on the Rights of Women	6
French Declaration of the Rights of Man and the Citizen	5, 6, 10
Instructions for the Government of Armies of the United States in the Field, General Order No 100, 24 April 1863 (Lieber Code)	14, 173
Magna Carta	3, 101
Universal Declaration of Human Rights	11, 17–18, 177
US Declaration of Independence	4–5, 10

Index

2020 Summit 147

ACT Greens 78, 94, 96
ACT *Human Rights Act* 41, 53,
  63, 73–107, 108, 111, 112, 115,
  116, 117, 118, 119, 120, 123,
  140, 141, 142, 144–45, 146, 157,
  158, 159, 161–62, 163, 164, 185,
  186, 187, 188, 189, 190, 192,
  193, 200, 201, 202
  consultation preceding 75–77,
    112, 151
  corporations, application to 82
  courts, impact on 66, 99–106
    role of legal profession
      105–106
    use of international
      jurisprudence 104
  declaration of incompatibility
    79, 99, 101
  direct right of action 80, 85–86,
    105–106, 186
  earlier proposals 74
  economic, social and cultural
    rights 76, 77, 78, 81, 157
  Executive, impact on 87–93
  Human Rights Commissioner
    80, 89–90, 92–93, 101, 105,
    119, 164
  human rights audits 92–93
  human rights culture 91
  interpretive provision 60–61, 79,
    83–85, 91, 99–101, 159
  Legislative Assembly debate on
    78–79
  legislature, impact on 93–98
  limitations on rights 82–83,
    95–96, 98, 185, 192
  Ombudsman 93
  opt-in provision 86, 162
  public authorities, duty on 80,
    85–86, 91, 162
  remedies 77, 86, 103, 106, 163
  reporting requirements 80, 91
  reviews 81, 83–84, 88, 157, 187
  rights protected by 80–81, 115
  scrutiny committee 80, 88,
    96–98, 188
  statement of compatibility 79,
    87–89, 96, 123, 158
Al-Kateb, Ahmed Ali 166
Alexander Maconochie Centre 90,
  188
Allan, James 60, 61, 200
Alston, Philip 45
American Revolution 3, 4
Amnesty International 140
anti-terrorism legislation 1, 42, 87,
  94, 95–96, 166
Antigone 2
Archer, Shelley 144
arms, right to bear 69, 75
Ashoka 2
Australia, approach to international
  human rights 20–22
Australian bill of rights *see* bill of
  rights, Australian
Australian Constitution see

Constitution (Commonwealth)
Australian Democrats
  ACT 78
  federal 32, 33
Australian Federal Police 103
Australian Labor Party
  ACT 74, 75, 77, 93
  federal 27–28, 30, 37, 42, 140,
    146–47
Australian Law Reform
  Commission 149, 199

Baker, Lisa 198
Behrendt, Larissa 75
Belconnen Remand Centre 93
Bentham, Jeremy 10
Berry, Wayne 96
bill of rights, Australian 24–34,
  35–36, 56–57, 146–69
  constitutional bill of rights,
    disadvantages of 154–55, 181
  constitutional validity of 155,
    160–61
  consultation process for 148–54
    accessibility 151–52
    education 150–51
    independent committee
      148–49
    media 153–54
    membership of committee
      149–50
    special interests 152–53
    terms of reference 150
  declaration of incompatibility
    160–61
  effect of 165–68
  human rights commission, role of
    164–65
  international human rights law,
    influence of 35–36, 56–57
  interpretive provision 159–60,
    201
  jurisdictional scope 155–56
  limitations on rights 157
  political leadership, importance
    of 148
  proposals for 24–34
  public authorities, duty on
    161–63
  remedies 163
  rights protected 156–57
  scrutiny committee 158–59
  statement of compatibility 158
bill of rights, generally
  'dialogue' bills of rights 51–54
  democracy and 34–35, 57–65,
    168–69
  human rights culture 63
  increase in litigation 65–66
  judiciary, role of 58–62
  Marxist criticism of 70–71
  models of 44–51
  relationship with responsibilities
    or duties 70
  risk of rights becoming irrelevant
    68–69
  'rogues' charter' concern 66–68
bill of rights, States and Territories
  dialogue between States and
    Territories 140, 144–45
  influence on Commonwealth
    legislation 145
  proposals for 41
  see also ACT *Human Rights Act*;
    Victorian Charter; Tasmania,
    bill of rights consultation;
    Western Australia, bill of rights
    consultation
Bjelke-Petersen, Joh 31
Bowen, Lionel 32
British Institute of Human Rights
  64
Broad, Candy 124
Burke, Brian 31, 33
Burke, Edmund 10
Bushell, Allison 51

Cain, John 109–10
*Canadian Charter of Rights and
  Freedoms* 46–47, 50–53, 82, 118,
  131, 161, 183
  dialogue metaphor 51–53
  notwithstanding clause 47, 52,
    118, 161
Carli, Carlo 129
Carnell government 74

Carnley, Peter 198
Carpenter government 144
Carr, Bob 42
Chaney, Fred 142, 149
Charlesworth, Hilary 75
Charter of Human Rights and Responsibilities 2006 (Vic) see Victorian Charter
Chartists 7
children, protection of 74, 80, 81, 115
Ciobo, Steven 42
Clark, Andrew Inglis 24, 174
Clark, Robert 128–29, 192
Cockburn, Alexander 25, 35
Connolly, Terry 74
Constitution (Commonwealth) 24–27, 28–29, 30, 32–33, 36, 38, 151, 154, 155, 160–61, 185, 200
    external affairs power 28–29, 30, 36, 38, 155
    referenda 26–27, 32–33
    rights in 25
    validity of federal bill of rights 155, 160–61
consultation process see bill of rights, Australian – consultation see also ACT Human Rights Act – consultation preceding; Victorian Charter – consultation preceding
counter-terrorism legislation see anti-terrorism legislation
Cox, Jamie 197

De Gouges, Olympe 6
declaration of incompatibility see ACT Human Rights Act – declaration of incompatibility; bill of rights, Australian – declaration of incompatibility; UK Human Rights Act – declaration of incompatibility; Victorian Charter – declaration of inconsistent interpretation
Dembour, Marie-Bénédicte 12
democracy see bills of rights, generally – democracy and

Department of Constitutional Affairs (UK) see UK Human Rights Act – review
dialogue bill of rights see bills of rights, generally – 'dialogue' bills of rights
Dinsmore, Andrew 194
Dixon, Sir Owen 25
due process see fair trial, right to
Dunstan, Don 42

Eades, Julian 197
Eastman, Kate 87, 95
economic, social and cultural rights see human rights – economic, social and cultural rights
education, right to 16, 50, 74, 81, 143
Engels, Friedrich 6
English Revolution 3, 17
Enlightenment 3
environmental rights 47, 78, 81
equality, right to 16, 24, 28, 46, 80, 115, 130
European Court of Human Rights 51, 98, 131, 190, 201, 202
Evans, Carolyn 121
Evans, Gareth 31, 109, 148
Evans, Simon 121
Evatt, HV 20, 26
expression, right to freedom of 5, 16, 27, 28, 45, 74, 81, 115, 117, 128, 131, 136

fair trial, right to 16, 81, 101, 103–104, 115, 116–17, 129, 135
Faris, Peter 134
family, protection of 16, 80, 98, 115, 166
Federation debates 24–26
Follett government 74
Foskey, Deb 94
Fraser government 29–30
French Revolution 3, 4

Galbally, Rhonda 111
Galligan, Brian 42

Gans, Jeremy 121
Gaze, Andrew 111
Gearty, Conor 60, 154, 184
Gelber, Katharine 140
Gibbs, Sir Harry 181
Glorious Revolution 3
Griffith, Samuel 24

Hargreaves, John 97
Hatzistergos, John 42
Hawke government 30
Hayward, Colleen 198
health, right to 16, 143
Heaney, Seamus 169
Henning, Terese 141
Hobbes, Thomas 4
Hogg, Peter 51
Holmes, Oliver Wendell 24
housing, right to 16, 81
Howard government 21, 34, 38
Howard, John 34, 55, 79, 139, 146
Hulls, Rob 110, 113, 148
human rights
    civil and political rights 6–7, 11,
        16, 17, 32
    collective rights 11, 16
    critiques of 10–12
    definition of 12–13
    economic, social and cultural
        rights 11, 14–15, 16, 17, 69,
        71, 141, 143 see also ACT
        Human Rights Act – economic,
        social and cultural rights;
        Victorian Charter – economic,
        social and cultural rights
    history of 2–8
    international protection of
        13–20
    justifications of 9
    universality of 9–10
Human Rights Act 1998 (UK) see
UK Human Rights Act
Human Rights Act 2004 (ACT) see
ACT Human Rights Act
Human Rights Act for Australia
    campaign 33–34
Human Rights and Equal
    Opportunity Commission

(HREOC) 38–40, 165, 176, 177
Human Rights Committee 37, 104,
    168, 176
human rights in Australia
    adequacy of protection 55–57
    community awareness of 1,
        139–40, 150–51
    protection of 36–40
Hutton, Lisa 197

Indigenous rights 11, 21, 46
international bill of rights 18–19,
    20
International Covenant on Civil
    and Political Rights (ICCPR) 18,
    20, 28, 29, 30, 31, 32, 33, 34, 36,
    37, 39, 48–49, 50, 70, 76, 81, 82,
    95, 113, 117, 155, 157, 165, 168,
    173, 176, 184, 185, 192, 201
International Covenant on
    Economic, Social and Cultural
    Rights (ICESCR) 18, 28, 29,
    34, 36, 39, 48–49, 76, 81, 155,
    177, 184
international humanitarian law
    13–14
International Labour Organisation
    (ILO) 8, 14–15
interpretive provision see ACT
    Human Rights Act – interpretive
    provision; bill of rights, Australian
    – interpretive provision; UK
    Human Rights Act – interpretive
    provision; Victorian Charter
    – interpretive provision
Ishay, Micheline 6

Jackson, Judy 141, 148
judicial review see bill of rights,
    generally – judiciary, role of
jury, right to trial by 24–25

Kant, Immanuel 9
Keating, Paul 37
Kelly, Elizabeth 75
Kennan, Jim 109, 110
Kennedy, David 10
Kons, Steve 141

labour rights 7–8, 15, 16
Lavarch, Michael 75
Layland, Penelope 75
League of Nations 8, 14, 173
Lees, Meg 33
Liberal Party
    ACT 74, 75, 77, 94, 187
    federal 29, 42, 146
liberty and security, right to 50, 81,
    95, 96, 102–103, 115, 131
life, right to 16, 50, 76, 80, 115,
    131, 152
Lincoln, Abraham 14
Llewellyn, David 142
Locke, John 3–4

MacIntyre, Alasdair 10
Mahathir Mohamad 172
Malik, Charles 172
Marx, Karl 6
McClelland, Robert 147
McCoy, Gerard 105
McGinty, Jim 142, 143, 144
Menzies, Sir Robert 35
minorities, rights of 8, 14, 16, 81,
    115–16
Montesquieu, Charles 5
movement, right to freedom of 16,
    28, 80, 115
Murphy, Lionel 28, 29, 42, 148

National Party 29, 142, 146
New Matilda see Human Rights
    Act for Australia campaign
Nicklin, Frank 42, 178

O'Connor, Richard 25
Ombudsman (Cwlth) 165 See also
    ACT Human Rights Act Victorian
    Charter – Ombudsman

parliamentary sovereignty see bill
    of rights, generally – democracy
    and Permanent Court of
    International Justice 14
privacy, right to 16, 28, 50, 80, 98,
    115, 128, 131, 166
property, right to 5, 50, 78, 116,

143
public authorities, duty on see
    ACT Human Rights Act – public
    authorities, duty on; bill of rights,
    Australian – public authorities,
    duty on; UK Human Rights
    Act – public authorities, duty
    on; Victorian Charter – public
    authorities, duty on

Qin dynasty 2
Quamby Youth Detention Centre
    90, 92, 94

Reformation 2–3
religion, right to freedom of 5, 16,
    24, 46, 50, 80, 115
religious groups and human rights
    152–53, 200
remedies see ACT Human Rights
    Act – remedies; bill of rights,
    Australian – remedies; UK Human
    Rights Act – remedies; Victorian
    Charter – remedies
Roosevelt, Franklin 26
Rose, Alan 199
Rousseau, Jean-Jacques 5
Rowell, Mat 197
Rudd government 21
Rudd, Kevin 147
Ryan, Susan 33

Second World War 15–16, 26
self-determination, right to 16, 81
Seselja, Zed 187
Shue, Henry 171
slavery 6, 8, 13, 16, 46, 50, 81
social contract 4, 5
Sophocles 2
speech, freedom of see expression,
    right to freedom of
Stanhope government 93
Stanhope, Jon 74, 75, 92, 148
statement of compatibility see ACT
    Human Rights Act – statement
    of compatibility; bill of rights,
    Australian – statement of
    compatibility; Victorian Charter

– statement of compatibility
States' rights 27, 29, 31, 34, 41
Stefaniak, Bill 77, 78
Stevenson, Alan 197
Stolen Generation report 40
Storey, Haddon 111, 149
Stott-Despoja, Natasha 33
strict liability offences 94–95,
    97–98, 102–103, 186
Sunstein, Cass 172
Symonston Temporary Remand
    Centre 93

Tasmania, bill of rights consultation
    141–42, 149, 158, 159–60, 197
Tasmanian Law Reform Institute
    141, 149, 159–60
Tate, Pamela 111, 193
Tomuschat, Christian 9
torture, right to be free from 16,
    50, 80, 115
trade unions, right to form 81
treaty system 19–20
Tucker, Kerrie 78

UK *Human Rights Act* 49–51, 52,
    53, 60–68, 84, 100, 101, 105,
    121, 122, 159, 160, 162, 163,
    164, 166, 201, 202
    declaration of incompatibility
        61–62, 160, 201
    Equality and Human Rights
        Commission 164
    impact on courts 65–66
        role of legal profession 105
    interpretive provision 60–61, 84,
        100, 101, 122, 159
    public authorities, duty on 121,
        162
    remedies 163, 202
    review of 63–65
Unger, Roberto 11
United Nations 16–17, 19, 20, 21,
    28
    General Assembly 17, 18

Victorian Charter 41, 53, 60–61,
    63, 84, 86, 93, 105, 108–38, 140,
    141, 142, 143, 144–45, 146, 151,
    152, 153, 157, 158, 159, 162–63,
    164, 187, 192, 193, 194, 195,
    196, 200, 201, 202
    commencement of 108, 114,
        123, 134
    consultation preceding 110–13,
        149–50, 151, 152, 153
    courts and tribunals, application
        to 119, 121, 193
    courts and tribunals, impact on
        134–37
    declaration of inconsistent
        interpretation 113–14, 118,
        127
    direct right of action 86, 111
    economic, social and cultural
        rights 111, 113, 119, 157
    earlier proposals 109–10
    Executive, impact on 123–28
    human rights certificates 125–26
    interpretive provision 60–61, 84,
        118, 136, 159
    Justice Statement 110
    legislature, impact on 128–33
    limitations on rights 116–17,
        120, 125, 130–31, 157, 192
    notice to Attorney-General in
        court proceedings 137
    Ombudsman 93, 119, 127–28,
        187, 194
    override declaration 114, 117,
        123, 127, 131
    public authorities, duty on 86,
        118, 120–21, 126, 136, 162–
        63, 193
    religious bodies, application to
        114, 120, 193
    remedies 118, 119, 122, 136,
        163
    reviews 119, 157
    rights protected by 115–17, 192
    Scrutiny of Acts and Regulations
        Committee 110, 117, 126,
        128, 129–33, 201
    statements of compatibility 117,
        123–26, 128, 129, 158
    Statement of Intent 111–12,

113, 122, 144
Victorian Equal Opportunity and
Human Rights Commission
118–19, 126–27, 133, 164
vote, right to 6, 7, 16, 28, 46, 117,
157

Waldron, Jeremy 62
Watchirs, Helen 92 *see also* ACT
Human Rights Act – Human
Rights Commission
Waterford, Jack 74

Webber, Jeremy 62
Weil, Simone 169
Western Australia, bill of rights
consultation 142–44, 150, 153,
158, 159, 198, 200
Whitlam government 28
Whitlam, Gough 42
Williams, Daryl 55
Williams, George 111, 112, 202
women, rights of 6, 8–9, 11, 200

Zifcak, Spencer 34